MOTHERSHIP
CONNECTED

American Music Series

HANIF ABDURRAQIB, JESSICA HOPPER, AND CHARLES L. HUGHES, SERIES EDITORS

Recent Titles

Niko Stratis, *The Dad Rock That Made Me a Woman*
Franz Nicolay, *Band People: Life and Work in Popular Music*
Tara López, *Chuco Punk: Sonic Insurgency in El Paso*
Alex Pappademas and Joan LeMay, *Quantum Criminals: Ramblers, Wild Gamblers, and Other Sole Survivors from the Songs of Steely Dan*
Bruce Adams, *You're with Stupid: kranky, Chicago, and the Reinvention of Indie Music*
Margo Price, *Maybe We'll Make It: A Memoir*
Francesca T. Royster, *Black Country Music: Listening for Revolutions*
Lynn Melnick, *I've Had to Think Up a Way to Survive: On Trauma, Persistence, and Dolly Parton*
Lance Scott Walker, *DJ Screw: A Life in Slow Revolution*
Eddie Huffman, *John Prine: In Spite of Himself*
David Cantwell, *The Running Kind: Listening to Merle Haggard*
Stephen Deusner, *Where the Devil Don't Stay: Traveling the South with the Drive-By Truckers*
Eric Harvey, *Who Got the Camera? A History of Rap and Reality*
Kristin Hersh, *Seeing Sideways: A Memoir of Music and Motherhood*
Hannah Ewens, *Fangirls: Scenes from Modern Music Culture*
Sasha Geffen, *Glitter Up the Dark: How Pop Music Broke the Binary*
Hanif Abdurraqib, *Go Ahead in the Rain: Notes to A Tribe Called Quest*

PETER BLACKSTOCK AND DAVID MENCONI, FOUNDING EDITORS

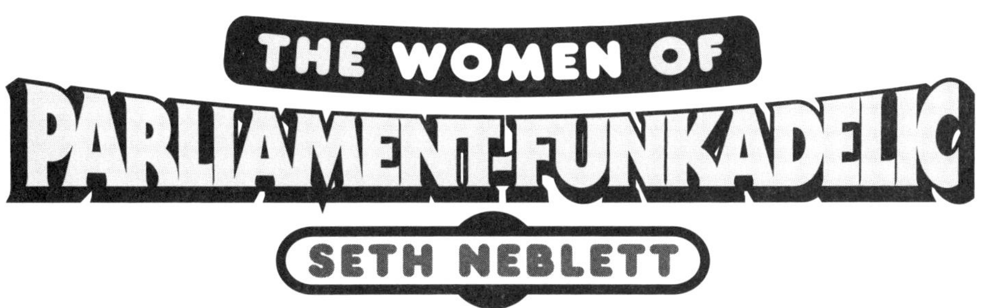

UNIVERSITY OF TEXAS PRESS AUSTIN

Printed in the United States of America
First edition, 2025

♾ The paper used in this book meets the minimum requirements of ANSI/NISO Z39.48-1992 (R1997) (Permanence of Paper).

Library of Congress Cataloging-in-Publication Data

Names: Neblett, Seth, author and interviewer.
Title: Mothership connected : the women of Parliament-Funkadelic / [interviews by] Seth Neblett.
Other titles: American music series (Austin, Tex.)
Description: First edition. | Austin : University of Texas Press, 2025. | Series: American music series | Includes index.
Identifiers: LCCN 2024056919 (print) | LCCN 2024056920 (ebook)
ISBN 978-1-4773-3267-2 (hardcover)
ISBN 978-1-4773-3268-9 (pdf)
ISBN 978-1-4773-3269-6 (epub)
Subjects: LCSH: African American women singers—Interviews. | Funk musicians—United States—Interviews. | Franklin, Mallia, 1952–2010. | Wright, Debbie, 1951–2017. | Hayden, Shirley. | Washington, Jeanette. | Silva, Dawn, 1951– | Mabry, Lynn, 1958– | Parlet (Musical group) | Brides of Funkenstein (Musical group) | P-Funk All Stars. | Funk (Music)—History and criticism. | African American women singers—Anecdotes.
Classification: LCC ML3527.8 .M67 2025 (print) | LCC ML3527.8 (ebook) | DDC 782.4216492/52—dc23/eng/20241223
LC record available at https://lccn.loc.gov/2024056919
LC ebook record available at https://lccn.loc.gov/2024056920

doi:10.7560/332672

CONTENTS

FOREWORD

FLIPPING THE PRISM ON THE MYTHOLOGY OF PARLIAMENT-FUNKADELIC

AYANA CONTRERAS

Eight years old and sitting cross-legged on the beige carpet of my grandmother's light-flooded living room, I sat with a small triangular prism in hand. Each angle exposed a new facet, and each facet produced a new ray of light against the pink walls and beige carpet. I think of this moment often when reconsidering what we collectively consider to be part of a variety of cultural canons that feel well established. What if we were to flip the prism to what we think we know about Parliament-Funkadelic, for instance?

George Clinton was a keynote speaker at the University of Southern California Thornton School of Music's 2024 Pop Conference. The conversation, titled "A Little Light Under the Sun: The Unstoppable Funky Genius and Cosmic Legacy of George Clinton," was quite timely, bearing in mind the 2024 tenth-anniversary revamped pressing of the 2014 book *George Clinton & the Cosmic Odyssey of the P-Funk Empire* by Kris Needs and word of an upcoming George Clinton documentary written by Ishmael Reed. In January 2024, Clinton even received a star on the Hollywood Walk of Fame. Additionally, Clinton was rightfully credited in a panel description by 2024 PopCon organizers as a "Grammy winner and Rock & Roll Hall of Fame inductee."

And yet (in perhaps characteristically funky dissonance), there was also a panel at the conference organized by Melissa A. Weber called "A Seat at the (Mother)Ship: The Reclamation of Women's Stories in Parliament-Funkadelic." Participants in the panel included P-Funk office manager Brenda Adams-Pierce, Lynn Mabry of The Brides of Funkenstein, P-Funk road manager Cheryl James, and *Mothership Connected* author Seth Neblett. The panel, which centered on the legacies of female members of P-Funk (none of whom were inducted into the Rock & Roll Hall of Fame in 1997 alongside their male Parliament-Funkadelic counterparts), put a fine point on the fact that this book is a necessary tool to flip the prism of P-Funk.

In the beginning, George Clinton was unassailably cast as the center of Parliament-Funkadelic: the charismatic cult leader of P-Funk, so sayeth the original mythology that introduced us to characters including Sir Nose D'voidoffunk (a.k.a. Sir Placebo), Rumpofsteelskin, Dr. Funkenstein, and the Starchild by means of lyrics and liner notes. In an April 1980 *Ebony* magazine profile of the songwriters and producers behind R&B's biggest acts, called "Unknown Millionaires of the Music World," Clinton was listed among luminary songwriting teams such as Philadelphia International's Gamble & Huff, Ashford & Simpson, and Motown's Holland-Dozier-Holland. Even though Clinton is nearly always listed as a cowriter of classic P-Funk recordings alongside the usual co-conspirators: bandmembers Fuzzy Haskins, Bootsy Collins, Bernie Worrell, Garry Shider, Eddie Hazel (who sometimes was credited using his mother's name, Grace Cook), perhaps tellingly, Clinton was listed alone in the *Ebony* piece, described as "the mastermind behind the Parliament-Funkadelic conglomerate that includes eleven acts." No other member of P-Funk was listed by name.

Eventually, the legends of individual players, from Hazel to Worrell, began to surface. Knowledge around the legacies of P-Funk's constellation of creatives was hastened by a succession of mid-nineties vault releases, such as *George Clinton's Family Series*, as well as via nascent internet chat rooms. But the trail was always clearer toward discovering the contributions of male members of the P-Funk All-Stars than those of the female persuasion. The Western convention of women taking their spouse's last name sometimes obscures the track toward finding their place in history, but in the case of Parliament-Funkadelic, their very identities, let alone their foundational roles, were, for the most part, initially omitted in the foundational mythmaking. Much of the previously published journalism detailing the P-Funk constellation continues to omit female perspectives.

WaxPoetics, the well-respected, decades-old cratedigger's magazine, dedicated its August/September 2006 issue to unpacking the myth of Parliament-Funkadelic. For the issue, they interviewed Clinton, Worrell, Bootsy Collins, Garry Shider, Billy "Bass" Nelson, cover artist Pedro Bell, Overton Loyd, Grady Thomas, Calvin Simon, and Fuzzy Haskins. One hundred pages of coverage, and not one woman profiled, merely mentioned.

Mothership Connected thankfully weaves together the narratives of these women, from members of The Brides of Funkenstein (founded by Lynn Mabry and Dawn Silva, defectors from Sly Stone's mid-seventies organization), to the ladies of Parlet: a more direct offshoot of Parliament that initially counted Debbie Wright, Jeanette Washington, and (Neblett's own mother) Mallia Franklin as members. The first female-led P-Funk project was Parlet's 1978 debut, *Pleasure Principle*. But before the release of that recording (and arguably after), femme energy was both conjured up and yet suppressed within the Parliament-Funkadelic subculture that masqueraded as being unequivocally progressive. Paradoxically, in P-Funk mythology, the Mothership is the source of everything, and yet the flesh-and-bone mothers were consistently miscast as intergalactic sex objects.

Upon examination of physical copies of Parliament-Funkadelic's early recorded output, a bevy of women more often than not graced the covers: as a psychedelic kaleidoscopic fever dream on the *Funkadelic* debut (1970); with hands outstretched skyward on the front and apropos uncovered ass gracing the flip of the gatefold sleeve on *Free Your Mind . . . and Your Ass Will Follow* (1970); screaming and buried in dirt on *Maggot Brain* (1971); and as a freaky Pedro Bell–penned hybrid-android nude complete with a control knob in place of her nipple on *Cosmic Slop* (1973). The cover models were rendered anonymous icons, uncredited in the liner notes.

The woman on the covers of both the debut self-titled *Funkadelic* album and *Maggot Brain* was fashion model Barbara Cheeseborough, who also graced the covers of *Essence* and *Harper's Bazaar* back in the day, but the model on *Free Your Mind* is debated. Even Parliament's 1974 album *Up for the Down Stroke* features George Clinton tripping the galactic light fantastically surrounded by three uncredited women. Women's voices played a pivotal role in the sound of the recording, and yet, though the cover image could be mistaken for a coed band, unfortunately not one woman is named on liner notes printed on the original record sleeves, be it model or vocalist, with the exception of Cathy Abel, the artist who illustrated the poster enclosed in original LPs of 1972's *America Eats Its Young*.

Despite their invisibility, female vocalists played an indelible role in the sonic character of the P-Funk sound as far back as the self-titled *Funkadelic* album, providing sweet and salty texture to tracks like "Mommy, What's a Funkadelic?" and "Good Old Music," and on cuts such as "Livin' the Life" on Parliament's debut album *Osmium* (1970), and the single "Breakdown" (1971), which was originally 45 rpm only. The signature, slightly acid background style is also evidenced on the 1960s sides by The Parliaments, the precursor male vocal group–centered configuration of the Parliament concept. For the record, the sound can even be traced back to some of George Clinton's earliest songwriting credits, such as on the marginally macabre track "Hold On," recorded by Ernie Harris in 1964. Harris, a consistent Clinton collaborator, later cowrote dozens of P-Funk–related tracks such as "The Goose That Laid a Golden Egg" for The Parliaments in 1968 and 1971's "Can You Get to That" for Funkadelic. In the case of "Hold On," the ladies' voices are foregrounded in the mix, weeping and wailing in a fashion that is antithetical to the prevailing tertiary manner in which R&B background vocalists were utilized at the time.

Among the women on record for the earliest true Parliament-Funkadelic recordings were sisters Pat and Diane Lewis, who, in addition to having their own respective solo careers dating back to the mid-1960s, were well-respected, prolific background recording artists on the Detroit scene. They provided vital harmonic flavor to Isaac Hayes's solo breakthrough, *Hot Buttered Soul* (1969). The Lewis sisters ultimately formed Hayes's backup ensemble, Hot, Buttered & Soul (with Rose Williams), and worked extensively with the arranger Dale Warren during this time. Though Pat Lewis, in particular, was credited for vocal arrangements as early as 1970 on Hayes's *The Isaac Hayes Movement* album (aligning with the then-contemporary industry trend for more robust liner notes on popular music) and had worked with Clinton dating back to the mid-sixties Parliament days, usually uncredited.

Likewise, Mallia Franklin and Debbie Wright (interviewed extensively in *Mothership Connected*) also participated in the recording of P-Funk material as early as 1970, according to Debbie Wright's interviews with Neblett, though femme backing vocalists weren't credited on a Parliament-Funkadelic album's liner notes until 1975's *Mothership Connection*. In reality, Franklin and Wright were merely acknowledged under a "Special Thanks" designation on the *Chocolate City* album, released earlier that year.

The evolution of women from anonymous contributors to credited members of the band, according to *Mothership Connected*, was precipitated by the Mothership Connection concert tour (also known as the P-Funk Earth Tour) of 1976–1977: It was decided by Clinton that their voices were too much a part of the sound to be omitted in live performance, while their looks would enhance the band's stage presence. Additionally, *Mothership Connected* does an extraordinary job of flipping the prism, if you will, on the recording process of the classic era of P-Funk (arguably 1970 through 1982) but centers on in-depth accounts of the conditions behind the making of the two Brides of Funkenstein albums: *Funk or Walk* (1978) and *Never Buy Texas from a Cowboy* (1979). Also discussed at length are the stories behind the three albums released by Parlet: 1978's *Pleasure Principle*, 1979's *Invasion of the Booty Snatchers* (on which Shirley Hayden replaced Debbie Wright), and 1980's *Play Me or Trade Me*. The book also delves deep into the 1960s sharkskin-suit-and-patent-leather mid-sixties era of The Parliaments from a fresh vantage point (primarily Mallia Franklin's), the acid-drenched early psychedelic late-sixties and early seventies period, the carnal, funky cocaine-fueled glory years, and the murky, freebase-devastated era of the early 1980s. All along the way, female voices and narratives are centered, with the city of Detroit serving as a tributary character.

But beyond the musical and aesthetic contributions of female members of Parliament-Funkadelic, this book hammers home the unique alchemic contributions of Mallia Franklin. In addition to providing years of backing vocals, lead vocals in the initial configuration of Parlet, and sustenance and lodging for a variety of members of the band (including George Clinton and his then-fiancée, Liz Bishop, during the early years of Funkadelic), she provided her knack for connection that could be considered to be a very high level of A&R work. Through multiple narrators, we learn that Mallia played a crucial role in bringing Junie Morrison and Bootsy Collins to George Clinton. Bootsy's band, the House Guests, along with his time working with James Brown, opened the P-Funk portal for Philippé Wynne—formerly a House Guest member and later a vocalist with The Spinners—as well as horn players Maceo Parker and Fred Wesley to join Parliament-Funkadelic. This chain reaction of essential band members in the seventies can be traced back to Mallia Franklin's initial introductions. In *Mothership Connected*, Bootsy's Rubber Band drummer Frankie "Kash" Waddy concedes, "Mallia has always been a connoisseur of good, funky people. I always give women credit for being processors. Mallia had a plan in her mind before any of us." That knack was proven invaluable again and again as a means to refresh the Parliament-Funkadelic sound with new levels of funkiness.

This book contributes mightily to expanding the lore of P-Funk, dramatically rendering the women of the organization in glowing color, flipping the prism to present diverse perspectives of the story. To that end, what's particularly compelling is how the respective recollections of the interviewees tapped for *Mothership Connected* stand in conversation (and sometimes, in conflict) with one another. But more than anything, the book succeeds in humanizing the funk gods, more fully rendering the goddesses, and drawing attention to their mortality and frailties, all while drawing our eyes to fresh facets of the ever-evolving P-Funk mythology.

MOTHERSHIP CONNECTED

PROLOGUE

ABDUCTED BY THE MOTHERSHIP

JANUARY 1978

It was a snowy night in Detroit, Michigan, when Parliament-Funkadelic, on the Funkentelechy, or Flash Light, Tour, made its way to the Motor City. My grandmother, Sarah Christine, held my hand as I stood rambunctiously in my little shirt and bow tie, ascending a ritzy hotel elevator. I was six years old and on my way to see Mallia Franklin—my mother, or "Mommy," as I called her back then. The elevator door parted, and I ran like a charging bull to get my arms around this woman who had become a long-lost love over my few years on Earth. She was gone mostly, moving to Los Angeles from her hometown of Detroit in 1974 to pursue her dream as a professional singer and leaving me, aged three, to be raised by my grandparents. She moved back to Detroit in 1977 to record her first album as a member of the Parliament-Funkadelic girl group Parlet. About four months after recording the Parlet album, she was gone again on tour as a part of the P-Funk caravan.

Mom was very emotional as she flung open the hotel suite's door. She showered me with kisses and hugs, saying, "My Bip Bip!," which she used to call me. High heels were strewn across her bed, outfits made of silk, fur, and leather spilling out of a suitcase, and tons of Parliament-Funkadelic goodies she'd rounded up for me during her travels. P-Funk was a brand, and their concert merchandise was really cool. Small plastic mini guns that shot little light strobes, glowing sabers, posters, and T-shirts waited for me.

The room got cramped as members of the P-Funk organization came by to say hello to my grandmother and me. Grandma was always like a matriarch to many of the guys, and they had serious respect for her. George Clinton, the ringleader of this musical circus, finally entered the room to say hi to "Moms," as he called her. One of the managers, Archie Ivy, was behind him, carrying a cardboard box. He set it on the table and tore it open. The box was filled with the first promotional copies of Parlet's debut album, *Pleasure Principle*. Mom yanked up the hotel phone. "Get down here! George brought our album." Debbie and Jeanette, the other two-thirds of Parlet, arrived moments later. Debbie, whom I had known all my life, hugged me as Jeanette pulled an album out of the box. She scoffed and said, "This don't look like none of us. And look how skinny they made Mallia!" In real life, Mom was built like Mae West. She was all hips, booty, boobs, and hair, with a small waist. When word spread around the hotel that the first copies of the Parlet album were in her room, it became a revolving door, with P-Funk members trying to get theirs.

About an hour later, P-Funk packed up and boarded their tour bus, coined "the Mothership," to the venue where they would perform that night. Grandma and I followed in her big orange Lincoln Continental, christened "The Stinkin' Lincoln" by the band. Almost everybody in P-Funk had been in The Stinkin' Lincoln at one time or another. We arrived at Cobo Arena, the Detroit waterfront's mammoth circular centerpiece that faced Canada, separated only by the Detroit River's choppy waters. I met Mom at the bottom when she descended the tour bus stairs. She peeled back a small badge that read "All-Access Pass" and slapped it on my shirt. We walked hand in hand through the backstage door to the dressing room marked "P-Funk Girls." I walked in, and everything was shiny: the costumes, the shoes . . . everything. I was immediately bombarded with hugs and kisses from my new P-Funk aunties, Lynn Mabry and Dawn Silva, the duo known as The Brides of Funkenstein. Music from the opening acts filled the echoing air, and marijuana and musk incense created a low fog under the dressing room's fluorescent light. The pungent fragrance and traces of expensive perfumes permeated my small nostrils. The mood was joyous as the ladies drank a hearty red wine and passed around a fat joint.

The tabletop was scattered with makeup, cassette tapes, money, a pill or two, hotel keys, jewelry, and the residue of a few lines of cocaine inhaled moments prior.

They discarded their coats and street clothes, relegating them to chairs, hangers, and garment bags, and slipped into their work uniforms—fishnet stockings, spandex bodysuits, silver bikinis, foxtails, and silver thigh-high boots. It was like watching superheroines preparing for battle, with wild manes of hair and long, intricate braids that reminded me of strands of onyx licorice. Their faces of different hues doubled as canvasses for shades of red, gold, silver, and little jewels of various colors. Crew and band members knocked on the large dressing room door to get some time with them before taking the stage.

Finally, a burly guy came in and announced, "Showtime, girls!" I followed behind my mother as the women were ushered through the echoing hallways. Their stilettos clicked on the stadium corridors' cement floor like a brood of stallions down a main city street as security guys with flashlights cleared pathways to the side steps of the stage.

My grandmother came up behind me to escort me to my seat in the audience. Mom kissed me goodbye, and I was on my way to the stadium filled with fifteen thousand strong. The arena went black before we reached our seats and erupted in screams. Instantly, light sabers purchased at the concession stands illuminated the sea of darkness. I had never experienced anything like this before. It was scary and exhilarating at the same time.

A large movie screen came down, and a cartoon started to play. It chronicled the story of Parliament's latest album, *Funkentelechy vs. the Placebo Syndrome*, and the interplanetary battle between Star Child and Sir Nose D'voidoffunk. The cartoon ended, the drummer counted off, and I felt the bass drum beat in my chest. The crowd thundered at the first beat through the massive amplifiers in the packed arena. After a chaotic prism of lights, flash bombs, and smoke, the horde of women made their way to the edge of the stage. The flock of beautiful creatures walked to the microphones and sang, "When you've taken every kind of pill . . . nothing seems to ever cure your ills." The crowd knew every word and chanted along. I couldn't see much, as height was a challenge for a six-year-old, but I caught glimpses through the transitional sways of the crowd.

"Can you see your mommy?" my grandmother asked.

"No!" I replied.

My grandmother lifted me and stood me on the back of the seat in front. "There she is!" In total wonderment, I saw my mom, Mallia, and my aunts, Lynn, Dawn, Debbie, and Jeanette. They all looked like angels in silver and black, blurred in white light. They sang and danced as their leader, George Clinton, appeared in a big, puffy Rolls Royce.

Moments later, Garry Shider flew above the awestruck crowd, shooting a giant laser gun. The vocalists started singing the hymn about an hour into the funk music extravaganza, "Swing down, sweet chariot, stop, and let me ride." One of the band's lead male singers, Glenn Goins, gave a spirit-filled emotional testimony of the coming of the Mothership. The audience heard a growl from above, and their roar reached a thunderous peak as a massive silver spaceship descended from the rafters.

The marriage of excited screams and the vibration of the ship's huge exhaust pipes filled the belly of the arena. Dry ice and lights created a glowing fog as thousands of fans clapped, pointed, and yelled, "I see it! I see the Mothership!" Onstage, the singers and musicians threw up their hands in worship as a tornado of smoke revealed the infamous Dr. Funkenstein—at the top of the ship's staircase. Dressed like an intergalactic pimp in a floor-length white mink coat, matching bebop hat, and long black wig, the doctor—George Clinton—strolled down the steps of the space chariot as fans yelled in sheer exhilaration.

To millions of Funkateers, this event was as holy as the Second Coming. Funkateers, or "Maggots," are to Clinton and Parliament-Funkadelic what the KISS Army is to the rock group KISS, or Deadheads are to the Grateful Dead. The enormous silver Mothership ascended to the rafters, and my little mind was blown as I realized my mother did this for a living.

After the show was over, we went back to the dressing room. Mom changed out of her costume and into her "ordinary" clothes. For P-Funk, ordinary was not ordinary at all, just a bit less outrageous. With burgundy platform boots, feathers in her hair, and a beige-and-white mink coat with a fluffy white fox collar, we hit the corridors of the arena. A pocket of Funkateers backstage mobbed my mom with requests for autographs and photos. I was confused and a bit protective.

I looked at my grandmother and asked, "Why do all these people want pictures with my mommy?!"

One of the fans waiting their turn answered, "Because she's a star."

I wasn't quite sure what a *star* was, other than those in the sky, but it was apparent that it was something important and extraordinary. After the last photo was taken, my mom grabbed my hand, and we walked toward the tour bus.

I looked up at her, flashed a big, proud smile, and said, "You're a star! But you're my mommy, too, and I love you."

That brutally cold night in Detroit changed my life forever; this was the first time I saw my mother with totally different eyes. P-Funk had been a part of my life since birth. I had a front-row seat to the music, pageantry, love, drugs, dys-funk-tion, and chaos of the world of P-Funk. Some things I witnessed firsthand, some peripherally, and others through conversations with the people involved. P-Funk, from my point of view, was a collection of episodes. Some were beautiful, and some were not so much. It was a combination of joy and pain, excitement and disappointment, fame and failure.

P-Funk's larger-than-life leader, George Clinton, is very different from the rainbow-haired, platform-wearing, bizarre freak of nature the masses consider him. I know him as a mortal. To me, it's Uncle George who gave me a spare twenty dollars for my birthday. Back then, George would take vows that he wouldn't bathe until a particular song or album was complete, so the funk would be powerful. On my eighth birthday, he dropped that twenty-dollar bill on the floor by his bare feet, and I had to pick it up by that stinky foot. That was too much funk for my eight-year-old nose to handle. I can still conjure that smell up in my mind today.

P-Funk was a group of men and women who laughed, loved, created, binged, purged, starved, and believed as one in "The One," the extra-hard thump of the bass and simultaneous crash of the cymbal at the beginning of every bar that holds the funk together and allows it to spread universally. As the years passed, members disappeared and reappeared at different junctures in their lives. Some members moved on with their careers; some left the organization feeling unfulfilled or betrayed by the movement they gave so much to. Some left only to return to what they had known for so long. A few simply refused to go, patiently waiting. Many today are still chasing their piece of the funk. It leaves people to wonder:

What was ultimately the payoff?

Was it the feeling of love and community?

Was it the promise of fame and fortune?

Was it to be a part of a musical and cultural phenomenon?

I think it was a combination of all those things—and more.

Parliament-Funkadelic was more than just a hit-making group of musicians and singers; in many ways, P-Funk was like a musical-spiritual cult. Almost every member, past and present, would say an element of spirituality and cultlike mentality flows through the organization and its music. Whatever your job was, you were and will forever be a member of Parliament-Funkadelic, no matter how hard you try to shake it or leave it behind. Dr. Funkenstein is the prophet, the Mothership is the spiritual symbol, and the funk is the Almighty. Funkenstein's creations in the form of musical clones were idolized as prominent immortals with degrees of power based on their P-Funk Holy Grail positions.

Uncle George has given up the multicolored hair and cartoon bed sheets for a cleaner look. He married the much younger Carlon Thompson, who inspired him to clean up his act, literally and figuratively, and leave hard drugs behind, for the years of rock and roll living were taking their toll on his body. Fronting a younger version of P-Funk comprised of children, grandchildren, and a smattering of members from the group's heyday, George announced his retirement in 2022 but continues to perform.

The female members of Parliament-Funkadelic, who composed The Brides of Funkenstein and Parlet, were, along with Bootsy Collins, the most successful groups to come out of the P-Funk Empire. The women sang and contributed to all the organization's in-house projects. P-Funk positioned itself to take over radios, stages, and psyches like a plague of rhythmic infections. The group's messages of archaeology, politics, science fiction, and unadulterated humor and freedom were successful. In an era of sex, drugs, rock and roll, detouring through disco, and cresting on punk and new wave of the eighties, this critical "female" piece of the music history puzzle is as important as any other. Possibly the greatest female story of funk and rock that you've never heard . . . until now.

This book chronicles five women's personal journeys, told in their own words. They are my mother, Mallia Franklin; Debbie Wright and Shirley Hayden of Parlet; and original Brides of Funkenstein members Dawn Silva and Lynn Mabry. They reveal their stories of survival, how they got there and made it through, what it took to be a woman out front in the music industry at a time when misogyny was the expectation, how they handled being a star, a sex object, a powerhouse, a puppet, an abuser, but also the abused, a woman but still a girl. Their stories, which can finally be told, are compelling and complex.

Everyone who lent their voice to this book has their own "truth" and experience, including me, as a product of Parliament-Funkadelic. But as the writer, I am not here to decipher what is real and what is not. My job is

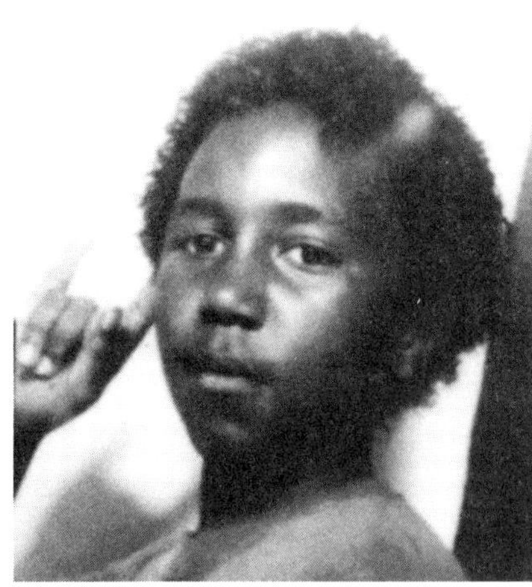

Author Seth Neblett "giving up the funk" at nine years old, in 1980.

to take the reader's hand and guide them through this incredible journey of funk, fame, failure, and survival through recollections of those involved.

As a person who didn't consider himself an author, I had no intention of being the writer of this book. I wrote this book out of necessity. This process started as a possible documentary with notable director Paul Justman in 2003, who was riding on the success of his 2002 film called *Standing in the Shadows of Motown*. He was a novice at best in Parliament-Funkadelic, outside of George Clinton and Bootsy Collins (who appeared in his *Motown* film). I knew the importance of the women of P-Funk and their impact on the group's sound, vision, and popularity overall because I witnessed it. After our first meeting, Justman knew there was something special about these stories. He said, "Everybody may not get the funk, and some don't know the music. But these ladies' personal stories are universally relatable." After meeting with various film companies, Paul said in 2004, "Seth, the only way we can get a documentary sold is if you have a book." From that point, a book was the new focus, but it was plagued with many false starts.

In 2006, after relocating to Los Angeles from Detroit, I aired my gripes about wrong authors, missed opportunities, and this frustrating book process over dinner with my mom (Mallia) and my godfather, Bootsy Collins. Surprisingly, Uncle Bootsy looked at me and said, "Why don't you write it? You know the story. You would know what's real and what's not. You're the one!" With my mother nodding in agreement, I pushed forward as the writer. I took on such a task because the story was essential to me personally. I have often felt that I was one of many sacrifices on this journey. I also knew that this story would be relevant to millions of fans and, hopefully, the masses at large when they discover the hope, love, despair, and, in some cases, the beauty of this remarkable testament of music and survival.

Over the years, I'd done a few interviews with my mom and a few of the other women for various projects, but I began conducting interviews for this book in 2006. I started with the women: Mallia, Shirley, Dawn, Debbie, Lynn, and their road manager and confidante Cheryl James. I then contacted the necessary people to provide insight into these women's stories to convey them in a balanced, multifaceted, and honest way. What culminated was a collection of memories, opinions, and commentary on the women's journeys, and ultimately, the P-Funk history as a whole, from the women themselves; the group's creator, producer, and Svengali, George Clinton (interviewed in 2007–2009); and songwriters, musicians, and producers William "Bootsy" Collins (2010), Bernie Worrell (2007), Ron Dunbar (2014–2016), Ron Ford (2007), Garry Shider (2008–2009), Donnie Sterling (2013), Gary "Mudbone" Cooper (2014), Ted Currier (2018), and Sly Stone (2008). I spoke to some of P-Funk's most influential contributors, Frankie "Kash" Waddy (2009), Gary Hudgins (2019), Gordon Carlton (2009), Starr Cullars (2021), Belita Woods (2009), Linda Shider (2007), DeWayne "Blackbyrd" McKnight (2010), and Jerome Ali (2018). I interviewed people on the business side of P-Funk, publicist Tom Vickers (2016); record promoter Henry Mayers (2021); and office staff and road managers at Clinton's production company, Thang Incorporated: Ron Brembry (2010), Bruce Peterson (2019), Andrea "Andi" Thomas (2009), Brenda Adams-Pierce (2014), and Leslie "Blonda" Vocino (2013). Also, I spoke to former business manager Robert Mittleman (2014), Mallia Franklin's sister, Jenifer Franklin (2010), and George Clinton's former fiancée, Liz Bishop (2019).

I thank you all for sharing your stories about this "moment in time." It is invaluable. We have since lost some people who lovingly gave their memories and recollections to this book. Thank you for sharing your voices. I'm grateful that almost everyone I contacted was willing to contribute their good, bad, and indifferent memories to this story. Some P-Funk members declined to participate for their own reasons. I respect their decision and love them no less, as they are and will always be part of my dys-funk-tional P-Funk family and this story.

To a child who grew up in the world of P-Funk, a line from one of their greatest hits, "One Nation Under a Groove," sums up the Parliament-Funkadelic experience best, as it is a pledge of undying allegiance.

"Do you promise to funk, the whole funk, and nothing but the funk?"

CHAPTER 1

AMERICA EATS ITS YOUNG

What is funk? Depending on your dictionary, "funk" is everything from a person's mood to the stench of sex. Ironically, Parliament-Funkadelic and its music are a kaleidoscope of every definition of funk. Its songs, cover art, and stage shows have always been layered with messages of sex, silliness, drugs, rebellion, politics, and partying. For music fans, funk is a genre many know, but only a select number of listeners have dared to dwell in. Funk is and has always been an acquired taste, and the history of funk is much more complicated than the roots of rock and roll or punk. Like all genres, various artists have touched on funk over different musical landscapes, with Parliament-Funkadelic hailed as the funkiest of all time. Any successful writer, producer, musician, and music lover who has ever been questioned, "Who are the funkiest artists ever?" would unequivocally respond, "Parliament-Funkadelic."

Most music historians affirm that funk started with the Godfather of Soul, James Brown. He cultivated the most crucial ingredient in funk music—"The One." The collaboration of sanctified gospel vocals, African beats, and bass thumping became the main ingredients of modern funk music. James Brown built the foundation. He planted the seeds of funk. Sly Stone pollinated popular music with the sound, but George Clinton

Rosalind Mallia Franklin at the age of thirteen in Detroit (1965).

and Parliament-Funkadelic watered the seeds, watched them grow, and took funk higher than ever. They evolved the musical harvest of "funk," as we now know it, and grew Parliament-Funkadelic into the biggest (literally) and most popular funk group in music history. As the Godfather of Funk, George Clinton's story is widely chronicled in media, magazines, documentaries, and his memoir, *Brothas Be, Yo Like George, Ain't That Funkin' Kinda Hard on You?* To understand the journey of the women of the P-Funk collective, Parlet and The Brides of Funkenstein, some knowledge and history of the group and its leader is required.

The success of Parliament-Funkadelic undoubtedly began with George Clinton. He has strategically been the group's focus for the past sixty years. The musical and social phenomenon known as P-Funk started innocently enough as a doo-wop quintet known as The Parliaments (named after the popular cigarette brand) in 1956. Born on July 22, 1941, George, a singer and budding songwriter who originally hailed from Kannapolis, North Carolina, formed the group in Plainfield, New Jersey. Clinton says he was born in an outhouse when his mother thought she had to use the bathroom, lending to the legend of his funky beginnings. Inspired to sing by Frankie Lymon and the Teenagers, Clinton worked in a barbershop, where he cut hair in the front room, allegedly sold drugs out of the back door, and quaffed the crowns of many popular soul singers like Jackie Wilson, Otis Redding, and The Fiestas. By the sixties, George ended up in Detroit, Michigan, after years of writing songs, personnel changes in The Parliaments, small record deals, and unproductive starts.

Also known as the "Motor City," Detroit is a metropolis built on the automobile industry's back. Detroit was one of the first cities where the government expanded fair housing and jobs for all races. Assembly plants were a critical reason so many people of color migrated to the Midwest from the South in the forties. By 1965, the Motown Records phenomenon became as important to the city's identity as the cars that made it famous. It was just a walk for the city's youth or, at most, a bus ride to the steps of the studio and offices of Hitsville, USA, on West Grand Boulevard. Motown Records and its artists were the most important musical movement in the country. The Supremes, The Temptations, and Smokey Robinson made many Black teenagers' dreams of success in popular music more than just a fantasy. The Motor City symbolized a place of Black prosperity.

George Clinton and the other members of The Parliaments (Clarence "Fuzzy" Haskins, Ray Davis, Calvin Simon, and Grady Thomas) came from New Jersey to audition at Motown. They signed a five-year contract with the label. As soon as the ink dried, the label said The Parliaments' style was too similar to The Temptations but not as polished. The label put The Parliaments on the shelf and released no music from the group. Clinton worked as a songwriter with Motown, but the position was not as fruitful as he had hoped. He soon parted ways with Motown and got The Parliaments a new record deal on a local Detroit label, Revilot Records. In 1967, The Parliaments' single "(I Wanna) Testify" hit the top five on the Billboard Soul charts. At that point, Berry Gordy sued Revilot for using The Parliaments' name because the group was still under their five-year term with Motown. Not threatened by Motown's legal actions, Clinton and The Parliaments continued to perform their hit record in the Midwest.

One of those performances was on a chilly night in late 1967 in Detroit. One of the most prominent Black sororities, Delta Sigma Theta, hosted its annual Jabberwock fashion show. This event was one of the most significant social outings of the year. The legendary Masonic Temple auditorium was filled to the rafters with the city's Black elite. The audience applauded in the theater, which was adorned with long, red velvet drapes and gold columns, as beautifully dressed models of every shade paraded down the aisles from the theater's rear. Detroit's jewel was Motown Records, and their biggest stars like Mary Wells, Marvin Gaye, and Martha Reeves & The Vandellas occupied most of the front row because Berry Gordy always wanted his acts to be pictured at these black-tie affairs in the newspapers.

That night at the Masonic Temple was also the beginning of a relationship that would forever change the direction of funk and music history when fifteen-year-old Mallia Franklin introduced herself to the evening's entertainment.

MALLIA FRANKLIN Joyce Thomas was the best friend of my parents, Godfrey and Sarah Franklin, and vice president of the Detroit chapter of Delta Sigma Theta. The Deltas were among the country's most influential Black sororities. My dad was an elite. That's why I pledged to be a Del Sprite, little sisters to the Deltas. We were going to debutante balls and those kinds of affairs. My sister was one of the models that night at Masonic.

Joyce hired a doo-wop group as the event's entertainment. Halfway through the affair, the emcee approached the microphone and said, "Ladies and gentlemen, put your hands together for The Parliaments!" A host of singers took the stage in bright orange sharkskin suits with oceans of processed waves crowning their heads. They were a typical male singing group like The Temptations or the Four Tops. "(I Wanna) Testify" was their hit single.

My sister and I stood on the side of the stage and watched The Parliaments perform. My eyes gravitated to a tall, fair-skinned young woman standing behind the curtain. She looked like she could have been our sister. I walked up to her and introduced myself.

"Hi, I'm Mallia Franklin."

She extended her hand and replied, "Hi, my name is Liz Bishop."

Liz was from Buffalo, New York, and was the girlfriend of the group's leader, George Clinton. She was stunning, tall, and well dressed, with long, wavy hair and a big floppy hat. She was beautiful, with a beautiful spirit to match. Liz introduced us to George. And George introduced us to the rest of The Parliaments, Grady Thomas, Ray Davis, and Fuzzy Haskins. The fifth Parliament, Calvin Simon, was in the Army and overseas fighting the Vietnam War. I met him when he returned to the States in 1969.

George Clinton then introduced me to their musicians, Billy "Bass" Nelson, Eddie Hazel, Tiki Fulwood, Tawl Ross, and Mickey Atkins. There were actually two Mickeys, a Black Mickey and a white Mickey. George said that if one Mickey couldn't do a gig, he could always call the other. That would be a philosophy George would live by for decades . . . always have a spare. The band members were younger than the singers in The Parliaments. They were teenagers, closer to my age. At that time, the band of musicians didn't have a name. They were just called "The Parliament band."

When my father, Godfrey, met George that night, he shook his hand

and said, "That's a good song, young man . . . but that's a loud suit you got on." My father said there was something special about The Parliaments, especially George.

LIZ BISHOP (GEORGE CLINTON'S EX-FIANCÉE) George and I got together in 1967 in Buffalo, New York. When I met him, I worked at a school for children with disabilities and moonlighted at a nightclub. The Parliaments came to the club . . . that's how we met. George and I got together, and I left Buffalo with him. Over time, my main contribution to George and his career was to inspire him and keep everything together while he pursued his dreams.

The Parliaments were traveling around to their gigs in a little van. Nobody had any money at the time. All we had was peanut butter and crackers to eat usually. They did shows here and there. Eventually, we ended up in Detroit so George and The Parliaments could further their careers as performers and recording artists at Motown.

GEORGE CLINTON Mallia was damn near a baby when we met her. She was young. She and her sister, Jenifer, were really *grown* to be as young as they were. They always hung out with us at the clubs and studio, and, eventually, Mallia started singing with us. I think Jenifer started seeing Billy Bass, and Mallia started dating our drummer, Tiki Fulwood. Most people don't know that Mallia is a damn good drummer. Tiki taught her everything he knew, and she had his drum lingo down.

MALLIA FRANKLIN We all connected instantly, and a special friendship blossomed between Liz, George, and my family. I had no idea that meeting this group of people would profoundly change my life.

I was born Rosalind Mallia Franklin in Detroit on "The One"—on March 1, 1952, to an interracial couple. My mother, Sarah Christine, a self-proclaimed hillbilly from the mountains of Tennessee, was a very smart and sensible woman. Losing both of her parents in a car crash at twelve years old, she was raised by her grandmother, then an aunt, until she graduated from high school. My mother was a mix of a Caucasian father and a white and Native American mother. She could have easily been a movie star with her dark, flowing hair, olive skin, and statuesque figure. Mom went to Bowling Green State University, where she got heavily involved in union organizing.

By age twenty-two, she was one of the first female union organizers in history. Mom was the international representative for the Office Workers Union. She organized the insurance agents, bank workers, engineers, clerical employees, social workers . . . every field in white-collar industries. She was the first woman president of their local union in Detroit, one of the first women on the Executive Board of International Unions, and the Congress of Industrial Organizations (CIO) executive board. Mom was the first national co-chair of the political action committee (PAC) of the CIO in 1944, working closely with the vice president of the United States, Henry Wallace, under President Franklin D. Roosevelt. Vice President Wallace created the first independent ticket . . . the Progressive Party. By thirty-five, Mom sat across conference tables, discussing union politics with the likes of Jimmy Hoffa.

In those days, you were considered a communist if you were liberal. Mom had a “red file” with the FBI for being suspected of communism. Agents did surveillance, especially on my mother’s ties to the union. The file was filled with pictures of us, surveillance notes on where we lived and went to school, and newspaper clippings on my mother. It was unbelievable how much information they had on my family, starting in the forties and continuing into the sixties. She was finally given her FBI red file in 1992. She wasn’t a communist, but Mom became so powerful in the unions and politics that Michigan Congressman John Conyers and UAW [United Auto Workers] Vice President Douglas Fraser were references on her résumé.

Mom cross-sectioned into blue collar, helping to unionize the automotive workers of the “Big Three” (Ford, Chrysler, and General Motors). That’s how she met my dad.

My father, Godfrey, was suave, charismatic, and extremely handsome. He was Black and Cuban. My father was one of the first appointed Black foundry supervisors for Ford Motor Company in Detroit when he met my mother, in 1948. My mother represented the United Auto Workers and came in as his superior. They spent many hours strategizing and organizing the workers. My father was married and had a son, Michael, from his first marriage and a second son out of wedlock, Jerry. His feelings for my mother were so overwhelming that he divorced his first wife to marry her in 1950. He lovingly referred to her as his “Beauty Box.”

The fact that such a powerful white woman married a Black man was almost unheard of back then. To most white people, she was just a “nigger lover.” My mother always said that in “White America’s” eyes, she was no longer a white woman when she married a Black man. She was never treated with the same respect. She was ostracized by most of her relatives when she married my father, all except an aunt and uncle. My mother told me many stories of expensive union galas they would attend in lavish hotels. The hotel would allow my mother to stay, but Dad had to stay in the run-down colored hotel across town. Mom would always attend those big union functions, beautiful and elegant, with her handsome Black husband on her arm. She never slept in those lavish hotels. She chose to stay at the colored hotels across town with him. "If he can't stay here, I *won't* stay here!" she said.

Rosa Parks became one of my mother's best friends after relocating to Detroit from Montgomery, Alabama, after being arrested on that life-changing day in 1955 for not giving up her seat on the bus. I was eleven years old when my family marched with Martin Luther King Jr. in June of 1963 at the Detroit Walk to Freedom that traveled down Woodward Avenue to Cobo Arena, a venue where I would grace the stage years later with P-Funk. We walked alongside the Queen of Soul, Aretha Franklin's father, Reverend C. L. Franklin, and Walter Reuther, a family friend and president of the UAW. Even today, it is still unbelievable that I was a part of that kind of history. MLK delivered a passionate speech after the march. It was a more detailed version of the "I Have a Dream" speech that Dr. King would deliver a few weeks later in Washington, DC.

As an interracial couple, my parents symbolized the Civil Rights Movement on the front lines. They hoped their daughters would be just as active. They didn't want me and my sister, Jenifer, to go through that . . . all that racial bullshit. [My half brother] Michael eventually joined the Nation of Islam, Muhammad Mosque Number One in Detroit.

Our parents gave my sister and me the best that life offered. We had beautiful clothes and went to the best schools. Our family took vacations all around the country, Canada, and Mexico. We were spoiled brats. I was, for sure. I knew early on that I would be a singer. And my parents knew it, too.

Growing up in Detroit in the sixties was like witnessing musical history. I listened to Black radio and watched the Motortown Revue shows at the Fox Theatre. My mother entered me into singing contests, and I won the WCHB Detroit Parks and Recreation talent show at twelve, singing Mary Wells's "My Guy." The first prize was a recording contract with Motown Records. Because of my age, my father declined the deal.

Although my father turned the Motown contract down, a singer-songwriter named Barrett Strong believed in my talent and became a mentor to me. Barrett was one of the first artists on Motown Records, and he had their first hit song, "Money (That's What I Want)." He and his

Mallia's mother, Sarah Christine Franklin (center), *and civil rights leader Rosa Parks* (right) *in 1978 in a Detroit newspaper.*

writing partner Norman Whitfield wrote iconic songs like "War," "I Heard It Through the Grapevine," "Cloud Nine," "Just My Imagination," and "Papa Was a Rolling Stone."

I was an alto-soprano, and my dad's dream was for me to become a concert pianist and opera singer. Ironically, my white mother was on the opposite side. She accepted and encouraged my choice of wanting to sing popular Black music. Although my mother was white, she was more accepting of certain aspects of the Black culture than my dad was. My mother had more faith and hope for the Black entertainment business than my father.

Dad loved all kinds of music. Classical, jazz, everything from Buffy Saint-Marie to Nancy Wilson. My mother liked country music. She liked Hank Williams, Roger Miller, Minnie Pearl, Loretta Lynn, Johnny Cash, and the Grand Ole Opry. My daddy was conservative in his lifestyle. He was considered bourgeoisie and always felt indifferent about that popular "Black music thing." He feared I would become a dope addict, a hoe, or a lush. Because in his generation, that's what he saw with Black female singers like Billie Holliday and Etta James. If my father had had more of an open mind about the fact that I wanted to sing Black music, it would have made a difference in my life. His thing was, "All niggas can dance and sing."

My parents moved to one of Detroit's much more influential neighborhoods. We lived on Oakman Boulevard, where all the houses were various colors of brown and red brick. We were on Oakman when the Detroit riots jumped off in 1967. Daddy had guns out, sitting in the living room with lights off. We were convinced that the rioters would come down Oakman and burn it to the ground.

I knew that my sister and I were different because we were mixed. My father called us "quadroons." A person with one-quarter Black ancestry. I was the girl who looked white but had the demeanor of a Black girl. I could flip over to any side that I wanted. But I chose to be what I was . . . me. I was dealing with all different classes of people in public school, and I got along with everyone, although my sister and I were considered well off by most. My parents sat us down to watch the 1959 film *Imitation of Life*, the story of a Black maid and her daughter who start working for a successful white actress. The maid's daughter, who appears white, does not want to be Black and passes as Caucasian until her mother shows up, unveiling her true race, to her embarrassment. My parents told us, "Girls . . . you never want to live like that. Don't deny any part of yourself." They knew that by being interracial, we would face these problems someday.

JENIFER FRANKLIN (MALLIA FRANKLIN'S SISTER) My sister and I had real identity issues being mixed race in the fifties. It was a real struggle to be accepted. We often went to extremes to prove we were "Black enough." Mallia was the beautiful one. The perfect mixed little girl with an olive complexion, dark eyes, long black hair, and perfect teeth, and all the little boys loved her. They cried for mercy when she sang and won her first talent show at Butler Park at twelve.

Our mother bought her a baby grand piano, paid for lessons she never wanted to take, and spent thousands on clothes and costumes. My mother wanted to send her to a private school, a Juilliard prep school. Our father disapproved of the money our mother was spending on my sister, and their marriage suffered because of it.

MALLIA FRANKLIN When I was fourteen, I met a prominent Detroit talent agent named Dick Scott. He was Berry Gordy's personal secretary and office manager at Motown. He had been Berry's right-hand man for years.

We met Dick through a family friend, Louise Tapps. Her husband, Shelton, was a union rep with Daddy. Louise did a lot of the makeup and hair for Motown. She had a huge beauty salon on Livernois Ave., a street that was called the "Avenue of Fashion." Louise did the wigs for the Supremes, Marvelettes, Martha Reeves & The Vandellas . . . all the Motown girls.

Dick believed in my talent, and by the time I was fifteen, I was doing matinee shows at prominent Detroit supper clubs like Menjo's. I'd usually work with a three-piece rhythm section, singing standards like "Misty," "Autumn Leaves," "Nature Boy," and "Alfie." Every standard there was. My parents loved Dick Scott because he saw much more for me than just R&B music. He saw me on Broadway . . . in movies . . . Dick was a visionary. In 1968, Dick wanted me to star in the first Detroit production of the musical *Hair* because he was also choosing talent for the Broadway adaptation and wanted to get me a starring role. That was the direction that my dad really wanted me to pursue. But I wasn't convinced, so I declined. No telling what my career would have become in hindsight.

By my teens, my parents enrolled me in an all-female boarding school in Pennsylvania. It was one of the best classical music conservatories in the country, and the expensive tuition included room and board. There were no Black faces on the entire campus when I was there, not even the cooks or custodians. It was very different from the environment that I was used to. I never hid the fact that I was Black. I played James Brown's "Say It Loud, I'm Black, and I'm Proud" all day as the girls peeped their heads in the door to see who was in my dorm room. I decorated my room with Black art and threw African dashiki prints over my bed. The first year at school wasn't bad. I generally got along with everyone. I had four or five good white girlfriends there. My roommate, JoAnne, also became a great friend. Because there was racism, she was bullied because she was Jewish. She asked the faculty if she could room with me because I had a four-student suite all to myself. Her request was granted. Having her there turned out to be a blessing for both of us.

A white-looking Black girl and a Jew were basically the same to our dorm mother. We were the school's misfits in her eyes, and I knew that she couldn't stand me. Our dorm mother looked like Mrs. Santa Claus. She was short, chubby, and her hair was snow-white in a bun, with little round glasses and the bluest of eyes, and I felt that she hated every Black drop of blood in my body. I would try to be nice and polite to her daily, but she was always strict and never looked me in the eye. I would cheerfully say "Hello" and ask her about her day. She would sternly respond, "Just keep walking, Rosalind." My presence was offensive to her. It wasn't the skin I was in, but it was what I represented. I was a mixing of the races. I wasn't one or the other. I wasn't just a "nigger." Passing as white? I never thought about it. To me, that was never an option. Everything about my identity was Black . . . my accent, singing voice, demeanor, and timing. In the school's one hundred and fifty year history, I think I was one of the first African American students—one of two—but I appeared as white as the students and faculty . . . and that was a first for them. I wasn't *obviously* Black.

The fact that I was mixed was a closely guarded secret by the school. I was oblivious but found out at the semester's first school dance. The girls were always shipped to the military and college affairs. So the boys would come to our dances from various military schools and college football teams. Boys were coming from Virginia and all the surrounding states. The dorm mother said, "Rosalind, now you just go ahead and dance . . . but don't tell them anything about you."

I didn't understand what that meant.

I didn't have a problem dancing with the white boys. They were the only option because Black boys weren't allowed at the dances. They jumped up and down, doing a dance called "The Frug." I was on the dance floor, doing all the latest dances from Detroit: the Philly Dog, the Jerk, the Mashed Potato, the Pony, and the Twine Time. I remember one of the white cadets dancing with me. He said, "Wow, you've got the moves. You dance like a Black girl!" When I innocently replied, "I *am* Black," he didn't want to dance with me anymore. Everyone wanted to dance with you if you were white and danced Black. But if you *were* Black, they didn't want anything to do with you. His face went flush. He turned around and walked off, leaving me on the dance floor. He went over to his buddies, and they started pointing, laughing, and mouthing the word "nigger." I was embarrassed and left the dance in tears. The dorm mother was angry. I wasn't supposed to say anything. It was too late; the secret was out.

I called my parents and told them what happened, and they hit the roof. Daddy called the dean that night and insisted on speaking with him. He told him I needed Black boys to dance with at any function from that night forward. He was not going to let his daughter be humiliated again. My dad's attitude was that I had to be a trailblazer. "You've got to show them that you are *better* than they think you are!" The school begrudgingly honored his request at the next dance, but there were never more than a handful of Black boys in attendance. They didn't really like this agreement because what my father was doing through me was integrating their dances and social functions. The faculty began seeing exactly what they didn't want to see: race mixing.

When the dorm mother reluctantly started inviting Black male teenagers to the dances for me to dance with, I danced all night. I wasn't leaning against the wall. I was sweating buckets, laughing, and having a blast. My Caucasian girlfriends started dancing with the Black male students. That wasn't supposed to happen. One of the girls, a pale blonde with a "Sassoon" haircut and blue eyes, fell hard for one of the Black students. A relationship developed. The girl would sneak out and go on dates with the male student. Eventually, she got caught, and the school blamed me. The girl's parents and the dorm mother said I was a troublemaker. THE DEAN CAME DOWN ON ME when I was alone at a private meeting. The parents of the girl were there . . . but not my parents. They made these decisions without talking to my father or mother. The girl and I were forbidden to speak and associate anymore . . . period! They eventually took her out of school.

When my parents found out about this private meeting, they went nuts. They were in Pennsylvania by the morning. My parents marched straight into the dean's office and told him they would have every civil rights leader they knew surrounding the school with picket signs within twenty-four hours. The dean refunded half of my tuition just to get my parents out of his office. My parents packed my bags, put me in the car, and I was on my way back to Detroit.

My parents refused to cower to racism, and I resentfully returned for the next semester, and it was more of the same. I felt real, unabashed prejudice. But I did take advantage of my free weekends. I would go to Buffalo, New York, to visit Liz Bishop's family, or sometimes I would go to Philadelphia and stay with Tiki Fulwood's [Parliament's drummer] family on Napa Street. Tiki was the drummer at the Uptown Theatre in their house band when he wasn't out with The Parliaments. When I returned to school, my roommate, JoAnne, wanted to hear every detail. She loved to listen to my stories about the music scene and nightlife.

During that second semester, another white female student got pregnant by a Black boy, and when it got out, the administration chastised me like it was my fault. The dorm mother said I was responsible for her having a "nigger baby." I was miserable, and my parents were consistently at odds with the administration. The school didn't pay any attention to what was happening. The country was changing. Many of the students were outwardly attempting to evolve with the times. But the school's faculty wanted nothing to do with it. As part of the MLK Civil Rights Movement,

George Clinton in the Apollo Theater dressing room in 1970.

my parents usually took a nonviolent approach to race issues. Their strategy toward racism was very different than my generation. We were drawn to Malcolm X and "by any means necessary." After two years of hell, I decided I was not going back, and I ensured they didn't want me to return either.

JENIFER FRANKLIN Mallia acted out to prove her "Blackness." By her teens, she started engaging in Black militant activity in Detroit. She threatened to bomb the private school in Pennsylvania and was expelled.

MALLIA FRANKLIN My parents felt they lost a lot of money, and my duty was to stay at that school and fight for my civil rights. Maybe it was, but I just wanted to sing a song, not change the world. The acts of blatant racism at that school damaged me so much that I tried to prove just how Black I was for the rest of my life. I WAS TOTALLY OUT OF CONTROL when I came home. I would sneak out of the house in my mother's cocktail dresses, heels, and furs and go to bars and fraternity parties.

I was enrolled at Chadsey High School in Detroit for my senior year. Being primarily Black was a stark contrast to what I had just experienced. But it was an environment I welcomed because I felt more in touch with my Black heritage. My biggest regret was that I dropped out and didn't graduate.

One night, my sister, Jenifer; my best friend in high school, Pat Greene; and I attended a Kappa Alpha Psi fraternity party. A few Kappas were hanging with the local chapter of the Black Panthers. There was a cross-culture in Detroit with young Black men who were either militant, building cars, or becoming doctors or lawyers. The Black Panthers crashed the party and took it over. They made us get on the floor, spitting their philosophy, trying to get new Panther recruits. I'm unsure how my mother found out, but I saw her standing in the doorway of the party. Because Mom was white, the Panther at the door wouldn't let her in. She opened her purse and pulled out a pearl-handled revolver. She pointed it between the guy's eyes. He immediately threw his hands in the air.

"Don't shoot!"

Mom said, "I just came for *mine!* Move out of the goddamn way!"

Waving the gun in the air, she screamed, "Mallia! Jenifer! Pat! Let's go!" We got off the floor, ran over to her, and walked out of the party. My mother would become the person who got me out of many tight spots for most of my life.

CHAPTER 2

FREE YOUR MIND . . . AND YOUR ASS WILL FOLLOW

By 1968, George Clinton and The Parliaments had a steady gig at the 20 Grand Nightclub. One of Detroit's most popular stages in the sixties and seventies, the large venue sat at the intersections of West Grand Boulevard and Woodward Avenue. The singers and band lived at the 20 Grand Motel next door. But with no steady income stream, George struggled to keep a roof over everyone's heads. The 20 Grand was one of the city's most famous venues. There was a bowling alley, a fireside lounge, and a large upper-floor hall called the Gold Room, where singers like Little Stevie Wonder, the Supremes, B. B. King, and Chuck Jackson would perform. One of the other regionally popular groups that often played at the 20 Grand was a Louisville, Kentucky, band called the Nite-Liters.

MALLIA FRANKLIN The Nite-Liters were a band brought in by Harvey Fuqua and his producing partner, Vernon Bullock. Harvey was a former member of the doo-wop group the Moonglows in the fifties. He was married to Berry Gordy's sister Gwen and worked for Motown. The Nite-Liters would become a band called New Birth in 1970. I met their drummer, Nathaniel "Nate" Neblett, or as the band called him, "Nebs." I was sixteen when I met Nate; he was twenty-three. Nate and I started dating, and my father was livid. My parents and I were already at odds about what happened in Pennsylvania, and now I was dating a grown-ass man. I was angry and rebellious and ran away from home to be with Nathaniel but returned shortly after with some coaxing from my mother.

My family moved into a larger six-bedroom home in a beautiful city called Highland Park, a small city within the city of Detroit. My parents both took positions with the mayor, Robert Blackwell. To help George Clinton keep a roof overhead, I asked my parents if George, Liz, and their baby, Barbarella, could live there until George got on his feet. Because of their fondness for George and Liz, they allowed it. My parents didn't ask for any rent. Their only request was for Liz to give them a hand around the house and watch over us when needed. They lived with us for about a year.

LIZ BISHOP George and I barely kept everything together when Mallia's parents offered us their home. We lived in an apartment over their garage. Our daughter, Barbarella, was only about a year old. The Franklins respected George's and my privacy as long as we respected their home. I loved Mallia's mother so much. I looked at her like she was my *own* mother. It's true; I did look like her daughters, Mallia and Jenifer, and she accepted and loved me like her own.

As the free love movement exploded in the late sixties, styles started to change. I was one of the first to really embrace that wild and funky hippie style, and I started dressing differently. Mallia used to tease me all the time about my outfits.

She would say, "Liz . . . you got see-through clothes on! Where did you get that from?"

She thought I had a lot of nerve to wear some of those outfits, but she also loved my confidence because she was coming into her own as a young woman. I had a transparent green jumpsuit that she loved and would always wear. Mallia was always different and funky, but I know I influenced her style. She was my little sister, and we loved each other like family.

By 1969, George and The Parliaments were making a change, musically and otherwise. I didn't understand this *new* psychedelic music they were creating. Everyone thought that I was *so* hip, but I was innocent. I smoked a little marijuana but wasn't into the acid and hard drugs like George had gotten into. He was a *lot* wilder than I was. The transformation from the doo-wop Parliaments to Funkadelic's psychedelic look and music happened while we lived with Mallia and her family.

MALLIA FRANKLIN The sharkskin suits were retired, and The Parliaments started tearing up jeans, buying stuff from thrift stores, and tie-dyeing their clothes. Liz couldn't have a crazy hat or cool outfit in the closet because George would take it and wear it onstage. She helped George a lot with his look back then. George started cutting stars and moonbeams in his hair, wearing dashikis to the floor, no shoes, and love beads. My parents didn't mind, but my father always made him wear shoes at the dinner table.

Mom tried to teach George things about finance. How to buy property and things like that. She helped him with financial institutions and taught him how to get through loopholes. My father taught him a lot about being a Black man in power and politics.

George had been in Detroit for a couple of years, but living with us took him to a new level. When a promoter or investor came to pick him up, he came out of a big house with an iron fence and two new Lincoln Continentals in the driveway. It made him appear a lot bigger than he was at that time. It looked prestigious, and I know it helped his image as an entertainer.

George, Liz, and I would go down to the 20 Grand Motel to take the guys in the band money. I always hung in Eddie Hazel, Billy "Bass" Nelson, and Tiki Fulwood's room. They would have two beds and a mattress on the floor.

The Parliaments' band of young musicians now had a name . . . it was Funkadelic [coined by bassist Billy "Bass" Nelson]. George and The Parliaments played catch-up with the psychedelic look and lifestyle because the younger guys in Funkadelic were already on that psychedelic-hippie path.

With issues still looming with Motown and the Parliament name, Funkadelic became the Parliament's alter ego. The 20 Grand became a testing ground for their new psychedelic look and sound. I was fortunate enough to witness this wild new approach . . . even George coming out naked under a sheet and shaking his penis in everybody's faces. They gained a reputation in Detroit and the surrounding cities as an innovative live act.

Black rock musicians like Sly and the Family Stone and Jimi Hendrix led the pack in music. All races accepted their progressive looks and sound and crossed racial lines. They were rock and roll stars as big as the Who or the Doors. George was more attracted to the rock and psychedelic bands coming out of the Detroit scene. Funkadelic's music and performance weren't mainstream, and by '70, they started gigging with groups like MC5 and Iggy and the Stooges. Those groups were the leaders of what would evolve into the punk movement. Funkadelic's sound wasn't just rock like Jimi Hendrix or crossover like Sly; it was a culmination of all influences.

I first recorded with George and Funkadelic at Golden World Recording Studio, where I met the owner, Ed Wingate, and his son, Charles. I also met Martha Reeves, Lois Reeves, and Sandy Tiller, who showed me how to be a good background singer and the importance of harmony and blending.

Keyboardist Bernie Worrell joined Funkadelic. What a valuable and irreplaceable addition he was. He was a genius, classically trained. Like the other guys, he ended up at the 20 Grand Motel when he got to Detroit from New Jersey. The motel was everybody's hangout spot. Then we would go next door and watch the bands perform.

One night, while hanging out with the guys at the motel, Bernie and his wife, Judie, introduced me to a girl around my age. Her name was Debbie Wright. She was so cool, and we got along right off. It was a music sistership at first sight.

DEBBIE WRIGHT I went to the 20 Grand restaurant on my school lunch break. I was in the tenth grade, so this was 1968. I sat in a booth and put some money in the jukebox. I was the only one in the whole place, so I started singing. The song playing was by Gladys Knight & The Pips. Three guys walked in. They watched me for a minute, then walked over and started singing with me.

When the record ended, they said, "So you sing?"

I said, "No!," because I was taught by my mother to never talk to strangers.

They said, "If we call you for a session, would you do it?"

I reluctantly said, "Maybe."

Honestly, I didn't know what a session was. I thought a session was standing on the corner, crooning under the streetlight. I asked, "What are your names, and what's the name of your group?"

"Ray, Fuzzy, and Grady . . . the name of the group is The Parliaments."

They gave me their number, and I went back to class. After school, I ran home to Momma and told her that I had met these guys, and they wanted me to do a session.

"What's a session?" I asked.

She said, "That's when you sing on a record. What's the name of the group?"

ABOVE *Debbie Wright at the age of sixteen (1967).*

RIGHT *Bernie Worrell, a pregnant Debbie Wright, and George Clinton in Detroit (1970).*

I said, "The Parliaments."

Surprised, she said, "The Parliaments? 'Testify'? Debbie, that's a well-known group!"

I called the guys back, and we became friends. They became very close to my whole family. My mother would pick The Parliaments up at a hotel in Highland Park and bring them to dinner or if we had cookouts or parties. George loved my mom. On Saturday mornings, he would jump in her bed and watch cartoons. Eventually, I started doing sessions with them.

I came from a musical family. In the 1930s, my grandfather Horace Sirmans was the original bass singer for the gospel group the Flying Clouds of Detroit. He sang with them for over a decade. When my Momma was about eight and her siblings got of some size, my granddad quit the Flying Clouds and trained them to sing. They did shows as the Family Jubilee Singers with groups like the Dixie Hummingbirds, Clara Ward and the Ward Singers, and others. When they went to Chicago, they would always stay with Mahalia Jackson.

I sang in school talent shows but didn't take music seriously until I was a teenager. Like many girls in the sixties, by high school, I started getting wild. That's when the drugs and drinking came in. I was smoking marijuana and dropping pills . . . red devils, yellow jackets, and debs.

Although we were both young, Mallia and I started hanging out in nightclubs all over the city of Detroit. We would sit at a table and sing so loud that sometimes the band would just come over to our table and give us the microphone.

I would go and sing at the studio with Funkadelic. Golden World Recording Studio was the place where they recorded most of their early Westbound stuff. I recorded many of those first Funkadelic songs and didn't get credit for them. When Mallia and I started recording with Funkadelic, we were seventeen and eighteen . . . we're talking early 1970. I was pregnant then with my son, Charles, with my boyfriend, Zachary Slayter, the drummer from the group McKinley Jackson & The Politicians.

MALLIA FRANKLIN Golden World Recording Studio with George was my introduction to recording and singing semiprofessionally. We sang with Pat and Diane Lewis from Hot, Buttered & Soul usually. They were seasoned singers, and we learned a lot from them. Being in those early sessions was a beautiful thing. Debbie and I witnessed a lot of P-Funk history being recorded in those first sessions. We saw and heard things that we would never forget. One of the most memorable was Eddie Hazel's incomparable guitar solo on "Maggot Brain."

We hung out a lot with Funkadelic down on Plum Street. Plum Street was all Black in the past, and you could get any illegal thing you wanted there, but it had turned multiracial by '69. The hippies opened businesses and shops with clothes, incense, and love beads . . . the love, peace, and "flower power" theory. You could still get drugs or anything you wanted down there; it was just that you didn't have to be Black to go there anymore. It was now Detroit's Haight-Ashbury District.

Funkadelic's 1970 self-titled album was the first for Armen Boladian's Detroit-based Westbound Records, establishing the group as a funk, rock, and acid-head trip. That same year saw the release of their second album, *Free Your Mind . . . and Your Ass Will Follow*. This album would be the first to feature keyboardist Bernie Worrell. Motown legend Martha Reeves and singers Telma Hopkins and Joyce Vincent (who would be known internationally as Dawn, the female duo behind singer Tony Orlando), and Hot, Buttered & Soul (Pat and Diane Lewis and Rose Williams) also sang on the Westbound recordings.

MALLIA FRANKLIN After the first couple of Funkadelic albums were released, the guys played on a show with George's hero, Sly Stone, in November 1970. Sly and the Family Stone performed at Cobo Hall, and Funkadelic played behind a singer named Ruth Copeland. Ruth was from England. She wrote songs with George and used Funkadelic as her backing band on her albums and as a live unit when she performed. Thanks to Ruth, the show at Cobo was the biggest Funkadelic had done up to that point.

After the show, my sister, Jenifer, and I went to Sly's hotel room with George and Liz. Sly's brother, Freddie Stone, and bassist Larry Graham were there with Ruth Copeland's husband, Jeffrey Bowen, a producer at the label that Ruth was signed to, Invictus Records.

Jeffrey was originally from Philadelphia, a member of the Gambel, Bell, and Huff camp before moving to Detroit and working with Holland-Dozier-Holland and Invictus. I knew that George and Jeffrey had a contentious relationship. George was irritated that [Jeffrey] got Funkadelic members to come over and do sessions at Invictus without his permission.

Everybody in Sly's room was drinking and smoking weed. George told Sly I was a good singer. Sly asked me to sing for him. I obliged and sang a song. I think it was "All Along the Watchtower." When I finished, Sly looked at me and said, "Girl . . . you can really sing! But you should sing rock and roll. Singing for the white crowds will get you over."

SLY STONE I love my people, but any time you are considered a *Black* singer that mainly caters to us Black folks, it can hold you back. It's crucial that white people understand that you are successful. I love my brothers and sisters, but it ain't no great thing for them to be the *only* ones to like my music because we're on the same side of the block. If you're on the same block, you're going to like the same music. But if you can cross the street to another hood, meaning the *white* hood, and make some noise there, then you're really doing something.

I suggested that Mallia needed to sing rock. I saw her being the next Janis Joplin. Mallia was a teenager at the time. She had the talent, and, more importantly, she had a "look" that *white* people would wholeheartedly accept. She had all those qualities going for her. I knew that she could thrive on that side of the block. The white-rock side.

GEORGE CLINTON Sly Stone met Mallia's sister, Jenifer, that night, and he liked her a lot. Jenifer and Liz would sneak and go to see Sly and Larry Graham. They started hanging out together, and Jenifer would bring Sly's demos back to me to hear before they came out. She would say, "This is going to be on Sly's new record, and he wants to know how you like it."

Sly and Jeffrey Bowen had a love-hate relationship. Jeffrey met Jenifer that night, too, and he wanted most things Sly wanted, and Jeffrey wanted Jenifer bad. I didn't see that one coming. Jeffrey and Ruth Copeland split up, he started dating Jenifer, and she [Ruth] ended up with Sly.

Once I got out of the Motown contract, Jeffrey, who was working at Invictus Records, said, "Let's resurrect the 'Parliaments' name." The label had artists like Freda Payne, Glass House, and the Chairman of the Board. We changed the name from "The Parliaments" to just "Parliament" and went with it. After we recorded *Osmium* with Invictus, Jeffrey slowly realized he couldn't control us like the other Invictus groups. He tried to stop us from gigging and making money. Jeffrey is the one who kept us from performing as Parliament. We started saying that we were the Funkadelic *backup* singers. We couldn't be in front, but we could be background singers for our musicians. That was the only way we could work and make any money, and he was upset with us.

That's how the Parliament-Funkadelic "name thing" *really* happened. It was because of Jeffrey Bowen at Invictus Records.

We got sick of Jeffrey's shit, and a couple of us kidnapped him from Mallia's house one night. We put a pillowcase over his head, bopped him over the head a few times, and threw him in a van. Jenifer was crying because she thought we were going to hurt him.

He recognized my voice and frantically said, "George! Don't do this, baby boy! Don't do this! I'm sorry, man! I'll leave you alone. I won't give you no more problems!"

Jeffrey was terrified. We thought that it was funny as hell. We held him hostage for a while to fuck with his head. We weren't really going to hurt him. Eventually, we let him go, and he let Parliament go from Invictus Records.

CHAPTER 3

HOLLYWOOD SQUARES

In the 1994 liner notes of a collection of Bootsy Collins's greatest hits, *Back in the Day: The Best of Bootsy*, Collins said, "Finally, we wound up in Detroit, but we had run out of money. Our luck turned when we met a singer named Mallia Franklin at the Love Club. Thank God for Mallia. She and her mama had a storefront with several rooms upstairs, and they put us up while we tried to get work around Detroit. Then Mallia took me to meet George Clinton."

In George Clinton's 2014 autobiography, *Brothas Be, Yo Like George, Ain't That Funkin' Kinda Hard On You?*, he wrote: "One night in Cincinnati, Mallia Franklin, one of the vocalists with Funkadelic, told us that we had to go see some young musicians. She said they looked like us, with the same style and the same attitude. The two musicians that she wanted us to meet were a bassist named William (Bootsy) Collins and his brother, a guitarist named Phelps Collins."

Though Clinton's and Collins's recollections of their first meeting may differ, it is no mistake that this great meeting would forever change the face of funk music. Bootsy, his brother, Phelps ("Catfish"), and drummer Frank Waddy had been playing with the JB's, James Brown's band, and they brought their JB discipline and theory of "The One" to George and

Parliament-Funkadelic. Bootsy would become one of George Clinton's most influential musicians and a primary collaborator, penning some of Parliament-Funkadelic's biggest hits, including "P-Funk (Wants to Get Funked Up)," "Up for the Down Stroke," and "Flash Light." Keyboardist Bernie Worrell was usually the third ingredient in the funk hitmaking "stew." They cultivated a sound that would take P-Funk up the music charts and catapult them out of the pockets of hippie fans. This new sound would take them to popular, mainstream radio.

MALLIA FRANKLIN By 1971, I was pregnant by Nate Neblett of New Birth. My father never embraced our relationship. He thought Nate was just another "broke-ass musician" with nothing to offer a baby or me. My parents had already "handled" a previous pregnancy by Nate when I ran away at 16. Dad wasn't thrilled and would ensure we were married before my son, Seth, was born. In contrast, my mother loved Nate.

Nathaniel was out on the road with Martha Reeves & The Vandellas when I went into labor. He'd stopped touring for a while because I had so many false alarms. When he went back on tour to make some money, I went into labor. Martha was playing in a casino in Vegas. When Seth was born, my mother called Martha's manager, and he told Nate while [Nate was] walking to the stage. Martha announced to the crowd of three thousand that Seth had arrived, and everyone cheered. Nate used to say that Seth had a charmed life from the beginning. Our marriage didn't last long because he didn't want me to sing anymore. He wanted me to be a wife and mother full-time. I wasn't willing to do that.

I stepped back into performing when Seth was a few months old. One show was at the Sepia Theatre in 1971 in Toledo, Ohio. The headliner was a singer named Gloria Taylor, who had a few regional hit records in the Midwest. A young William "Bootsy" Collins played behind her with the band, the House Guests. The band included Bootsy's older brother, Phelps "Catfish" Collins; Frankie "Kash" Waddy; Clayton "Chicken" Gunnels; and Randy Wallace.

They were entirely in another world from the bouffant hair and prom-gown vibe that Gloria had going on. They were funky, fresh, and had a concept that was a winner. I kept being drawn to this guy Bootsy, thumping his bass and playing tambourine with his foot, never missing a beat in the background. I was saying to myself, "Wow! George needs to see and hear this because Bootsy and these guys need to be on the front burner,

The Complete Strangers in 1972. Front row, left to right: *Frankie "Kash" Waddy, Phelps "Catfish" Collins, and William "Bootsy" Collins. Other members included Rufus Allen, Clayton "Chicken" Gunnells, Randy Wallace, Steve Tucker, and Gary "Mudbone" Cooper.*

burning down the house, not on the back burner, just simmering." I knew George was just the crazy guy who would see my vision for Bootsy.

After the show was over, I introduced myself to them. We all hung out that night and discussed our ambitions of breaking into the record business. Bootsy said, "At this point, we're just trying to keep a steady gig." I asked them if they had been to Detroit. At that time, Detroit had a bustling nightlife and tons of clubs with live entertainment, like Ben's Hi Chaparral, Watts Mozambique, and the 20 Grand. They told me they had gone to Detroit a few times to back up The Spinners. Phillipé [Wynne] had just left the House Guests and joined The Spinners. Phillipé's cousin, G. C. Cameron, left The Spinners, and Phillipé took his spot.

I said, "Y'all remind me of Funkadelic. Do you know who they are? Have you ever met George Clinton?"

Bootsy responded, "No. Who's that?"

I said, "I know George. I can hook that up for you if you want to meet him. I think you *should* meet him."

A couple of weeks later, with my newborn son, Seth, lying in the passenger's seat, I hit I-75 in my parents' station wagon and drove to Cincinnati, Ohio. The House Guests put their instruments in the back and piled into the car, and I brought them back to Detroit with me. Like P-Funk, the House Guests and I became family, and, like George and Liz, the House Guests moved in with me.

By 1970, my mother owned a specialty advertising business, Program Products, on Detroit's east side. She had accounts like American Motors, Ford, Chrysler, and Kelvinator. She was now the first female president of the Michigan Specialty Advertising Association and the first female member on the international board of the National Specialty Advertising Association in Washington, DC.

Mom made promotional items for political campaigns and companies, including Westbound Records. She produced products for groups like the Ohio Players . . . ashtrays, pens, and other merchandise. She also made buttons for the "Free Angela Davis" movement. Seth and I lived in a large apartment on the second floor of the building. Bootsy and the House Guests moved in, and we all lived together like a family.

WILLIAM "BOOTSY" COLLINS Mallia was the one that turned us on to George and Funkadelic. If that meeting hadn't happened, I don't know what the *funk* would be going on with me right now. I know I would have been doing something, but it worked out just like God had written the script. Mallia saw the vision and was that piece that connected us with George. She invited us to stay with her in her mom's building. Our whole band stayed upstairs. That was deep in itself. You had all these crazy-looking dudes, Mallia and her new baby boy, Seth. He was the first baby that I ever held in my life, and Mallia had to teach me because I was scared to hold him.

Mal was like one of the guys. She was aggressive . . . but she was a chick. She had both angles of the spectrum covered. She knew how to be a lady, but at the same time, she could do the "dude" thing too. She knew how to not be in the way but also how to get aggressive and be in the way when needed. Mallia was so open with everything. Whatever she had was ours, and her momma, Christine, was the same. That is what allowed us to survive and thrive in Detroit.

MALLIA FRANKLIN Bootsy and the guys were with me for some months. My son, Seth, loved for Uncle Bootsy to give him rides on his shoulders. All the guys took turns giving him "horseback" rides. At a time when I was a young single mother, these guys—Bootsy, Frankie, and Catfish—helped raise my son. Seth was the product of two musicians, and he always had musicians around, some of the greatest, so he got that naturally. I mean, Sugarfoot and Billy Beck from the Ohio Players would babysit. Funkadelic might have been on tour in England when I brought Bootsy to Detroit . . . or on their way overseas. I didn't get in touch with George right away, so Bootsy and the guys stayed with me for a while.

Some time passed, and I finally got in touch with George. I told him that I had a group that I wanted him to check out. I set up a gig for the House Guests at a club on Detroit's west side called Woody's Soul Expression. The mighty Soul Expression was truly Detroit's psychedelic shack. The owner, Woody Bryant, was a good friend of mine and George's. Woody had an apartment upstairs with large transparent plastic bubbles set in the living room floor so he could see what was happening in his club at any given time. The largest bubble was over by the stage. Before George would even meet Bootsy and the guys, he wanted to look at them first.

George arrived that night and went directly upstairs to Woody's place. When the House Guests hit the stage, George went over to the big bubble and looked down.

He said, "Yeah, Mal, they look real good."

I looked at him and said, "Those are Funkadelics, George . . . and Bootsy, that's your star. Shit, he can play tambourine with his foot!"

He smiled at me and showed me those two front teeth. By the time Bootsy got into their second song, George had gone downstairs to check them out up close. I followed behind him. He was totally into it. When George likes something, he gets excited. They were extremely tight and disciplined because they had come from James Brown. It was also great that they had horns, making their sound big. That was something that Funkadelic didn't have at the time. Bootsy was a showman but was always content with being a band member. He was so unique in his bass playing. He would use guitar pedals on his bass to create crazy but innovative sounds. I always called Bootsy "the Jimi Hendrix of bass." After two songs, George knew my instincts were right and told me to bring them to the house the next day. George started calling me "the Geiger counter" because my instincts were so good that I could *feel* how funky someone was *or* wasn't.

WILLIAM "BOOTSY" COLLINS Mallia took us to George's house to meet him the next night. I knocked on the door, and it creaked open halfway. The place was pitch black. It was like we were walking into a haunted house or something. I instantly heard the music from *The Addams Family* in my head. It was spooky. Plus, I was probably high and trippin' on something too. We walked in and went into the living room. I could see things glowing from a black light on the table.

I said, "George, are you in here?"

Mallia pointed and said, "He over there."

I turned to the left and saw something strange. "Am I trippin'? Dang . . . what's that in the corner?"

I saw something white, and it was glowing. It looked like a ghost. I got closer and realized George was dressed in a sheet in the corner. Then I looked down; he was wearing big rubber chicken feet like Foghorn Leghorn. I said to myself, "This mug is out of his mind! That's the kind of dude I want to be with."

That was it. From that day, we were in Parliament-Funkadelic. Mallia was *my* Mothership Connection.

GEORGE CLINTON Mallia brought everybody around. She would always have somebody interesting to meet. She'd say, "George, he's a Funkadelic, George!" That was her rap. When I saw Bootsy, I said, "Wow, I didn't know we had an extra man in the band." He already looked like a Funkadelic. When it was time to expand, he was the first person I called. First, Bootsy played with us, then his brother, Catfish, and the rest of Bootsy's band. Bootsy then brought Fred Wesley and Maceo Parker from James Brown.

FRANKIE "KASH" WADDY (DRUMMER) Mallia has always been a connoisseur of good, funky people. I always give women credit for being processors. Mallia had a plan in her mind before *any* of us. She saw the vision. George was in the market for something new and different, and, for whatever reason, he was ready for another band. When George finally got a chance to see us perform, he got it. He saw the direction that he wanted to go in. We had horns and dynamics, and we were doing arrangements. We came from that military type of training with James Brown and the JB's.

Most people don't know we had the opportunity to be Jimi Hendrix's band. If that had happened, Jimi might still be alive now, *or* maybe we would be totally out of our minds . . . who knows? We chose not to do that. He wanted us to quit James Brown, and he would hire us immediately. I wanted to do it, but the other guys didn't, so we stayed with James. Jimi was ready for more of a Black-oriented act. We would have been the band Buddy Miles, and those guys became . . . the Band of Gypsys.

Mallia's mother, Christine, was a powerful woman in Detroit, and Mal

Invictus producer Jeffrey Bowen and Mallia's sister, Jenifer (right, top row), *and some of the Invictus Records clan in 1971, including Ron Dunbar, Brian Holland, Detroit radio personality Martha Jean the Queen, Lamont Dozier, Eddie Holland, General Johnson, and Danny Woods of Chairman of the Board.*

didn't have to worry about anything financially. We lived with her in *two* different places. We went from her mom's business on the east side, which was like a crash pad, to Mallia's house on LaSalle Boulevard. She had her own house and car by twenty. And what I still remember was that they matched . . . Black and white. She and I had gotten *very* close. We became an item. Her husband was pretty much out of the picture by then. She ensured we didn't starve and had somewhere to lay our heads. She knew everybody and could get in touch with anybody. Mallia was the keeper and connector.

MALLIA FRANKLIN Invictus producer Jeffrey Bowen became a more significant part of my life when he left Ruth Copeland and started dating my sister, Jenifer. When I moved to LaSalle Boulevard on Detroit's west side, Jeffrey's first wife, Nancy, and his son, Jeffrey Jr., lived across the street. He was with Nancy before Ruth, and Nancy and I were great friends. When Jeffrey left Ruth and got with my sister, Jenifer, he had some guys take Ruth's expensive touring equipment and bring it to my house. Jeffrey had all her instruments, amplifiers, and sound system set up in my basement.

My house on LaSalle became the "Funk House." Everybody would come and hang out. They came to play on Ruth Copeland's sound system. The Ohio Players, Earth, Wind & Fire, Michael Henderson, Ray Parker Jr., New Birth, Ricky Rouse, the Dramatics, Enchantment, Ollie and Ray, the ADC Band, and the Undisputed Truth were some of the friends and talent that came over to the "Funk House." It was truly a house of love and music. P-Funk was always there, and Jeffrey and some of the Invictus staff were usually there. The vibe was always cool, and everyone's ego was left at the front door. People would be cooking in the kitchen. Some would get high around the dining room table and drink wine and beer in the living room. Some had "free love" with girls in one of the bedrooms, but most would be having an all-night jam session in the basement. They would take turns playing with each other and vibin' musically. That was a beautiful thing. There were some great musical collaborations in that house. It brought a lot of legendary musicians together and started some great friendships. I was always the one who brought people together, and that became one of my strongest gifts as time went on.

A friend of mine, Robin Russell from New Birth, brought his drums to my house. He replaced my former husband, Nate, as their drummer when Nate started playing behind Martha Reeves and the Supremes with Jean Terrell. Robin was also touring with Little Richard all over the world. They went to China. When he returned, he brought his drum kit to my house. When he unpacked it, I heard a loud shriek. I asked Robin what was wrong. He pointed at the bass drum. I looked in and saw a breathing lump of white and yellow scales. He didn't know that an albino reticulated python had crawled into his bass drum and was smuggled back to the United States.

If I hadn't been a singer, I would have been a veterinarian because I had an uncanny way with animals. I coaxed the large snake out of the drum with pieces of raw chicken. She became my pet, and I named her Coco: short for "Cocaine." She was a musical snake. Anytime Bootsy would play Jimi Hendrix, the snake would stand straight up, knocking the screen off the top of the giant aquarium I kept her in. She would wiggle . . . she would dance, but only to Jimi Hendrix. We would all be high, sitting around the dining room table, watching Coco dance. That freaked out bassist Larry Graham [of Sly and the Family Stone] when he was at my house. The first time Larry saw Coco dance, he literally fell out of his chair and ran out of the house and down the block. We all laughed so hard.

The 1972 release of the Funkadelic album *America Eats Its Young* introduced Bootsy Collins as a songwriter and the House Guests' members as new Funkadelic recruits. The acid-induced influences of Funkadelic's music were starting to diminish by the 1973 album *Cosmic Slop*. With blaxploitation films like *The Mack*, *Boss Nigger*, *Black Caesar*, and *Super*

Fly telling tales of drugs, pimps, whores, revenge, and Black street life in urban theaters all over the country, Funkadelic brought the Black ghetto experience to its records. Songs like "Trash A-Go-Go," about a man prostituting his girlfriend, and the album's title track, about a mother selling herself to feed her kids, became commonplace for the group.

Cartoon illustrations by Chicago-born artist Pedro Bell were distributed across Funkadelic album covers from *Cosmic Slop* forward. Otherworldly landscapes and bizarre comic strips illustrated in colored markers set the tone for the music contained within. Depictions of females in orgasm, as mindless sex robots, prostitute aliens with milky nipples, and twisted freaks with perfect breasts and genitalia were familiar visuals on the album covers. In the cartoons, as in the music, women as glorified moneymakers, generally as whores, added to the misogynistic culture. With tunes like "Nappy Dugout" now a part of the P-Funk repertoire, it was clear the women's liberation movement had yet to reach the land of Funkadelica. Bell's freaky visual conceptualizations of the group's world, scattered across gatefold glossy cardboard, became almost as important to the album's sales as Funkadelic's music.

In 1973, during a pivotal point in his career, Invictus Records producer Jeffrey Bowen left the slowly crumbling record label when Berry Gordy offered him a position with the new Los Angeles–based Motown Records. Since his split with ex-wife, Ruth Copeland, in 1971, Mallia Franklin's sister, Jenifer, had been in a relationship with Jeffrey. He asked her to move to Hollywood to begin his new life with Motown. Gordy allowed them to live in his first Hollywood residence on Sunset View Drive in the Hollywood Hills. Jeffrey would write and produce records on Jermaine Jackson, Smokey Robinson, the Commodores, David Ruffin, and The Temptations. He was also a ghostwriter and producer of hit songs by Switch and Rick James. Following her sister's lead, Mallia would leave her son in her parents' care, pack up her car, and drive to Los Angeles with dreams of breaking into the music business.

GARRY SHIDER (GUITARIST) We always knew when we were in Hollywood because we would look up and see Jenifer. She was modeling at the time, and there was a big billboard of her right on Sunset Boulevard in a sexy outfit of leather and feathers. It was for North Beach Leather. They did a lot of shit for rock stars. I would point up and say, "We in Hollywood! There's Jenifer!"

MALLIA FRANKLIN In 1974, Jeffrey invited me to live in the Gordy house with him, Jenifer, and his sister, Candy, who aspired to be an actress. The house was pure Hollywood, with a pool, a deck overlooking the city, and a triple gold Rolls Royce in my sister's name in the driveway. At that time, Jeffrey produced songs like "Shaky Ground" for The Temptations. He used Funkadelic musicians like Eddie Hazel and Billy "Bass" Nelson on those recordings. They would stay at the Gordy house in LA to work for Jeffrey.

Jeffrey put me in circles to meet influential people in the music industry. He taught me the importance of being seen and networking and took Jenifer and me to many Hollywood parties. My first was at the Beverly Hills penthouse of Motown executive Suzanne DePasse. Her place was huge. I believe it took the whole top floor of the building. Everybody was there... The Temptations, Diana Ross, Marvin Gaye, and a sixteen-year-old Michael Jackson... everyone who moved with Berry to Los Angeles.

Suzanne was very warm toward me. I told her how Jeffrey was helping me with my career, and she gave me some advice. She said, "It's great that he wants to help you. Jeffrey is a hitmaker. But don't let your family connections get in the way of your career path."

She told me that the music business was all political. I was thankful for Jeffrey's opportunities, so I didn't agree with Suzanne then. I wouldn't have been in Los Angeles if it hadn't been for Jeffrey and Jenifer.

There was a big buzz about George Clinton and the Parliament name again. After leaving Invictus, George signed a new recording contract. In 1974, he put out Parliament's first album, *Up for the Down Stroke*, with Neil Bogart on his newly formed label, Casablanca Records. George's long-standing relationship with Neil blossomed while he was an executive at Buddha Records. They were good friends, and Neil was receptive to George's crazy concepts. Parliament would be the second act signed to the label after the rock group KISS.

After being in Hollywood for about six months, Bootsy called me. He was complaining about George. He said George was supposed to get him a record deal, but he was concentrating on other things. Bootsy wanted me to hear the songs that he had done, so he played them for me over the phone. By this time, Bootsy was working with Gary "Mudbone" Cooper, Joel "Razor Sharp" Johnson, Robert "P-Nut" Johnson, and Fred Wesley and the Horny Horns, the guys that would become the Rubber Band. He played songs like "Physical Love" over the phone. The music was light-years ahead. He asked me if Jeffrey had anything going on in LA because he was discouraged waiting on George. They weren't making any money.

Jeffrey met Bootsy previously at my house in Detroit. Jeffrey had a big ego and could be a snob, and he told me that he thought Bootsy was "country," with that gold tooth in his mouth. I called Jeffrey to the phone to hear some of Bootsy's music. He heard it and knew it was great. Even though Bootsy didn't pride himself as a singer more than a musician, he had that star quality that couldn't be denied. He was unique. Jeffrey heard the music and told Bootsy he'd take it to Motown and get him a record deal. He sent for Bootsy in a matter of days.

Somehow George got wind of Jeffrey's plan and didn't like it at all. Jeffrey attempted the same thing when he wanted to team Funkadelic's Eddie Hazel and Billy "Bass" Nelson up with a young male singer named Howard Hewitt, who became famous as the lead singer of Shalamar. Along with bassist Donald Baldwin and keyboardist Truman Thomas, the five of them would form a group called Kingdom Come. George heard about that plan and broke that up. He promised Eddie a solo record deal and got one on Warner Brothers.

WILLIAM "BOOTSY" COLLINS I went to LA to check Jeffrey out. I was like, "Wow, this is awesome!" I was in a torn situation. I wanted to be with George, but at the same time, Mallia had introduced me to Jeffrey Bowen, and he had it going on at Motown. We weren't really doing anything with George . . . just gigging here and there. We were still scuffling because there was no consistent money coming in.

I think the thing that turned me off about the whole thing was when Jeffrey took me up to his house on the hill. He took me out on the balcony, where you could see all of LA. He turned to me and said, "All of this could be yours." I don't know what it was, but I didn't want *any* part of it when that rap came out of his mouth. I realized how much I loved being with George because that was the first person Mallia introduced me to, and we just clicked like brothers. Money didn't mean that much to me. It was more about the relationship that I had with George. Mallia knew it, but, at the same time, she knew we were scuffling and all trying to make it.

Jeffrey was the kind of guy who would get something when he wanted it. He had a *thing* about George, and George had a *thing* about him. It became more about, "Who's going to get Bootsy?" George wasn't having it. He said, "Bootsy's in my group, and I don't care what you say or do. Bootsy's mine!" Honestly, I probably wouldn't have gone with Jeffrey anyway. My heart was so set against whatever Jeffrey was putting down on that balcony. He was after hitmakers; I didn't feel I was a hitmaker at that time.

I just wanted to play music. George was the one that I felt like I could let my true self out [to], and he encouraged that. He allowed me to play what I felt. That, to me, was more important than making lots of money.

GEORGE CLINTON We had just finished *Chocolate City* and were in the middle of recording *Mothership Connection* on Parliament. I talked to Bootsy on the phone, and he snuck out of Jeffrey's house. He was scared as hell to leave because Jeffrey had put a real head trip on him. I was like, "Damn, what are you scared of?" When I got to LA, Bootsy had already checked in to the Holiday Inn on Hollywood and Highland. One of my managers, Cholly Bassoline, and I went over and kidnapped Bootsy from the hotel. He was even scared to leave the damn hotel. He went to Cholly's house at the top of Kings Road and Hollywood Boulevard and stayed with him for a while. Bootsy returned to Detroit, and we started putting his first album together, *Stretchin' Out in Bootsy's Rubber Band*.

MALLIA FRANKLIN When Bootsy left Jeffrey's house, Jeffrey was royally pissed off. He accused me of knowing about George's plan of stealing Bootsy back, even accused me of having some part of it. Jeffrey was so angry that he put me out of the Gordy house. I instantly flashed back to what Suzanne DePasse said about not letting our family ties ruin our working relationship.

I moved into a motel on Sunset Boulevard in Hollywood and started looking for gigs in LA. After a few auditions, my first gig was opening for a well-known LA female impersonator named Sir Lady Java. "Transgender" is what she would be called nowadays. We didn't use that word in the seventies . . . we'd say "transvestite." She was a beauty. She performed with legends like Redd Foxx and Lena Horne. Lady Java was famous in the Black entertainment community, and all the Black superstars came to see her perform.

Then I joined Joe Kincaid and the Soul Brothers. After that, Pop Cycle, then Jay Schlesinger and Excess Baggage. That was the start of what turned into a great career in Los Angeles nightclubs for me. I started making a name for myself as a lead singer. I sang in every nightclub . . . the Fontana, Rock City, and Tiffany's, from the Amber Light Lounge to the Continental Hyatt House, from Filthy McNastys in the valley to Alias Smith & Jones in Orange County.

In hindsight, Jeffrey throwing me out of the Gordy house was a blessing. It forced me to grow. But Jeffrey would still use me for session work.

He was mad, but he wasn't *that* mad. And eventually, he got over it.

CHAPTER 4

CROSSWORD PUZZLE

In the summer of 1975, Motown producer Jeffrey Bowen began production on an album with Sly Stone's sister, Rose Banks, for the label. Sly wrote and produced some songs with Bowen and Rose's husband, Bubba Banks.

By 1975, with a slew of hit songs under his belt, Sly Stone was considered music royalty and one of the highest-paid Black singer-songwriters in the industry. In June, Sly married model-actress Kathy Silva in front of thousands at Madison Square Garden in matching sequined outfits designed by Halston. They separated in 1976 after their son was mauled by Sly's pit bull, Gunn. Kathy told *People* magazine, "I didn't want that world of drugs and weirdness."

Dawn Silva (no relation to Kathy), a background singer for Sly and the Family Stone since 1974, accompanied him to the sessions for the Rose Stone-Banks recordings in Los Angeles.

DAWN SILVA Sly was recording Rose's album in the studio at Marvin Gaye's house. Marvin lived in a mansion off Barham and the 101 freeway in Hollywood that Berry Gordy bought when Marvin married his sister Anna Gordy. Sly and I stayed in the guesthouse by the pool while they were recording Rose's album.

Dawn Silva and Sly Stone in 1975.

I remember the first day that I met Mallia Franklin. I walked into the studio as Mallia sang in the vocal booth. I saw this girl hitting some serious power licks. I thought to myself, "Damn, she can sing!" I thought she was white until she said, "Jeffrey, roll the highs off this bitch and turn me up!" I took a second look, and realized that maybe she wasn't.

Mallia came over every day to record on Rose's album with Jeffrey. She would come out and sit by the pool with me. We would smoke a joint and have lunch. So, for about five days in a row, we really got to know each other. She was singing weekly at the Starwood on Melrose and invited me to see her perform. Unfortunately, I wouldn't get the opportunity.

Sly got a chance to produce some songs for Diana Ross. I'm not sure how the Diana Ross thing happened. I think Jeffrey hooked it up. Of course, Diana would be excited about the great Sly Stone producing a record for her.

A few days after Mallia and I met, we went to the studio, and Sly told us to go in the booth and put background parts down on the hooks of one of Diana's songs. We were in there for about an hour stacking. There was no sampling back then. We were doing one track after the other. We were close to the end when Miss Diana Ross walked into the studio. We were in the booth singing, so Mallia and I couldn't hear what she and Sly were saying, but judging from the body language, I could tell that the conversation escalated to a place where Diana wasn't pleased. Jeffrey pushed the intercom and told us to come out of the vocal booth. We came out, and I heard Diana say the parts were too strong . . . too aggressive. She wanted to sing them herself and told Sly to take them off.

Sly said, "I'm not taking off nothing!"

Diana said, "If you don't, I'm leaving."

Sly said, "OK . . . bye!"

She stormed out, and Jeffrey panicked and ran after her.

The next thing I knew, the Diana Ross project was over for Sly Stone.

Kathy, Sly's estranged wife, somehow got on Marvin Gaye's property one day, looking for Sly. You had to go through a lot of security to get back there. But she got back there. I remember seeing her walking up the long driveway with her sister. They were coming to kick my ass. They were both Amazons . . . over six feet. Kathy was pointing, "There's that bitch right there!" I guess she found out I was there with Sly and was coming to confront me. Kathy always thought it was more than what it was. I understand. Sly was definitely not faithful. He always had other women. So I can see how that made her insecure.

Everybody thought Sly and I were together. I was more eye candy than anything else. We never really had a relationship. He liked taking me around. Sly was so big then; it was a feather in my cap to be seen with him. We were great friends. Sly had all of his other women. He was a free spirit.

MALLIA FRANKLIN I didn't have a problem with Sly's wife, Kathy. She and my sister, Jenifer, were very good friends. But Kathy found out that Dawn was staying in the guesthouse with Sly and was coming up there to "beat that ass!" She brought her sister, April, with her. Kathy's sister was messing around with the director Orson Welles at the time. He was paying for her place and keeping her living a nice lifestyle. I wouldn't have gotten involved if it was a one-on-one situation. But I wasn't going to let it go down like that. "You're not bringing your sister so you can both jump on Dawn. So I guess we all fightin' in this motherfucker!"

DAWN SILVA They were some big bitches, over six feet. I was a fighter. I wasn't scared, and I had backup. Mallia kicked off her platform shoes and said, "Y'all not fuckin' with nothin' over here." I kicked off my shoes and picked one up by the chunky heel to use as a weapon. Mallia and I stood there in a stance, ready to fight. They looked surprised and realized they didn't want the confrontation after all. They talked shit and walked away. Mallia slapped me five, and our friendship from that point was etched in stone.

My journey with Sly Stone started in 1974. My friend Michael Samuels was a friend of Sly's. He called me one day and asked if I wanted to meet Sly at the Record Plant. I said, "Sure!" We jumped in his car and headed to Sausalito. The Record Plant was a famous studio. Everyone from Stevie Wonder to Fleetwood Mac recorded there. When we arrived, the band and singers recorded in what was known as "the Pit." It was an office space transformed into a recording studio just for Sly. It was round like a coliseum and sunk ten feet into the floor. The studio was surrounded by plush shag carpet.

They were working on a song called "Crossword Puzzle." Sly's sister, Vette, was one of the background singers. She was hoarse and couldn't hit the top note. As Vette made a few more attempts, I heard a voice from the darkness say, "I need those top notes, Vette!"

Vette replied, "I'm hoarse. We can do the top notes tomorrow."

The voice in the darkness said, "I need those top notes now!"

My friend Michael said, "Dawn can hit those notes."

The voice in the darkness said, "What are you waiting on?"

My eyes got wide, and my heart started beating fast. I nervously got up from the seat, and my knees were shaking. I didn't have a clue about

Mallia Franklin performing at a nightclub on the Sunset Strip in 1975.

what I was supposed to do. I walked to the top of the pit with the other background singers, and they didn't look pleased. I approached the microphone, standing about ten feet back.

Vette said, "You have to stand closer to the mic than that!"

I was introduced to the other two girls, Lucy and Tiny. They, along with Vette Stone, were the group Little Sister.

Vette asked, "Have you ever sung in the studio before?"

I said, "No."

"Well, here's the part," Vette said.

The tape rolled, and I sang the part as if my life depended on it. The other girls were glaring at me. Suddenly, the tape stopped, and my heart started to pound in my ears. I didn't realize at the time that I was over-singing my parts.

Tiny said, "Maybe you need to back off the microphone after all. Take one of the headphones off your ear so you can hear. A good background singer has to know how to blend." I learned that the voice in the darkness was Sly Stone when he yelled, "What is this? Vocal lessons?! Let's get this done now!"

I followed Tiny's advice and removed the left headphone from my ear. After a couple of attempts, the harmonies started to flow, and we got the parts down on tape. After the session, I was handed $300 in cash. Michael tapped me on the shoulder and said, "Sly wants to meet you." He led me down a hallway and opened a door. Sly was lounging on a mattress shaped like a swollen tongue. Large teeth framed the bed. Lying on that mattress were four women surrounding him, one of whom was a band member and mother of his daughter, Phunne, Cynthia Robinson. He looked at me and gave me a big smile. My first instinct was to turn around and run.

Through his big grin, Sly said, "Welcome to Sly and the Family Stone."

I thought for a few seconds, smiled, and accepted his offer. That was life-changing for me.

I was born in Sacramento, California, on January 2, 1951. I was an army brat, and our family bounced around the globe because my father, Lawrence Weber, was in the Air Force. He was a scientist working with German officers and civilians. He also supervised the refueling of B-52 bombers with liquid oxygen. My dad was one of the soldiers in Uncle Sam's army that they put on the front line through the treacherous mountains of Italy on the "Red Ball Express." He was decorated because he was one of the few to survive that mission.

Dad was stationed in Sacramento, California, where he met my mother, Mary Frances. My mother was a gorgeous woman and incredibly sensual. She won a couple of beauty contests when she was younger. After they married, she worked for the state's parole board at all the most infamous prisons, like Soledad and Vacaville. Our family grew up in an all-white neighborhood. I was one of those kids privileged enough to know the differences in music and have knowledge of classical *and* soul music. I was trained in classical music at my school and sang in the concert choir from seventh grade until high school. I was one of twelve but the only Black. I was always the lead singer and went through a lot of racial discrimination.

I had a strict Methodist mother and a Catholic father who worshipped and adored her. Growing up, my father tried to do anything to please my mother. It didn't matter if it was right or wrong. He did whatever he could to prove his love to her. Because she was very strict in her parenting, she would tell our father to spank us if any of us kids got out of line. By the time I was six years old, those spankings had evolved into hardcore abuse. It got to a point where my father would beat me so hard that my mother would have to scream at him multiple times to stop. I knew my mother was fully aware that my father would cross the line separating discipline from abuse. He was madly in love with her, and she played on his love. He would have done anything to please her . . . including beating the crap out of his kids.

As time went on, I began seeing their relationship differently. Affectionate moments between them were few and far between. My mom wasn't in love with my father anymore, so I didn't blame him as much for his behavior . . . I felt sorry for him. The irony was that my mother seemed to love my father less and less at the end of every beating. I held my mother responsible for playing on *our* fear of his beatings. The mental anguish of spending an entire day wondering if the beating would happen was far worse than the beating itself. I often wondered if they noticed I was becoming a bitter little girl. As I got older and stronger, beatings from my father turned into fights. I started fighting my father back when he hit me, which made things worse. Finally, when I was about thirteen, the physical violence between my father and me stopped.

My mother had a great body and sexy legs, and by my teens, I was built just like her. The only difference was that I had my father's golden skin tone. Like my mother, I also won beauty pageants as a teenager. As I matured, I became more aware of the power of my sexuality in life, and I learned to use it as a weapon. I was rebelling against my parents and all the beatings of my childhood.

When I was fifteen, my father took me to the Memorial Auditorium to see my first big concert. It was Sly and the Family Stone. The group was so invigorated, young, and hungry. I was mesmerized by their energy, clothes, and sound. Their music flowed from the stage, and I was hooked. I never actually thought about being a big star or singing professionally. My dream was to be a professional dancer and dance teacher. But I decided right then that I wanted to be a part of a popular group . . . something famous. I never would have dreamed that one day I would sing with the man I watched onstage that night at fifteen with my father, the great Sly Stone.

By sixteen, I wanted to get my music career underway, so I started a girl group with my sister and a friend in high school, called Windsong. We weren't great, but we would get local gigs here and there. It allowed me to get my feet wet as a singer and performer. My high school also had a full music department, and I took drum classes weekly. My mother thought I was beating on a practice pad every Wednesday night at school, but I wasn't. I would put on dark sunglasses that I lifted from her purse, wear my father's old military jacket, pick my hair out into a natural, and jump on my bicycle to ride down to 35th and Broadway. That's where they held the Black Panther "Free Huey" rallies.

At the time, the leader of the Black Panthers, Huey P. Newton, was in prison for the death of a police officer. I would stand in the crowd with my fist in the air, screaming, "Free Huey!" I watched the Panthers speak about the scurrilous government. But I didn't have a clue what it was really all about. I just thought it was a form of expression as far as Black identity. Blacks didn't have anything to identify with at that time, so I got into the Black Panther philosophy, read Malcolm X, and studied the concept of being a Panther.

I took a break from my life as a radical with the Panthers and married my high school sweetheart, Justin Silva. We had a child, our son, Justin Jr., who we called "Bubba." Like my father, my new husband was a military man and was shipped off to sea during the Vietnam War. When he returned, he was a different person. He was not the man that I married. He did bizarre things to me and became strange, paranoid, and mistrusting. Our marriage ended soon after his return from Vietnam. I continued to raise our son, and within a couple of years, I started my musical journey with Sly and the Family Stone.

After my first session with Sly at the Record Plant, the first show I performed with him on was Dick Clark's American Music Awards in February 1975, in Los Angeles. He gave me the address to his ranch in Novato, California. That's where he rehearsed. There were always celebrities at the ranch. The first day I went there, I saw a woman wrapped in a sheet descending the stairs. It was the legendary actress Doris Day. Sly was seeing her at the time.

By now, a lot had changed. Half of the original Family Stone was gone. Freddie Stone, Jerry Martini, and Cynthia Robinson were still around. His sister, Rose, was gone, and so were bassist Larry Graham and drummer Greg Errico. Sly replaced them with local Bay Area musicians.

I would go to Sly's ranch almost daily to rehearse for the upcoming awards show, but we never rehearsed because Sly was too high most days. I didn't know what I was supposed to sing when we got to the auditorium the night of the awards. I didn't even know what song we were doing.

Five minutes before going onstage, Sly said, "You sing all of Rose's parts."

I said, "All of her parts? What are her parts? I don't know her parts."

Sly said, "Every time I point at you, just sing!"

I got through the performance, but I was mortified. Unfortunately, the chaos of that night was a mirror of things to come. Shortly after the American Music Awards, members of the *new* Family Stone unit also began jumping ship.

I was still studying the Black Panthers' culture when I joined Sly and the Family Stone. I was fortunate enough, or so I thought, to finally meet the Panther's leader after his conviction was overturned and he was released from prison. I was invited to Huey P. Newton's penthouse at 1200 Lakeshore Drive overlooking Lake Merritt in Oakland, California. There were a few other girls there when I arrived. I immediately saw that Huey was high on drugs. His mentality and rhetoric were still institutionalized, drug-fueled, and abusive after his release from prison in 1970.

As the visit went on, Huey and the other soldiers told us girls what a woman's role in the Panthers *really* was. That role was to produce little soldiers. Huey said it was our duty for each woman to birth an army of children. He would pick the soldiers that the women would have sex with. It was our duty to allow ourselves to get pregnant by them. These children would be educated in [the Panthers'] own private schools and trained in [their] military in a sovereign state independent from America.

In all the books and propaganda I read about the Black Panthers, I never saw anything that said I was supposed to be a sex slave and produce an army of children for the Panthers. I wanted to leave immediately. I tried to exit the penthouse, but the soldiers wouldn't let me go. They stripped me naked, and I had to watch Huey and the soldiers sexually use and abuse the women held up in the apartment for three days.

I finally managed to escape when a soldier at the door fell asleep. I wrapped myself in a towel and slipped past him. I ran down over twenty flights of stairs and hid in a garbage dumpster. The concierge of the building saw me desperately trying to flee. I told him what happened. Horrified,

Dawn Silva and Sly Stone at CBS Studios in San Francisco in 1975.

he gave me twenty dollars and called a taxi. My sister Paula lived in San Francisco off Mission and 16th. Still wrapped in a towel, I jumped in the cab and was dropped off at my sister's place.

As soon as I arrived, I called Sly, and he came to get me in his Cornish Rolls Royce. When he arrived, I jumped in the Rolls and cried on his shoulder as he picked up his car phone and called Huey P. Newton.

Sly told him, "You can't have this one. This one belongs to me. I need her shit out of your apartment NOW!"

I knew that Huey had a lot of respect for Sly, and if anyone could get the things I had to leave behind, he could. A day or so later, some of the Panthers brought my purse and clothing in a brown paper bag down to CBS Studios in San Francisco. After that horrific experience in Huey's penthouse, my days as a Black Panther were over.

SLY STONE A couple of weeks after I met Dawn . . . Huey Newton . . . uh, I need to be careful about how I say this. She ended up with a group of activists: brothers that I loved. I won't go into too much detail, but I was the one that got to her in time under the circumstances. She was one of the finest girls I had ever seen, and I liked to be with pretty girls who could sing. Somehow, she ended up with Huey and the Black Panthers. I think through a lawyer that she was seeing. Dawn led them to believe that her intentions were parallel to theirs. When she realized how serious they were about their methods and beliefs, it was too late for her to run away. Dawn called me, and I got her out of that situation with Huey Newton.

CHAPTER 5

FAMILY AFFAIR

Sly Stone's legendary songs, including "Stand," "Family Affair," "Thank You (Falettinme Be Mice Elf Agin)," and "I Wanna Take You Higher," are irreplaceable threads in the tapestry of modern music. However, by 1975, the Family Stone, who had risen to the top with Sly in the sixties, was defunct, leaving Sly's brother Freddie and horn players Jerry Martini and Cynthia Robinson as the only holdovers to cohabitate with new musicians and singers.

Missing the feeling of creating and recording with his family, Sly called his cousin LaTonya Mabry, whom he affectionately called Toni. As they talked, she filled him in on the musical activities of her daughter Lynn.

Recently crowned Miss Berkeley High, Lynn Mabry was gigging regularly with ex-Santana member Coke Escovedo. Sly wanted her to sing on his next album, *Heard You Missed Me, Well I'm Back*. LaTonya and Lynn accepted his invitation and drove to the first session at the Record Plant. "I believe in nepotism," Sly said. "That means that you get your family working the best you can. Because my cousin Lynn could sing, and her mom, Toni, was my favorite cousin, I had to take her with me. It was the right thing to do . . . it was the only thing to do."

Lynn Mabry in 1975, homecoming queen of Berkeley High School.

SLY STONE When the original Family Stone was together, I could see that while the sincerity was there, as time went on, they had no reason to be loyal to the Family Stone or me anymore. They were young artists, all talented, and now loyal to themselves. Before that, we were younger and hungrier. Loyalty to each other was a part of our daily activity. The band had another attitude about it, and I understood where they were coming from. There was no loyalty in the Family Stone anymore. They were moving in another direction, away from me.

LYNN MABRY I remember the first day recording with Sly at the Record Plant. He introduced me to everyone like a proud papa. He told everybody I was his cousin and would sing with him for a while. As we walked around the room, Sly introduced me to the musicians, engineers, and such. Sitting close to the control board was a girl with a big smile and dimples the size of saucers. She reached out her hand to me and said, "Hi, I'm Dawn." She was very nice and welcoming immediately. I wasn't sure what her relationship with Sly was—"Was she his woman?" She let me know that they were "very close." It was evident that she had a sincere fondness for him, and I could appreciate that. Little did I know then that she would become one of my best friends, a musical collaborator, and the one who would be an intricate component of my entering this new endeavor called the entertainment industry.

DAWN SILVA I remember meeting Lynn for the first time differently. We were at Sly's ranch in Novato. She was wild, funny, and a bit naive. I fell in love with her the first day that I met her. I was happy that she would be recording and touring with us. When we finally got an opportunity to sing together, our voices had an instant blend. Not long after Lynn arrived, Virginia Ayers was the next young lady who came into the fold. She was a beautiful girl with an incredible personality. The three of us clicked instantly. Not only were we not bad to look at, but our personalities gelled. Sly loved having us around him all the time. He called us the "Perfect Vocal Blend."

LYNN MABRY I was born Peggilyn Mabry on March 21, 1958, in the small waterfront community of Vallejo, in Northern California. My mother, LaTonya, whose birth name was Beulah Anna, was the youngest of six. Being the baby, she was inevitably rebellious, opinionated, and creative.

Her parents were raised Pentecostals in the Church of God in Christ. With this came stringent spiritual beliefs. My mother, a self-taught piano player, was selected as their church's pianist. Although my mom believed in God, she had her own perception of Christianity from the start. She felt uncomfortably inundated with the religious trappings forced upon her by her parents and generations before them.

My father, Elmer Bob Mabry, was the oldest of eight children, raised by devoted parents in Crowley, Louisiana. Even as a young boy, my father knew early about responsibility, having worked on a rice farm at age seven, proudly keeping the crows away from the paddy fields. In his junior year of high school, my dad left to join the army. He was initially stationed at Travis Air Force Base and later deployed to Okinawa, Japan. After retiring from the military due to an injury in the line of duty, he returned to California to begin a new life.

When my dad returned to the States, he reconnected with my mother. They had met before, while he was in the service. He swept my mother off her feet, and they were married within the year. My mom shared that she was drawn to my dad for many reasons beyond his good looks and charm. They had a spiritual connection, but, more importantly, as she longed to escape the trappings of her strict family home, marrying my dad was a suitable way out. They moved to San Jose and rented a small duplex to settle in and start their family. I entered the world shortly after. My dad, searching for work, secured a job at a photography studio. It sufficed for a while. However, his sultry and striking speaking voice eventually landed him a gig as a disc jockey at a local radio station. Staying close to his spiritual roots, he became his church choir director. My mother landed a great job as the executive secretary to high-ranking Colonel Parker at the former Presidio Military Base in San Francisco.

With their new baby girl, this loving couple, a two-income family, began living what a seemingly perfect life was . . . but not for long. My very strong-willed and opinionated mom and dad began to separate like oil and vinegar, with his possessiveness and low tolerance for frustration. As time passed, they discovered that they had nothing else in common besides the church and me. Aside from her beauty, my dad's love for my mom was seemingly rooted in his need to be cared for. Since he'd been his family caretaker for so long, I believe his desire for it to be reciprocated created this patrician scenario. While each hoped the marriage would work, there was no way for it to grow under the circumstances. In the end, a price would be paid by all.

Evidently, their faith in God wasn't enough to maintain their relationship as husband and wife, and they divorced. My father's calling was not to be a bachelor, and soon after their divorce, he married again.

As my mother began juggling her new roles as a single parent and independent woman, we moved to the Bay Area of Northern California. Fearing she wouldn't be the best mother she could be alone; she asked my grandmother for advice, [who] told my mom that she didn't condone single parenting and felt it was vital for me to live in a "complete" Christian family household, convincing my mother to have me stay with her sister (my aunt) and husband for a while. I was five years old when my mom packed me up and drove me to their home in Bakersfield, California. Little did I understand how these early years would be the catalyst to orchestrate my paths.

What I thought would be a summer vacation with my aunt, uncle, and three cousins in Bakersfield turned into a living situation that lasted for years. Month after month, year after year, my little mind wondered if I would ever be with my parents again. As a child, I was inquisitive, sensitive, and adventurous. My aunt and uncle, the pastor and "first lady" of Morningstar Church of God in Christ, fearfully exposed me to their faith. I was taught that if you disappointed God, "you will burn in hell!" I never wanted to disappoint God. The only thing keeping me hopeful was that my mother was doing everything she could to get me back. My dad would occasionally come, bringing everything from the most amazing bear hugs to what I thought was the biggest bicycle he could find me. I could digest that my dad had moved on with his life and new wife, but I couldn't understand what took my mom so long to come to Bakersfield and take me home.

Four years in this foreign place had passed, and I was about to receive the greatest gift I could ever hope for. My mother finally came to take me home. It was like Christmas one thousand times over. I had anticipated this reunion every day for four long years. I was eager to start living a new life with my mom in a new city: San Francisco.

From Victorian homes to modern high-rises, the blend of architecture was as unique as the city's long periods of fog and vision of Alcatraz seen across the bay while crossing the Golden Gate Bridge. I was now a resident of what became the core of America's counterculture. Artists, writers, musicians, and hippies were outside my front door. I was genuinely excited to live in such an environment of love and freedom. We moved into a beautiful, high-rise apartment. Every day, I strived to leave my days in Bakersfield in the past. But my fear of abandonment resonated in my mind, and it was expressed in overcompensation. My primary objective at this point was to please my mother. That personality trait would continue for the remainder of my life. I always wanted to please and accommodate her, and anyone else, for that matter. Being a servant was something I saw in my mother, and I became fascinated with her. She was a beautifully poised woman. In my eyes, she was like a movie star, and I wanted to be just like her. My mother had a very eclectic group of friends... male, female, straight, gay, politically involved, military, Black, white, and otherwise. I had a sense of the world in my living room every week.

My mother was very open and a true reflection of our liberating times. She was also a very liberated parent. I remember celebrating my thirteenth birthday and my mother planning a beautiful day for me. This day was even more exciting because she let my friends and me smoke marijuana under her supervision. She was integrating me into her new and adventurous lifestyle, and her lenient rules offered me a lot of freedom.

Other life events were about to take place that changed everything for me. One of my mom's close male friends volunteered to babysit me one evening while she went on a date. It wasn't an unusual request, as he had previously watched me. As we watched TV on the couch, he reached over and pulled me closer to him. It was strange, but I thought nothing of it until he gently rubbed my shoulders. Now I was getting uneasy. He stretched out on the couch, facing the television, and positioned my small frame strategically in front of him. Slowly pulling me closer, I began to feel the heat from his breath on the top of my head. His hands then moved to lower places on my body. What was confusing was that I had feelings and reactions that I had never felt before. It was an unfamiliar sensation. I was very uncomfortable and knew in my heart that something wasn't right. What was on TV became a blur. "Is this behavior OK?" I was afraid and confused. I lay there motionless until he was finished. There was fondling but no penetration.

When it was over, he asked, "Are you OK?"

Confused, I said, "Yes."

He responded, "You know I love you. You're my girl, but you can't say anything to your mom. This is between you and me."

Was it normal to have such secrets? I wasn't sure. From that night, I was very guarded when I saw him. I was ashamed and didn't want my mother to know what had happened. He would come by our home for occasional visits or get-togethers that my mom would host. I didn't want her to see me acting differently toward him. I wasn't afraid of him but didn't want to sit or stand close to him again. I didn't want to hug him because I thought it would encourage him, so I put on the charade like everything was OK, but it wasn't.

About four months later, it happened again with another friend of my mother's . . . a woman. The pattern was the same as how I was being touched before. She placed me on top of her. The same feelings were aroused in my body, but in my mind, I was confused.

"How is this happening again?

Why am I feeling this way again?

What am *I* doing to have this happen to me?"

Afterward, she lowered her head in shame and apologized. This was the second molestation within a few months. It made me question who I was as a little girl and why I was such a target. The rest of my mother's friends and boyfriends never laid a hand on me. They were people of integrity. This understanding made those who took advantage of me stand out even more like monsters.

Years later, I chose to forgive them. In doing so, I could finally share those incidents with my mother. Understandably devastated, she wanted to kill them. She asked that I forgive her for unknowingly allowing them to have the opportunity to hurt me. I was blessed that I could forgive my abusers, but it took my mother years to forgive herself.

We left San Francisco and the memories of all that happened behind and moved across the bay to Berkeley. The hippie movement was in full swing, and I was a hippie at heart. The women's liberation movement had exploded, and the entire Bay Area was a hotbed of social change and progress. Although I'd already experienced more than the average fifteen-year-old girl, I began to come into my own by my junior year in high school. I started dating an older guy by the name of Charles. He graduated three years before me. He had an apartment and owned a car. He was very handsome, but, more importantly, he truly loved me and wanted to always take care of me. He enjoyed buying me new things and loved my mother as any young girl would hope for. I thought that I had found Mr. Right. But my Prince Charming was living with his own demons. As our relationship blossomed, I realized he supported himself and his lavish lifestyle by selling drugs. I initially thought it was exciting. He introduced me to substances I had never heard of . . . like chocolate mescaline and windowpane acid.

Charles often heard me sing along with songs on the radio and always complimented my voice. One day, he heard a radio advertisement that a

Lynn and her mother, LaTonya Mabry, in 1974.

musician from the Bay Area, Coke Escovedo, was auditioning for a backup vocalist. He suggested that I audition. I was so impressed by Charles thinking I was good enough to audition that I agreed to do it. Music and singing, in many ways, allowed me to express myself. Singing was the echo and secrets of my childhood; hearing certain melodies spoke to my soul, and the lyrics often gave me hope. It was a way to release my inner struggles constructively, but I didn't see it as a profession. My life's ambition was to be a psychologist. I wanted to understand the workings of the human mind. What makes people different? What made abusers abuse?

I auditioned for Coke Escovedo and was hired. For the first time, I saw something positive in my talent that was appreciated and respected. It was a gift God gave me, and I didn't even have to try . . . it came naturally. My first gig with Coke was at King Richards Night Club in Oakland. The owner of the club was Coke's manager at the time. I was allowed to perform onstage but sequestered in the owner's office between sets because I was sixteen. It was the only place where I could hang out legally. I was a junior in high school, and with homework in tow, I would study there until it was time to perform. That continued until we started performing at larger venues, opening for acts like Earth, Wind & Fire featuring the Emotions.

Coke had gigs at King Richards every weekend. I was still singing with him when I did my first sessions with my cousin Sly Stone at the Record Plant. After the first session with Sly, I recorded with him regularly. I was with Sly recording on a Friday night, when I looked at the clock and realized how late it was. I had to be at the show with Coke. With the session running late, I told Sly I needed to leave immediately to make the gig.

He abruptly said, "No! We're not done yet, and I need you to stay and finish the track we're working on. You need to call them and tell them you can't come."

I said, "Sly, there's no way I can call to say I won't make tonight's performance." It was unprofessional, and I wanted to keep my gig with Coke.

Sly said, "I'll call him myself and inform him that you won't be showing up."

We took a break from recording and went to the studio office to deal with the situation. Sly insisted that I call Coke's manager. I hoped receiving a call from the great Sly Stone would soften the blow, and some grace would be provided to me. I reluctantly dialed the manager's phone number and handed the receiver to Sly. Coke's manager picked up.

"This is Sly . . . Sly Stone. I'm calling to let you know that Lynn is working with me tonight, and she won't be able to make it to the gig."

Coke's manager told Sly, "Tell Lynn that she will not be welcomed back if she doesn't show up. She can stay with you permanently!"

That response pissed Sly off. After a short pause, he started screaming into the receiver and slammed it on the desk. I looked at him in disbelief and said, "Did I just get fired?" To this day, I'm still not sure if he was upset because he was defending me or because his ego was bruised. Maybe it was a little bit of both. That fateful phone call ended my career with Coke Escovedo but cemented my position with Sly and the Family Stone.

As Lynn Mabry was integrated into the new Family Stone, she and Dawn Silva became Sly's confidantes, companions, and caretakers. They were thrown into a vortex of excess from day one and forced to sink or swim in a pool of music, money, and drugs. They assisted and observed him trying to recover his former glory as a chart-topping juggernaut. Lynn and Dawn had hope and could see a new horizon for Sly. Unfortunately, Sly's addictions kept him from seeing the rays of sunshine himself.

DAWN SILVA There were so many different types of venues that we were playing with Sly. We did dates with Dr. John and a lot of TV shows like *Midnight Special*. We even played the Grand Ole Opry with Loretta Lynn. We did the shows that most Black artists weren't [on] . . . maybe only Ray Charles and Charlie Pride. Sly leaned on Lynn, Virginia, and me because we encouraged and inspired him. He always wanted us around.

His drug use was out of control and shows became harder and harder. We never knew if Sly was going to show up. Or if he did, would he be too high to perform? There are so many stories that I could tell about Sly and drugs. One stands out in my mind. I went to his ranch one evening, and Sly was passed out. His safe was wide open, and there were thousands of dollars lying all over the floor. There was cocaine and drugs everywhere. His jewelry and rings were scattered all over the tables. I picked up all the money and jewelry and put them in his safe. I then took all the cocaine and threw it in the garbage. I stayed at the ranch to watch over him, and he slept for two straight days. When he woke up, he wanted to get high again. He crawled out of bed and started looking for his drugs. He came storming down the hallway, wanting to know what had happened to his cocaine. I told him that it was in the trash.

He said, "Why would you throw it away?!"

"Fewer drugs to kill yourself with," I said.

He replied, "Who made you the drug monitor?"

I think he knew I didn't want anything bad to happen to him. Sly had a beautiful spirit. He was a wonderful person. I loved him, and it hurt me to see him hurting himself, his career, and his legacy.

LYNN MABRY Once I started touring with Sly, I finally saw the degree of his addiction. He and I would buck heads a lot because I had a kinship with him. We were family, and I was always very outspoken with him, especially about his excessive drug use. By then, I was old enough to know how you must care for yourself, and I took a vested interest in caring for him. We

Sly and his girls: Lynn Mabry, Virginia Ayers, Dawn Silva, and Sly Stone on Midnight Special in 1976.

would perform on TV shows, which was a struggle each time because of the drugs. I'm sure I stepped over the line many times.

I would say things to him like, "You don't need to be smoking that," or, "You can't go out there with your hair looking like that."

The biggest issue was that I would say these things in front of others in our organization, which embarrassed him. Eventually, he fired me for speaking my mind about his drug use. He fired me several times, replaced me, but always called and asked me to come back. Once Dawn and I got closer, she understood and supported the stand I took with him. We were trying to get him back on track. We both wanted him to be reintroduced to the world as Sly Stone . . . bigger and better than ever.

I remember when Dawn and I were in Kansas City performing at Arrowhead Stadium. We were with Sly in his suite. The room had about four R&B heavyweights that were there to visit him. I remember Barry White, Teddy Pendergrass, Eddie Kendricks, and others. They were excited to see him. He was excited to be around these guys and about to go further than he needed to. As we lounged around, Sly disappeared into his bedroom and emerged with a bag of PCP. He started lacing his joints with it.

I thought to myself, if he smokes this PCP, we will be in trouble because we have a show to do.

I told him, “You don’t want to smoke that.”

“What are you talking about?” he refuted.

“It gets all funky and comes out your poop hole,” I jokingly said.

I tried to give Sly some advice in a funny way and not be so blunt or offend him. I wanted him to be the best he could be, but I also wanted the others in the room to see him in his best light. I wasn’t trying to hinder him. I would often dump some of the drugs behind couches, down toilets, or take them with me so he wouldn’t use them. I loved Sly and was trying to take care of him. I didn’t want to upset him, but it didn’t work. He got so angry that he fired me again and hired a singer named Lady Bianca in my place.

Some time passed, and he called me back. Lady Bianca was gone, and Sly asked me to return to the group with Dawn and Virginia. That was right before Sly was booked on the Mothership Earth Tour with Parliament-Funkadelic in the fall of 1976.

CHAPTER 6

MOTHERSHIP CONNECTION

In 1975, George Clinton described Parliament's new album *Chocolate City*, the group's second for the Casablanca label after 1974's *Up for the Down Stroke*, as "taking Black people to places that you don't normally see us." The White House was the first stop. Clinton proclaimed boxer Muhammad Ali as president, with a federal cabinet that included Richard Pryor, Aretha Franklin, and Stevie Wonder. Clinton's prophecy of a Black "commander in chief" was over three decades prior to the election of Barack Obama as the forty-fourth president of the United States. The *Chocolate City* album established Parliament as a commercial force, selling 150,000 copies in Washington, DC, alone.

The P-Funk organization grew in popularity, recognition, and revenue with every album. Backstage Management, who was handling the group, was run by a big P-Funk supporter, Cholly Bassoline. Cholly would be immortalized in a Funkadelic song in 1978, "Cholly (Funk Get Ready to Roll)." He crafted multiple record deals for Clinton with his partners Robert Mittleman and Ron Strasner.

ROBERT MITTLEMAN (BACKSTAGE MANAGEMENT) Cholly Bassoline had been a fan of George's for years when he came out with the first Funkadelic album in 1970. He sought George out and got him to sign with Backstage. Cholly's partner was Ron Strasner, who had a management company called Ron Strasner & Associates. They started managing George right before he signed with Casablanca Records. Ron Strasner & Associates became Backstage Management when I came aboard in 1975.

After Neil [Bogart] at Casablanca signed Parliament, the other original Parliament guys, singers Fuzzy, Calvin, Ray, and Grady, started to feel that their positions in the group were in question. George was the guy who got the money, and everybody else was on salary. Even when they were The Parliaments in the early days, George was the leader. George was the creative force of the group. He was a genius at that time, for sure.

Ron made the deal for Parliament over at Casablanca with Neil Bogart. George contemplated creating other acts and his own production company at that time. Ronny gave him some valuable advice.

He said, "You don't want a production company with one record label because every loser counts against a winner. So we'll make deals with different record companies that want a piece of George Clinton and P-Funk." Ronny made about six or seven record deals for George over time.

I often helped the band [members] out, especially if they were considered "valued" members. George paid the band members something like two hundred and fifty dollars weekly. It doesn't sound like much. In 1975, it was something, but hardly enough to become rich. When George would get a big royalty check, we would give the band members nine to eleven thousand each. That was to anyone that George felt was an *important* member of P-Funk.

Who did George consider important? There were eight to ten guys in the group at that time and really no leaders. For sure, Glenn Goins was a leader, Garry Shider, maybe Jerome Brailey. Who else was a leader? Boogie? Michael? Bernie? They were great musicians but, in my opinion, not leaders. P-Funk was not a bunch of chiefs and no Indians. They were *all* Indians, and there was only one chief . . . and that was George Clinton.

By late 1975, Parliament's musical focus shifted from the Black power messages of *Chocolate City* to a conceptual hybrid of Egyptian mythology, street swagger, and space travel. Their third album for Casablanca would be the landmark *Mothership Connection*. Clinton and Bootsy Collins have previously told the story of the record's inspiration: They experienced an unearthly visit from an extraterrestrial that would change them forever.

While traveling in a car together, they described a flash of light nearly paralyzing them. A fiery laser beam hit the vehicle's hood, morphing into what George called "a red liquid that looked like drops of mercury." After that experience, they firmly believed that life existed on other planets.

George's fiancée at that time, Liz Bishop, recounts the event. "I was in the car with them when they had that legendary 'visit' from aliens. Bootsy was driving. George was in the passenger's seat, and I was in the back seat behind him. I saw bright lights, like cars were coming straight toward us. George shuddered and said to Bootsy, 'Did you see that?' Bootsy was hesitant at first, like he was processing the situation. He then said, 'Yeah, yeah . . . I saw it.' I was there. I witnessed the whole thing."

As with *Chocolate City*, Clinton wanted to take Black people where they had never been seen before. George noted that the only Black person in space was Nichelle Nichols, who played Lieutenant Uhura on *Star Trek*. When Clinton brought his initial ideas for the *Mothership Connection* concept to Casablanca Records President Neil Bogart, he was enthusiastic and gave Clinton the funds needed for the Mothership to take flight. According to Clinton's autobiography, Bogart's wife, Joyce, wanted to call the album *Landing in the Ghetto*, with the concept of a spaceship coming from outer space to save poor Blacks in the inner city. Clinton's ideas were much more universal than just the urban underprivileged. He wanted to spread his vision of "musical afro-nauts" across the galaxy.

The musical-cosmic odyssey of *Mothership Connection* was a revolution that many Black people still quote, teach, and live by. Because Clinton believed that fictitious characters like Mickey Mouse lasted longer than people, he created several characters and a funk theory that resonated with its fans. P-Funk lingo spawned the Funken Cyclo-P-dia, with a glossary chockful of terms like the Bomb, Funkentelechy, Pinocchio theory, Cro-Nasal Sapiens, ego munchies, splank, psychoalphadiscobetabioaquadooloop, and super-groov-alistic-prosi-funk-staca-tion. This ideology created a movement that millions of fans, known as Maggots and Funkateers, follow loyally.

With the release of the *Mothership Connection* album in December 1975 and its instant success, the funk spread further than anyone could have imagined. The record went platinum, a feat that no Parliament or Funkadelic album had yet accomplished. The single,"Give Up the Funk (Tear the Roof off the Sucker)," inspired by David Bowie's song "Fame," according to cowriter Jerome Brailey, reached number five on *Billboard* magazine's Soul charts and number fifteen on the pop charts.

Clinton quickly crafted a sequel, *The Clones of Dr. Funkenstein*, which hit record stores in July 1976. As the title suggests, Clinton constructed an alter ego in the self-proclaimed scientist, prophet, and pimp, Dr. Funkenstein. The doctor was the cool ghoul with the bump transplant, the big pill, the Mad/Glad scientist, the master technician of clone funk, and the outer space tribal leader of the descendants of the Thumpasorus People. The *Clones* album went gold, riding on the sheer velocity of *Mothership Connection.*

After the massive success of both records, the group was slated on their biggest arena tour ever. Momentum was high for the maiden voyage of the Mothership Connection/P-Funk Earth Tour in October 1976. Inspired by arena rock groups like Pink Floyd and Queen, Clinton had Casablanca Records invest a quarter of a million dollars in props and costumes. The funk opera included a full-sized, forty-foot silver spaceship, laser beams, flashing lights, explosions, and a gleaming gold pyramid. Jules Fischer, who did stage sets for the Rolling Stones, David Bowie, and Parliament's label mates, KISS, designed the massive props.

The P-Funk Mothership Earth Tour became one of the biggest ever executed by any Black music group. The only Black act to come close to the Parliament-Funkadelic theatrics was Earth, Wind & Fire, with their Egyptian-inspired regalia and Vegas-style magic tricks. EWF had the glitter, but nobody had a Mothership. Pulling the massive show off every night would take four trucks, seventy-five roadies, and a camper.

The band's outrageous style was just as crucial as its music. They dressed in acid-funk-inspired clothes from thrift stores, costume shops, and custom pieces constructed by a friend to the band, Detroit designer Tom "The Leatherman" Wojciechowski. Tom also created most of the leather stage wear for Bootsy Collins. Clinton had extravagant higher-end pieces designed by emerging New York costume designer Larry LeGaspi. LeGaspi had designed flamboyant stage costumes for KISS and space couture for the female "Lady Marmalade" singers Labelle.

Although Mallia Franklin and Debbie Wright sang on Parliament's first album for Casablanca Records and on early Funkadelic albums on Westbound, they didn't receive their first credits until *Chocolate City* (1975). By the time the Mothership was set to fly, they would be in Clinton's sight as possibly the first female additions to the all-male band.

GEORGE CLINTON Why was *Mothership Connection* so big? We'd just finished doing *Chocolate City*, and Garry Shider and I were at Woody's Soul

Expression in Detroit. Woody, the owner, and I were friends. We were all in his office, and he offered us some cocaine. We snorted it, and I realized it wasn't cocaine.

I said, "Aww, man! This ain't cocaine; it's PCP!"

I told Garry, "Don't move! Lay down on the floor right where you are. The high will only last about ten minutes. But if you move, you got eighteen hours of this shit!"

There was a self-motivation record playing in the background called "Success." It was one of those subliminal records that worked on your subconscious while you slept. As we went under on this PCP, the record spoke to us about success.

Then I heard in my ears, "You in heaven, nigger! You in heaven, and you gonna pay me for this!"

I said to myself, "Oh, man. We got some rotten shit!"

About fifteen minutes later, I was coming out of it, like waking up from anesthesia. The sound came back to my ears, and I could hear people talking.

Still lying on the floor, I looked over at Garry and said, "Are you alright?"

He said, "Yeah."

"Don't move yet," I told him.

When I finally came out of it, I told Woody, "That was some dirty shit to do to us."

After that happened at Woody's, we started recording songs that would be on the next album . . . which was *Mothership Connection*. That record was so big that it went right out of the ballpark, bigger than anything we'd done. It was to the moon from that point on. I had to ask myself, "Did that record about success have anything to do with us being so damn big so quick?"

When we started planning the Mothership Connection Tour, we knew it would have to be a big show . . . like Broadway. It was the biggest tour that we had ever done. Because Bootsy's solo record took off, Bootsy's Rubber Band would be the opening act.

DEBBIE WRIGHT I was singing with a local group in Detroit called The Second Coming. It was an all-white band. We did Top 40 gigs in the city to put a little money in our pockets. But I was starting to feel stuck. *Mothership Connection* was all over the radio. P-Funk was doing well, and I knew I needed to talk to George. One day, while I was cooking and doing housework, I picked up the phone and called down to United Sound Systems, where P-Funk was recording. I asked the receptionist if I could speak to George. She put me on hold, and about thirty seconds later, he picked up the phone.

I said, "George, I need to talk to you. It's important."

He said, "OK. Jump in a taxi and come down here. I'll pay for it."

A friend of mine, Jeanette Washington, was on her way to my house. I met Jeanette through my little brother Jim, who was a drummer. She was a singer in his band, Stiheem. She was a young girl, maybe sixteen at the time. Jeanette arrived shortly after my conversation with George. I told her that we needed to go down to the studio.

She said, "What's a studio?"

I said, "You are about to find out."

Jeanette was a nice girl. Still naive about life. She had some issues with her family, specifically her mother, who was very religious, and step-siblings. Her mom was a minister and had a storefront church. She wasn't the nicest to Jeanette, and I think Jeanette was looking for a way out of her situation. She was often unhappy, and I always told her I would try to help her if I ever got a real break.

We jumped in the taxi and went down to United Sound. We walked into Studio A, where George, Bootsy, and Garry Shider listened to rhythm tracks. Jeanette sat on the couch, and George and I went downstairs into the lounge to talk. I told him I was tired of being in Detroit and needed steady work.

He smiled and said, "You can ride the Mothership. We are going to New York to start rehearsals in four days. Can you be ready?"

I said, "I can be ready in *two* days!"

I carefully asked, "George, can you use another girl?"

He said, "Yeah, I guess we can."

I responded, "What about the girl I brought with me . . . Jeanette?"

"Can she sing?" he asked.

I said, "Is my word good enough?"

He nodded, "Yes."

I replied, "She can sing."

We went back into the studio, and George introduced himself to Jeanette. He started telling her that he wanted to hire her for the tour. He gave her information about when we were scheduled to leave and when rehearsals began. I don't think she heard anything that he said. She believed that George was playing a joke on her . . . just talking shit.

GEORGE CLINTON We always had girls singing on the albums, but they were *never* in the band. We had to start re-creating the sound on the records. We were crossing over as a band, and I knew that females would give us a more crossover look and appeal. Debbie and Mallia did all the Parliament stuff, so they were the first girls on my mind when it was time to tour. Mallia was in Los Angeles with Jeffrey [Bowen], but Debbie was still in Detroit. Debbie brought us Jeanette Washington. It was great timing for her. Jeanette just happened to be in the right place at the right time.

Debbie and Jeanette were young and innocent enough to get into the characters we were putting together. They didn't have any ego, none of that at first. They were ripe and easy to adapt to the Parliament-Funkadelic situation. They were energetic and looked the part . . . like two bookends. My only reservation was that I wasn't sure if they were old enough to be on the road in such a big way or mature enough to handle that kind of success.

GARRY SHIDER When Jeanette Washington came around, she was a little uneasy at first. I don't think she was trying to be a singer on any real professional level. Jeanette was a church girl, a total square at that time. She wasn't even feeling this *funk* shit at all; she was scared of it. George sent me to her house to talk to her mom because of her age. She was sixteen at the time. I remember sitting in the kitchen, talking to her mother, and telling her we wanted Jeanette to tour with us. I assured her we would take care of her and keep her safe. I could tell that her mom just looked at it as a financial thing. She wanted to know how much it was paying. She felt Jeanette could bring some money into the household, so she was OK with her going.

DEBBIE WRIGHT A few days passed, and I called Jeanette to head to the airport to catch our flight to New York to start rehearsals.
Her mom answered the phone and said, "She's not home. She's in Flint [Michigan]."

I couldn't believe my ears. "What? What is she doing in Flint? Tell her my limousine just pulled up, and I'm leaving for New York."

I flew to New York without Jeanette. Later that night, the phone rang in my room. It was Jeanette sobbing, "You left me!"

I'm drinking champagne and saying, "Girl, stop crying! I told you George was serious, but you didn't believe him."

I went and got George; he talked to her and calmed her down. He told

Jeanette Washington and Debbie Wright backstage during the Mothership Connection/P-Funk Earth Tour in 1976.

her that he would send her another plane ticket. She was in New York the next day.

Rehearsals for the Mothership Connection Tour took place at Stewart Airport in Newburgh, New York. It was an airplane hangar. We rehearsed in the hangar because the props were so big. IT WAS SO OVERWHELMING when I saw the Mothership hanging from the rafters for the first time. Then there were other big props, like the puffy silver car and the giant pyramid. I knew I was about to be a part of something unbelievably big. It was like a dream come true, and it happened within a week. One day, I wondered where my next loaf of bread was coming from, and the next day, I was in New York rehearsing for a major tour. I can understand how Jeanette may have felt. It could be hard to believe such a big twist of fate could happen like that.

George explained that we needed to be in costume during the show. We had to put our own look together. It had to be funky, sexy, and spacey. It was like Halloween in the beginning. Jeanette dressed like a kitty cat, and I dressed like an Indian. I had been hanging around P-Funk for years and dressed funky. I was a hippie, so it wasn't a big change for me. Jeanette had to find her balance of funk and femininity, but she got there and found her style. She was a church girl, and dressing funky wasn't how she was raised. She became uninhibited onstage and didn't have any hang-ups about wearing some sexier outfits. She had a nice, athletic body and didn't mind showing it. Maybe she was rebelling. It was like the church girl in a little box finally breaking out. I know that Jeanette and I added femininity to the group. It was like "Beauty and the Beast." Offstage, she dressed more conservatively. Deep down, she was still a church girl.

BERNIE WORRELL (KEYBOARDIST) Debbie and Jeanette definitely gave the crowds something to look at. That was one of their biggest contributions to the group, and it was an asset. They gave the show more *woo* for the eyes. Then, when they heard them sing, that was a plus. They were the ultimate *woo* to the senses. They were pleasing to the eyes and the ears, making a difference in the group's look, sound, and live shows.

GEORGE CLINTON We spent so much money on that tour; it was ridiculous. I had a big bag of white foxtails—$400 a tail. Jeanette would wear them in her afro. I also had a big white mink coat. It was a real mink, and that coat was expensive as hell. It cost me about $40,000. I had to stop wearing it because protest groups like PETA started really wearing people

Mothership Connection: Parliament-Funkadelic in 1976. (Left to right) *George Clinton, Garry Shider, Calvin Simon, Bernie Worrell, Grady Thomas, Cordell "Boogie" Mosson, Michael Hampton, Ray Davis, Fuzzy Haskins, Glenn Goins, Jerome Brailey, Debbie Wright, and Jeanette Washington. A Garry Shider–signed Casablanca Records promotional photo.*

out about wearing real animal skins. That coat was too damn expensive for PETA to fuck it up, so I had another *fake* mink coat made for the rest of the tour. I put the real one in storage.

DEBBIE WRIGHT The tour was a big success right from the start. On our first night, we were introduced by Casablanca's "first lady," Donna Summer. It was the best time of my life. We were on the road and living like lapdogs of luxury. George was buying us expensive clothes, taking us to dinners; [we were] staying at beautiful hotels and traveling all over the country. We had some great times traveling with the guys. They were protective of us as big brothers and got us anything we wanted. We were causing trouble, having fun, and living our dreams.

P-Funk's dazzling extravaganza, the Mothership Connection/P-Funk Earth Tour, launched in October 1976 and began a one-hundred-city invasion of mainly sports arenas. Night after night, the enthusiastic crowds screamed, clapped, and marveled. At the same time, chants like "Shit, goddamn, get off your ass and jam" and "If you ain't gonna get it on, take your dead ass home" were willingly recited by legions of fans.

In the colorful mass of male musicians and singers onstage, the two petite and effervescent young girls, Debbie and Jeanette, pranced, danced, and harmonized side by side with the charismatic Dr. Funkenstein. Both were tiny firecrackers onstage, [each] barely standing 5'2". Debbie, adorned in leather, fringe, and feathers, complemented Jeanette's black leotard, giant silver pacifier, and huge afro with Clinton's white foxtails hanging underneath. As George predicted, their presence softened some of the band's hardcore image and added some of the feminine tones missing from the group's live shows.

CHAPTER 7

FANTASY IS REALITY

Parliament-Funkadelic were headliners of the Mothership Connection/Earth Tour, and various opening acts shared the bill in different cities. P-Funk's offspring, Bootsy and his Rubber Band, was a mainstay. Other artists, such as Hugh Masekela, Santana, Mandrill, and George's hero, Sly Stone, would also perform. By 1976, one of popular music's biggest innovators, Sly Stone, was working hard to keep his career afloat when he joined the tour as one of its supporting acts.

On Sly's first stop in Houston, Texas, on Halloween 1976, Clinton invited all the acts onstage to celebrate in the last groove of the night, their top five hit, "Give Up the Funk (Tear the Roof off the Sucker)." Bootsy Collins and his Rubber Band came from the back to the stage's edge. So did the group Cameo. Sly Stone declined, but his trio of background singers—Lynn Mabry, Dawn Silva, and Virginia Ayers, dressed in elegant black evening gowns—came out to dance in the spotlight, feeling a need to represent Sly. They stood out as a touch of normalcy and elegance amid P-Funk's wild, outrageous costumes and demeanor.

GEORGE CLINTON When I first saw Sly's background girls, they were *really* good. All three of them came out onstage with us at the end of each show.

The tour made it to Baltimore, Maryland, and I was told by my managers that I couldn't leave the hotel. Everybody tried to make me stay in my room because someone crazy threatened to assassinate me. I got tired of sitting around and decided to go to the venue anyway.

I was waiting in the hotel lobby for a cab when Lynn Mabry came down on the elevator. The rest of the Family Stone had gone to the venue already. She walked up and asked if she could ride to the show with me. I'd had enough of sitting around, so Lynn and I caught a cab to the civic center. We had done maybe seven shows with Sly, but this was the first time I spent one-on-one time with any of his girls.

The cab drove Lynn and me around to the backstage door of the venue. We jumped out, and a weird guy walked up to us. He had rotten teeth in his mouth, makeup all over his face, and had on a ratty wig. He thought that he was Dr. Funkenstein.

Startled, I thought to myself, "Oh shit! This must be the dude!"

He smiled really big and said, "Folks think I look like you."

I scoffed and said, "You got everybody running around here scared, thinking that you are going to do something to me."

He said, "C'mon, man! You're my idol. I just want to go to the concert."

He walked into the backstage area with Lynn and me, and with a mouth full of rotten teeth, he smiled from ear to ear. I told the managers to get him a ticket to the show. He didn't want to kill me; he just wanted to walk in with me and see the show.

LYNN MABRY That whole Parliament-Funkadelic experience was something that I wasn't used to. I was into a little rock-'n'-roll . . . the Eagles, Rascals, Jimi Hendrix, but I wasn't living in that "funk" world. I must admit that it was fascinating and different. When I saw my first P-Funk show, it was unbelievable. The ship, the props, and the pageantry were nothing like Sly's show. I saw Debbie Wright and Jeanette Washington onstage with the guys and thought, "These girls are wild and crazy, but they can sing." Hearing their voices blend in with all the male singers was cool.

I remember Jeanette's big afro, silver eye shadow, and beet-red lipstick. Debbie had on a bone-straight, shoulder-length wig with a headband, and gold bangles up and down her arms. They were such a big contrast from Dawn, Virginia, and me. In the funk world, we were a lot more conservative and conventional. We were considered "snooty."

George started wooing me soon after we met, and we spent time together on the road. He wasn't necessarily my type, but something about him was intriguing. I was young, vulnerable, and impressed by his presence and ability to captivate tens of thousands of fans every night. He was skinny and kind of peculiar, but I was from Berkeley, so I enjoyed his quirkiness. He pulled out all the stops to impress me. He would take me on trips, buy me clothes, and supply endless drugs. If I needed some change, he would throw a bunch of hundreds my way. We had fun and enjoyed each other's company.

I saw firsthand how crazy Funkadelic was on the road. My first real taste was one night after a show. I laughed and talked with P-Funk members Jerome Brailey, Raymond Spruell, and Bernie Worrell in the dressing room, and a random girl walked in.

She said, "Is this the Funkadelic?"

The guys said, "Yeah, baby, we are the Funkadelic."

She said, "This ain't no Funkadelic. I'll show you Funkadelic!"

She stood in the middle of the floor and pulled her top off. She pulled down her pants and panties and had bumps and sores all over her butt. It was the skankiest thing that I had ever seen. One of the guys stood up and pulled his pants down. She lay on the ground, and one of the other guys unzipped his pants to mount her. I was in total shock. Right then, out of nowhere, George appeared, grabbed my hand, said, "You don't need to see this!," and snatched me out of the room. I was familiar with free love; however, I had never witnessed a groupie giving up that kind of *funk*. George tried to convince me that that behavior was not the norm. This, to me, was an introduction to the scope of the uninhibited nature of Funkadelic.

DAWN SILVA The P-Funk show was entirely different from what we were doing with Sly. A specific class of individuals was around when you were with Sly Stone. Even though it was wild and crazy in one sense, it was still elegant. Some people thought Lynn and I were superficial because we presented ourselves with class. That's the way that we were raised. The band members in P-Funk were interesting, looked crazy, and some guys smelled really bad.

When we first met the P-Funk Girls, Debbie Wright and Jeanette Washington, they were the total opposite of us. I grew up a debutante. Lynn was her high school's homecoming queen. The way we were raised, a lady didn't leave her house with a safety pin holding anything together or without having her hair and makeup done. Ladies didn't swear or smoke. Debbie and Jeanette did all the above. Some of the nastiest curse words came from those two girls' mouths. I had never encountered girls like that, and we hadn't ever toured with a band like Parliament-Funkadelic before.

Sly was rhythm and blues. He was rock and even country. He didn't have the whole Disney cartoon theory to go with his music as George did. P-Funk had the concept, the costumes, and the spaceship. Dr. Funkenstein and his clones, sent here to deliver the earth from the blues and the blahs. P-Funk gave the music an edge with the high energy of rock and the bottoms of the funk. As great as Sly was, he didn't want to compete with anyone *or* anything, and it didn't take long for him to feel frustrated. He felt that he now had to compete with a spaceship.

Our show in Baltimore turned out to be a disaster. Sly was playing piano and fell off his stool. He stood up and realized that he'd split his pants wide open. He turned around and walked off the stage. We kept singing, and the band continued to play. After a few minutes of stalling, it was apparent that Sly was not returning. Defeated, we ended his set and took the limo back to the hotel.

As we waited for the elevator, the Family Stone horn player, Cynthia Robinson, turned to us and said, "Pack your stuff. Tonight will be Sly's last show on the tour." Sly was expected to be with P-Funk for three months; we had only been there for maybe three weeks. Disappointed and trying to process this new information, we returned to our suite. We walked in the door, and the phone rang. A voice on the other end said, "This is Debbie Wright from P-Funk. Our guitar player Michael Hampton is turning twenty, and we're having a birthday party in George's suite. I want to invite you to come. It's room 1019."

Lynn and I decided to go to George's suite, but Virginia backed out. She was very reserved and the most conservative of us all. She wasn't a big fan of P-Funk's looseness and carefree lifestyle.

Lynn and I changed out of our gowns and headed to the room. We knocked a few times. The door finally opened, and a cloud of cigarette smoke laced with cocaine greeted us. I didn't see balloons, a cake . . . nothing. In my naive mind, I thought we were going to a *real* birthday party . . . but this was a P-Funk party. Debbie Wright saw us, came up, and formally introduced herself. She said excitedly, "Hey! Y'all made it!" She grabbed me by my hand and said, "The birthday boy sho' the fuck wants to meet you!" Debbie led me through the crowd of people, and we found Michael Hampton in the bathroom alone, playing his guitar. He looked up with a scowl on his face.

Debbie pushed me into the bathroom and said, "Here she is!"

I think she embarrassed him. I cheerfully said, "Happy Birthday."

He shyly and reluctantly said, "Thank you," looked down at his guitar, and continued to play.

I backed out of the bathroom, looking for Lynn, and bumped into the guitar player who wore the diaper onstage, Garry Shider. Actually, I smelled him before I saw him because his armpits were on fire.

He grinned at me and said, "Y'all need to be with the funk."

"The what?"

"The funk," he repeated.

"What's the funk?"

He said, "You'll see."

I nervously backed away from him. As I was getting out of the realm of Garry's body odor, another guy walked up and stuck his false teeth out of his mouth in my face. It was the keyboard player, Bernie Worrell. Yuck! I was outdone. I spotted Lynn over in a corner talking to George. We made eye contact, and she worked her way to the other side of the crowded room, insisting that I meet him. I wasn't interested. The room was two large suites that were connected. Lynn dragged me into the connecting suite. George was smoking a joint in the corner and listening to a rhythm track blaring through his big boom box.

Lynn gleefully said, "George, this is Dawn."

I put my hand out and said, "How do you do?"

George laughed, saying, "Y'all got to be the politest girls I've ever met."

Lynn and I were so proper that we amused George. He thought that we were funny. I had no idea that Lynn and George had been hanging out previously. But, by Lynn's strange behavior, I could tell she was high on something. George stuck his extended pinky fingernail out with a powdery substance on it that I thought was cocaine.

He said, "You want some?"

"No, thank you. I don't like cocaine," I replied.

He said, "It's not cocaine; it's green. You want some?"

"What's green?" I said.

He said, "It's just *green*."

I snorted the powder off his fingernail, and it blew the back of my head off. I was high as hell instantly and floating. I started hallucinating. I saw George's smiling face at every turn, saying, "Is it a green evening?" That went on for hours.

The next thing I knew, I saw sunlight streaking through the suite's curtains. I was finally starting to come down, but I had the biggest headache I'd ever experienced. I got myself together and found Lynn. We returned to our room and packed our bags to go home to Northern California. Somehow, Sly found out that we were in George's suite and told us that we couldn't have anything to do with "the funks" anymore. We were his employees, and he didn't want us intermingling with them at all.

I didn't find out what "green" was until much later. There was a P-Funk crewmember by the name of Jaggers. He was a chemist and created altered drugs for George to use on the road. I learned from Jaggers that the drug George had us snorting was something he called rat tranquilizer. He insisted that I stay far away from it. So that was my first meeting with George Clinton. That wasn't a very good first impression. Lynn and I headed back home, and that was the end of the P-Funk tour for Sly Stone.

LYNN MABRY I remember our introduction to "green" differently than Dawn does. I recall George and I planning a party in his suite for all the acts on tour, and that's where we tried it laced in a joint.

Nevertheless, the next morning, we flew back home to Northern California. I returned to the penthouse I was sharing with my boyfriend, Charles. He was now one of the biggest drug dealers in the Bay Area. He was so big that the police started trailing us all around the city. We would sometimes drive with pounds of cocaine in the trunk. I never dealt drugs; I was just his girlfriend. But I knew that if the cops pulled us over, that would have been the *end* for me.

Early one morning, as we sat in bed snorting cocaine off a Kleenex box, the Berkeley police rammed the apartment door open. Cops with guns drawn came into the bedroom and surrounded us. They grabbed me off the bed and escorted me into the living room. About twenty minutes later, Charles walked out in handcuffs. He looked me straight in the eyes and said, "Don't say nothing!" It was the most frightened that I had ever seen him. Strangely, it relieved me because everything had gotten very risky. I was taken to the women's jail in Emeryville and was placed in a cell with two girlfriends of Charles's drug associates, who had also been arrested in the sting. As we sat in the cell, one of the girls sighed and said, "I'm so tired of my man getting busted." She lifted her dress, pulled her panties down, reached into her vagina, and pulled out a half-empty medicine bottle of red pills. She opened it, stuck the pill bottle in my face, and said, "You want a red?"

I could only look at the bottle in disgust and say, "No, thank you." She took out a pill, put it in her mouth, and put the bottle back where she got it from.

I was transferred to the juvenile hall [detention center] in San Francisco because I hadn't reached my eighteenth birthday. I was given a prison uniform and escorted to my holding cell. As soon as the door shut, I began to vomit violently, realizing the seriousness of the situation. Unbeknownst to me, my mother was contacted and waiting outside the courtroom to accompany me to my hearing. Fortunately, the judge was forgiving.

He said, "Miss Mabry, after reviewing all the evidence, it looks like you were in the wrong place at the wrong time. I'm going to release you into your mother's custody. I suggest that you pick your boyfriends more wisely."

I was released, and Charles was convicted and sent to prison.

George Clinton stayed in contact with me after Sly left the Mothership Earth Tour. Parliament-Funkadelic was playing in the Bay Area in January 1977 at Oakland Coliseum. George called me and invited Dawn, Virginia, and me to the show. They were recording the *Parliament Live: P-Funk Earth Tour* album that night, and he wanted us to sing on microphones set up backstage. He had mics behind the huge Marshall amplifiers so people could sing without being in costume. Dawn and I went, Virginia declined. When the band got to their last song of the night, George called Dawn and me out onstage to sing with him.

The next morning, Dawn and I got telegrams almost simultaneously from Cynthia Robinson on Sly Stone's behalf. They read, "After careful consideration, your services are no longer needed by Sly and the Family Stone." Someone who worked for Sly was at the show, saw us onstage with P-Funk, and reported back. We were fired, and our days with Sly and the Family Stone ended.

That afternoon, Dawn and I went to George's hotel. We were both really sad. We showed him our telegrams of dismissal. He read them, looked at us, and said, "If Sly is serious about firing you, I'll hire you today!" In shock, we both said, "Really?" That was exciting because Sly didn't do much after the Mothership Connection Tour. A few weeks passed, and we got a phone call from George to come to Los Angeles to do some studio work. Dawn and I obliged, and Virginia again passed on the invitation.

DAWN SILVA Lynn and I drove from Berkeley down to Los Angeles and walked through the doors of Hollywood Sounds Recording Studio. George arrived shortly after with an entourage. I learned early on that George is easily bored with things and people. Lynn and I were new curiosities, so we entertained and excited him.

We were different from the P-Funk Girls . . . nothing like Debbie and Jeanette. We also had a connection to his hero, Sly Stone, and that intrigued him. Lynn, being blood kin to Sly, intrigued him even more. The two of us went into the vocal booth, and the first track was a Horny Horns remake of a Parliament song "Up for the Down Stroke." We sang layers upon layers of background parts and a sprinkling of leads. When we finished, George handed both of us a hundred dollars. He grinned at us and said, "See you tomorrow." I wanted to ask him if that was our per diem because if this was a union session, we should have easily made about $2,000 each. We finished the Horny Horns album and moved on to the next project, a solo album for the guitarist Eddie Hazel. Eddie was one of the most talented musicians I had ever worked with. Lynn and I spent about a week on Eddie's album. We were again paid one hundred dollars at the end of each session.

George moved us from the Hyatt to the Beverly Comstock Hotel in Beverly Hills. He called our room early one morning and told us to put on swimsuits and come join him by the pool. When we arrived, George was sitting there with a big smile on his face. He was wearing an orange, skintight leather outfit. I was thinking, "Why is he wearing a leather outfit at the pool?" A photographer was sitting at the table beside him.

George said, "Come on, girls, take a picture with me."

We said, "No, George! We just woke up! We haven't put on any makeup. Our hair isn't even done. We don't want to take pictures."

He said, "It's cool. It's just a picture for me."

A few weeks later, that picture showed up as a part of a feature story in *People* magazine on George and P-Funk, and I didn't know whether to be happy or to cry. I thought we looked ridiculous. We eventually finished the Eddie Hazel sessions and went back to Berkeley.

LYNN MABRY Not long after our first sessions, George wanted to take Dawn and me on vacation to Miami to go fishing . . . one of his favorite pastimes. He told us that it was an initiation for all new members. We checked in to a beautiful two-bedroom suite, put on our bathing suits, and George took us out on the ocean in a yacht for deep-sea fishing. The boat took us way out. We finally dropped anchor, and I noticed that everything got still. All I saw was water; there was no land in sight. Dawn and I started observing strange things floating in the water, like luggage, an orange, a

Dawn Silva, George Clinton, and Lynn Mabry pose by the pool at the Beverly Comstock Hotel in January 1977.

shoe, and pieces of children's clothing. George turned to us and said, "Hey girls, do you know where we are?"

We both looked puzzled and said, "No, where are we?"

He said, "We are in the Bermuda Triangle."

I was startled. We both were. It was a bit spooky, and I probably said a few curse words. We had heard stories about extraterrestrial beings and the paranormal abducting of ships and airplanes. I'm sure that's why George took us there in the first place. But ironically, there was great fishing there, and George loved to fish.

After a long day at sea, we finally returned to land. We got back to our hotel, and we were completely worn out. We had been out all day and had fish juice and saltwater all over us. George was *extra* funky because he hadn't bathed for several days.

The suite that we were staying in had a fully functioning kitchen. George said, "I'm going to cook some of the fish we caught today for you."

I thought, "Great! We can all get showered, and George will cook us a delicious fish dinner."

Dawn showers, then I shower, but George is not showering and smells awful.

George was in the kitchen, preparing to cook, and I said, "George, you need to take a bath."

He said, "Oh . . . naw, girl, it's cool . . . I'm good."

I said, "Nope! You aren't . . . and before you cook anything for me, you must take a bath! I'll even draw your bathwater."

I ran some water for him and even put bubbles in it. He finally got in the tub and took a bath. When he finished, he was *cleaner*. After he was done, I went to the bathroom and glanced in the tub. I was shocked. I called Dawn in to see what I was looking at. I think she gasped. We had never seen a tub so filthy. It was lined with dirt. I'm not talking about a little soap scum . . . but dirt! If there was ever a doubt in my mind, that night confirmed that George was funky . . . in his music . . . and on his body, too.

After the trip to the Bermuda Triangle, George Clinton became a bigger part of our lives. I was so impressed at how amorous he was toward us. In his eyes, Dawn and I were the best things since sliced bread, which was attractive to me. I was excited as a young lady to be pampered. George and I developed a personal and physical relationship, but I knew this wouldn't be lasting. I knew there were other women, and it was OK. We were having fun, and I enjoyed the perks of being appreciated.

CHAPTER 8

HARDCORE JOLLIES

With the P-Funk Earth Tour becoming a gigantic moneymaker for Clinton and Casablanca Records, a second wave of Mothership Earth Tour shows billed as "The Second Coming of the Mothership" was added to the band's roster. The venues became more massive, as did the revenue.

Without notifying any band members, George Clinton hired Lynn Mabry and Dawn Silva as permanent fixtures of Parliament-Funkadelic. That struck a nerve with others in the group, particularly with the original female members, Debbie Wright and Jeanette Washington. They learned secondhand that Clinton was using Mabry and Silva in their absence on projects in Los Angeles. The tension was thick when the duo stepped onto the band's tour bus, christened the "Mothership," with Clinton for the second round of shows in early 1977.

LYNN MABRY I always thought that George was inviting us into a family. It was all supposed to be a big party. We were under the impression that he treated everybody as well as he treated us. Dawn and I were the new girls, and P-Funk was a foreign land. We thought we would be embraced, but that wasn't the case, and many band members weren't happy that we were there.

Our relationship with the P-Funk Girls, Debbie and Jeanette, was superficial at best. They were apprehensive about getting close to us because they didn't know our motivations. They were "hardcore" from Detroit. You just didn't come in and be embraced. You had to earn their respect, love, and trust. Dawn and I were just happy to be there. We didn't have that feeling of being competitive at all. Dawn and I weren't tense until we noticed Debbie and Jeanette's tension toward us. We were young and immature, but Debbie and Jeanette thought, "Here come some new girls stealing our thunder, taking our joy, and singing our parts." At that time, that was a valid emotion.

Looking back, I know that George manipulated the situation where we, as women, didn't trust each other. Dawn and I would go to him with concerns, and he always reacted in laughter. That was hard for me. I went to the leader, someone I've had a *close* relationship with, thinking he would handle this tense situation. It was like he didn't even care. His response was usually, "Let it play out. It's no big thing." I was still a teenager and needed validation; we *all* needed validation from George.

WILLIAM "BOOTSY" COLLINS Now we got four chicks in the group? It was a shock at first. It had been just us guys for so long. Then we got Debbie and Jeanette, and now Lynn and Dawn. The good thing was that they weren't like *regular* chicks. That made it a lot easier. The more the girls were around, the more the guys started thinking, "Wow! They add some real polish to the act." Most of the guys started to accept it. But some guys in the group didn't like it at all. Not everybody was cool with these new women being in P-Funk.

GARRY SHIDER When Lynn and Dawn joined the group, I thought, "What's up with these California girls?" The whole group felt the same way in the beginning. It was like they came from nowhere, and it got my attention. It really got Debbie and Jeanette's attention because they saw Lynn and Dawn as competition. But competition was what George was all about. He did the same thing with the guys in the group. But it's a little different with women because they are more sensitive and emotional. I learned to love Lynn and Dawn as I got to know them. They were beautiful and had great voices and an unbelievable vocal blend.

I knew George was planning something. He always had a thing for female singers and girl groups. Maybe around 1976, after we signed to Casablanca, George talked to me about producing a girl group. We were thinking about Debbie Wright, Mallia Franklin, and my wife, Linda Brown, but nothing ever came of it.

LINDA SHIDER (SONGWRITER, VOCALIST, AND WIFE OF GARRY SHIDER) When Lynn and Dawn came into the organization, I wasn't feeling them at first because I had heard things. I heard that they were wild and that Sly's whole thing was kind of bizarre. There were whispers about them being with George sexually, and I didn't know if they were girls I wanted to be cool with. Once I got to know them, I realized most of it was rumors. They weren't anything like what I had heard. I have to say that Lynn and Dawn were very aggressive. I think George thought that as singers, Debbie and Jeanette had powerful vocals. Still, Lynn and Dawn had more stage presence, maybe even more physically attractive to some. They were different kinds of women than he already had with Debbie and Jeanette.

FRANKIE "KASH" WADDY We knew George was excited to bring Sly Stone's girls into the P-Funk fold. Initially, he wanted Sly to hear that he was treating *his* girls well. He spoiled Lynn and Dawn when they first came around. I think the limos, dinners, and private yachts were more to impress *Sly*. We were a bunch of horny guys, so the more girls, the merrier.

Like some of the guys, I looked at Lynn and Dawn in a different light. Debbie and Jeanette didn't really have relationships with the guys in the band. We would all have little flings, but they were never exclusive with band members; they were more like our little sisters. Lynn and Dawn came in, and the guys in the band wanted more of a romantic, exclusive relationship with them. They got a lot of attention, which caused problems.

DAWN SILVA I learned early on how things worked in the organization. It was our first payday, and I heard the secret P-Funk knock at my hotel room door. Before I could answer, I saw a white envelope slide underneath. I picked it up and looked inside. It was six hundred dollars and a gram of cocaine. I thought, "Why is there cocaine in my envelope?" I opened the door and saw P-Funk's road manager, Johnny Parent, slide an envelope underneath the door across the hall. I was the new girl in the group. I wasn't trying to break any rules, but I wanted my money, not drugs.

I yelled, "Hey! What is this?" He turned around, looking annoyed.

He said, "Oh, that's your salary."

"George said that Lynn and I were making seven hundred dollars a week. There's only six hundred in here."

He replied, "I know. I put a little extra *something* in there for you."

I said, "Oh, I get it; you're going to take a hundred dollars out of my salary and replace it with cocaine?"

He said, "Busted! I'll get you the other hundred, and you can keep the cocaine."

I said, "I don't want this cocaine!"

The bass player, Cordell "Boogie" Mosson, opened his door, heard me refuse the drugs, and gleefully said, "I'll take it!"

After that, Johnny Parent never slid another envelope under my door or tried to pay me in cocaine again. He needed to put my money in my hand and understood from then on that he couldn't pay me in drugs.

LYNN MABRY I had a big issue with Johnny Parent. He was a horrible road manager. I remember the tour bus taking us to a motel in Shreveport, Louisiana. Johnny told everyone to check in, and then he would call us down to the bus to get our weekly pay. As instructed, we checked in to the hotel, got our keys, and went to our rooms. Dawn and I had a room that faced the parking lot. As we unpacked, we heard the bus start. I glanced out the window, and I saw the bus drive away. The next gig wasn't for days, and we had no money. There was no way to get in touch with anyone. No plane ticket to get home; we were just stuck.

The motel room was horrible. It was infested with crickets. They would chirp and jump on our beds when the lights went out at night. It was bad.

We pulled a few pennies together and bought meals from a small country store nearby. We would purchase small boxes of cereal but didn't have enough money for milk. So we ate it dry. It was terrible. The only good thing about that experience was that we all came together in our time of need. It was a testament to the new kinship Dawn and I were building with the group. Johnny and the tour bus returned almost a week later to pick everybody up for the next gig. We confronted him.

He said, "I'm sorry. George didn't give me any money to give you, and I didn't know what to say, so I just left."

How cowardly. That was the day that I lost all respect for Johnny Parent.

Seeing wild things on the road with P-Funk didn't take long. We had all kinds of crazy things happen. We were in Washington, DC, and a woman came onstage with a short skirt. She pulled up her skirt and wasn't wearing any underwear. She stuck a lit cigarette up her butt and puffed it . . .

blowing smoke rings. There were times that George came out onstage with nothing on but a sheet, and strange women would crawl under it. I was young and immature, and that stuff grossed me out.

During the second leg of the Mothership Connection Tour, Debbie Wright confessed that she had fallen in love with Clinton and claimed they had a romantic relationship. After years of platonic friendship, she boarded an emotional roller coaster that would change her life forever. According to Debbie, the relationship developed during the first leg of the Mothership Earth Tour. Debbie's feelings for George and Clinton's relationship with newcomer Lynn Mabry caused an even deeper rift in the friendships between the P-Funk women.

DEBBIE WRIGHT I started having an affair with George while we were touring. I'd loved him since I was a teenager, and I still love him to this day. I wanted him because he was the *smart* one. He was like a brother, father, friend, and my man, all rolled up in one. By the Mothership Tour in '76, I wasn't a little girl anymore. I was a young woman in my twenties and wanted some of *his* funk. I don't know how he treated other girls, but he was good to me. It didn't last long, but I loved him. When I found out that he liked Lynn, I had a big problem with that. We were all young girls, and Lynn was the most natural target; I took many of my frustrations out on her.

GEORGE CLINTON Debbie and I never had a physical relationship. At that time, Debbie was jealous of any woman . . . even Jeanette Washington. Before Lynn was in the group, I remember Debbie coming to my hotel room and jumping in my bed. I thought that she was joking around. She knew Jeanette was coming to my room and wanted her to believe we were sleeping together. Debbie acted like she was really giving it to me. She did it because she thought I would try to hit on Jeanette. I looked at Jeanette like a baby sister; I had no intention of trying to sleep with her. When Jeanette came into the room, she saw Debbie in my bed. I was thinking, "Damn! Now Jeanette must think that this shit is for real." I thought it was messed up for Debbie to do that because she was messing around with Ray Davis then. I never slept with Debbie.

DAWN SILVA When George and Lynn hooked up, he flaunted his relationship with her. I can't even imagine how Debbie must have felt. She was a secret to everyone. They were sneaking around, and George was boisterous about his relationship with Lynn. Debbie would never admit it, but she was furious at George and started physically taking things out on Lynn. Debbie didn't bother me; we were always cool, but she really went after Lynn.

We were on the bus going to a gig, and every time Debbie walked past, she stomped on Lynn's toes. Every time Debbie stomped on her foot, Lynn would turn to me and say, "Dawn, did you see her? She just stepped on my foot." Lynn wasn't a fighter, but I was.

I said, "Lynn, if you let that girl step on your foot one more time, I'm gonna beat her ass and then beat *your* ass for letting her do it!"

Lynn said, "What am I supposed to do? She won't stop stepping on my foot."

I turned around and said, "Debbie, if you step on her foot one more time, I'm beating your little ass!"

Jeanette Washington had been looking for a reason to fight with me. She jumped up and said, "You got to go through me first to get to her!"

I had no problem with that. I said, "Come on, you little bitch!"

Jeanette sat down.

We kept our distance from them initially, but one night, I went to sing next to Jeanette onstage. She wasn't happy and jerked the mic stand, hitting me in the mouth with the microphone. She busted my lip, drawing blood, then barked at me, "You don't sing on that part! That's Debbie's part!" I didn't fight her. I decided to back away and dance to the other side of the stage. I told Johnny Parent, the road manager, what happened. He let George know, and Jeanette got off with a warning. The next night, she hit me in the back of the head with the mic stand.

I said, "You little bitch! I will beat your ass right on this stage if you touch me again!"

She boastfully responded, "Bring it!"

Johnny saw what she did and told her she would be fired if she touched me again. She stopped being physical, but then it became more *verbal* abuse. The reality hit Debbie and Jeanette that Lynn and I were there for good, and that horrible behavior continued for a while. The guys in the band treated us differently than them, which didn't help our friendship. We were always ladylike, and Debbie and Jeanette were rough around the edges. Of course, the guys probably intended to get Lynn and me in bed. Still, the approach was different toward Debbie and Jeanette. As time went on, things got worse. Jeanette had the nastiest mouth I had ever heard

Debbie Wright, Jeanette Washington, Lynn Mabry, Dawn Silva, and George Clinton bring the funk to the masses in Baltimore, Maryland.

from a woman. As mean as she was, I knew something was troubling her deeply. She always seemed so unhappy. I couldn't compete with her when it came to pure meanness, so I tried to be kind, and, after a while, she softened up a little bit. When the guys saw her being more feminine, they also treated her differently. I think Lynn and I were a good influence on her.

I realized later that all the confusion and discord worked to keep everybody in line. The girls weren't attacking George for what was happening; we were attacking each other. You couldn't just walk up and punch somebody, so you took your aggression to the stage.

LYNN MABRY I didn't take my relationship with George as seriously as Debbie did. I knew it was just a fling. I was young. I was doing cocaine, smoking weed, taking quaaludes, and drinking Martell. That's no excuse for any woman to be with another woman's man, but that was my reality at that time in my life. Debbie got to a point where she started separating herself from everyone. She only wanted to be with George. I believe she got so heavily into George to escape Dawn and me. And, in the end, it didn't help her. It would ultimately be to her detriment.

GEORGE CLINTON Lynn and Dawn came in, and Debbie and Jeanette were fucked up in the head about it . . . like they would get left out. Then Fuzzy, Grady, and Calvin [original Parliament members] left the group, which disenchanted the other members. The shit was building up and falling apart at the same time. We were approaching the biggest part . . . the best part of what we were doing. But it was also the hardest part; some people couldn't handle it. Everything was happening at one time. The moment that the shit was taking off was the moment when everybody got shook up.

In June 1977, the original singers of The Parliaments—Fuzzy Haskins, Grady Thomas, Ray Davis, and Calvin Simon—walked away from the P-Funk organization. Clinton bringing on Lynn and Dawn was the icing on a mounting cake of the original singers' issues with him, namely, popularity and monetary, since the group's massive success. Ray Davis returned to the fold in a matter of weeks, but the others stayed away for two decades.

The original male vocalists' exit gave way to a new, glamorous look and crisper sound onstage. Debbie and Jeanette had been usually relegated to one side and outnumbered by men on the front line. The addition of Dawn and Lynn now made the women a visual and vocal force. Alongside George Clinton and lead singers Garry Shider and Glenn Goins, the quartet of ladies stood center stage night after night, reinforcing a feminine presence in P-Funk that would be vital to the group's popularity and success.

CHAPTER 9

CLONES OF DR. FUNKENSTEIN

By June 1977, the "Parliafunkadelicment Thang" had become one of the biggest tickets in music. George Clinton wanted to use the group's popularity to create new stars to deliver profits to his organization. His vision included two girl groups, a duo, and a trio. Clinton said, "Each group must have the right combination of booty *and* talent. Some girls have more vocal abilities than others. But I surrounded them with the right amount of *booty* to make the group sellable."

With four female singers in tow, Clinton split them into separate sectors. Lynn Mabry and Dawn Silva entered studios in Los Angeles. Simultaneously, Debbie Wright and Jeanette Washington were escorted into studios in Detroit. Being one girl shy of fulfilling his vision, Clinton's plan was to reenlist Mallia Franklin, who had made a name for herself as a lead singer on the Hollywood nightclub circuit.

Clinton rounded up an entourage to hit Hollywood's streets during a Mothership Earth Tour stop in Los Angeles in June 1977. The most important man in tow was Casablanca Records president Neil Bogart. Neil expressed to George that he wanted the first P-Funk female group released on Parliament's home label, Casablanca Records.

Richard "Kush" Griffith (left) and Frankie "Kash" Waddy (right) of Bootsy's Rubber Band pose with Mallia Franklin in 1977.

MALLIA FRANKLIN By 1977, my following in LA was pretty big. Everyone came out to my shows. My musical friends like The Chambers Brothers; Earth, Wind & Fire; and Side Effect were usually in attendance.

I had a weekly gig at the Soul'd Out on Sunset Boulevard and Vine. A guy named Eddie Nash owned the club. He loved my voice, and I sang at all his nightclubs and private parties. He had some really popular clubs, like the Starwood in West Hollywood and the Paradise Ballroom. Like many nightclub owners of that time, Eddie was a gangster. He was found guilty of what would be called "The Wonderland Murders" in 1981.

George would send Raymond Spruell, one of his managers, to the clubs around LA where I would perform. I would look up, and Raymond would be in the audience. At every show, he would tell me, "George said he's coming for you." That went on for about six months. Parliament-Funkadelic was on the Mothership Tour and played a big show at the LA Coliseum. George called me to come down and sit in. I told him I couldn't because I had a gig with my band Above and Beyond at the Soul'd Out that night. We usually did three sets a night. Around midnight, I was onstage and heard a commotion in the audience. A group of bodies got closer, and I started to recognize faces. I saw George, Bootsy, Garry Shider, Frankie "Kash," Bernie Worrell, Gary "Mudbone" Cooper, Michael Hampton, and most of the guys from P-Funk walking toward me. Ironically, this night was when Fuzzy, Grady, and Calvin left the group.

At the end of my set, George met me on the side of the stage. He hugged me and playfully said, "You're abducted!" George finally made good on his promise. He pulled me over to a table where a sharp-dressed man in a black velvet jacket sat.

George said, "Mallia, I want you to meet somebody. This is Neil Bogart. He's the president of Casablanca Records."

He looked over at Neil and said, "This is Mallia. Whatcha think?"

Neil stood up and grabbed my hands in his. He looked at me with the biggest smile and replied, "There *won't* be a girl group on Casablanca Records without her."

I thought, "*What* girl group is he talking about?"

I was confused, but I smiled and accepted the compliment.

They stayed for the last set of the night, and at the end of every song, they would stand, clap, and whistle. George has the loudest whistle . . . nobody whistles like him.

After my show, we all sat at a big table, and Neil ordered bottles of champagne. It felt like we were celebrating something. I just wasn't sure what it was. George leaned over and said, "I want you to go with us up north to Oakland and San Francisco. We leavin' in the morning. I'll send the Mothership to get you."

I replied, "Certainly!"

GEORGE CLINTON I knew that Mallia could sing, but damn! She blew all of us away that night. She was even better than I remembered. I had never really seen Mallia perform with a band. She had become a real pro and a great frontwoman. Mallia had such a strong voice and could riff her ass off. Goddamn, she tore that motherfucker down.

She had a hot band too. I asked her horn players (Clay Lawrey, Darryl Dixon, and Valerie Drayton) if they wanted a gig. The Horny Horns usually toured with us, but they were Bootsy's horn players. Bootsy started to get bigger than us and was gigging on his own, and the Horny Horns went out on the road with him. That left Parliament-Funkadelic with no horns section.

MALLIA FRANKLIN The next morning, a huge tour bus called the "Mothership" pulled up in Long Beach in front of the house that I shared with my fiancé, Donnie Sterling, and his family. Surprisingly, I met my horn players on the side of the bus. I didn't know that George had offered them a gig too. But I was happy for them to get the opportunity.

I gave my suitcase to the driver and climbed up the bus stairs. The first face that I saw was Debbie Wright. She let out a scream and threw her arms around me. Debbie introduced me to the other female Parliament singer, Jeanette Washington. She said that Jeanette was cool, which was *cool* enough for me. "You sharing a room with me!" Debbie insisted. During our conversation, Debbie and Jeanette told me about the two new girls in P-Funk. It didn't take long for me to realize that they disliked them. Because Debbie was a friend and we were from Detroit, she wanted me to dislike them too.

"We Detroit girls! We got to stick together. Fuck those California girls!"

After about five hours on the road, we arrived at a hotel in Oakland, California. The group unloaded, and one of the road managers, Ron Brembry, handed me a room key. Walking down the hotel hallway, I saw George turn the corner. Two girls were walking with him. One on each arm. I thought, "Uh oh, these must be the girls I've heard so much about." We met up, and he introduced me to P-Funk's newest additions.

"Mallia, this is Lynn and Dawn. These are my Brides."

With big, warm smiles, they both said, "Hello."

My first thought was, "His Brides?"

I knew George was a wild kind of guy, so it wasn't far-fetched for him to have two wives. After a few seconds, I realized, "Oh my God. That's Dawn Silva!" Dawn and I hadn't seen each other since the days with Sly Stone and Jeffrey Bowen. She flashed a huge smile and said, "Hey, girl!" We hugged. Dawn always had the "legs of life"! I call her "Silva Sonic" because even her walk was powerful. Lynn was fun, beautiful, and carefree, with a beautiful tone in her singing voice that was distinctly her own. She and Lynn were really close. So it was all love as far as I was concerned. I had no reason to dislike them. I wasn't threatened. I had been in Hollywood for a few years and had that "Valley-Cali glamour girl–star" thing on me too. And, I didn't have the same territorial issues that Debbie and Jeanette had with them.

I did my first show with Parliament-Funkadelic that night but wasn't onstage; I sang behind the amplifiers. Afterward, I went back to the hotel room I shared with Debbie.

She said, "Girl, I'm with George now."

"What?! Since when?"

"A few months ago," she said.

A lot of things had changed. And that confession was surprising to me. George was always like a big brother to us.

She then said, "I got some bomb weed. You want to puff on this joint with me?"

I needed a joint after that revelation and never turned down good weed, so I said, "Hell, yeah!"

Debbie opened the nightstand drawer and pulled out a tied-up silk scarf. Inside was a ball of aluminum foil. She cracked open the foil, and the odor was so intense that it filled the room. Inside was the greenest, rankest weed I had ever smelled. I could tell it had been soaked in PCP. "Angel dust" or "sherm" is what we called it back in the day. She lit a stick of incense to try to mask the pungent odor. Debbie rolled up a joint with that stinky weed, fired it up, and passed it to me.

I reluctantly said, "Hell, naw, girl! You can have that shit! I don't fuck around with angel dust."

I had only one experience with angel dust. A friend of my bandmate Donald Tavie offered me a "cool stick." I thought it was a combination of tobacco and weed. I didn't know it was dipped in formaldehyde . . . that's what they make dust with. I smoked it, and I couldn't even feel the floor. In all the hallucinations, I saw rainbows. It was the craziest shit in the world. It was such a head trip that I vowed never to smoke dust again. As I watched her puff on the joint, I grew concerned. Debbie and I had done drugs together in the past . . . pills, weed. But I never knew her to smoke angel dust . . . ever.

After the show in Oakland, we loaded the tour bus and returned to Los Angeles. George, or "Bert," as some of us called him, never wanted to hurt anyone's feelings or make them feel left out, so he would send the road managers over to relay secret messages. While we were on the bus, George sent Raymond Spruell over to talk to me. "George wants you to return to the hotel with us in LA, but don't tell nobody." That was George's favorite line, "Don't tell nobody."

George got rooms at the Continental Hyatt on Sunset Boulevard in West Hollywood. About an hour passed, and I got a call from him to come to his suite. George's room was easy to find. All you had to do was follow the loud music and smell of weed. His new girlfriend, Stephanie, answered the door. I came in and sat down across from him, and he lowered the volume on his boom box. Puffing on a joint, he said, "I want to talk seriously about you joining P-Funk full-time." He then asked me how I felt about a girl group situation. I had never been in a girl group before. I was discouraged by people in the industry, even the P-Funk guys, from joining one. They said that girls were a problem and there was always a lot of drama. I knew I was strong on my own, and I gravitated toward fronting self-contained bands more in the vein of Chaka Khan and Rufus.

I pondered it overnight and saw George the next day. He said, "What you wanna do?" I told him I'd be down to do a girl group if it got me in the door.

George said, "Cool! So, do you want to be a Parlet or a Bride of Funkenstein?"

I said, "Shit! I don't know the difference. Put me where you want me to be."

My fiancé, Donnie Sterling, was a great bass player and songwriter in his own right. I met Donnie a year earlier at a club in LA called Alias Smith & Jones. I went to see a band I eventually joined, Above and Beyond. A group opening for them was called The Higher Evolution of Music (T.H.E.M). Donnie Sterling was the bass player. He was quiet and kind of strange to me at first. But we eventually ended up getting together. Donnie asked me to move out of my hotel on Sunset Boulevard and into a house in Long Beach with his family. He ended up eventually joining Above & Beyond as well. Donnie came to my room at the Hyatt that night and got his chance to meet George Clinton in person. I wasn't going to leave Donnie out in the cold. He was talented. And I felt a sense of obligation. So I asked George if I could bring him in as a bass player when that time came. George said that he was cool with that.

GEORGE CLINTON Donnie Sterling, he played every instrument. He was a good musician. He would have been a Funkadelic if it hadn't been for Rodney "Skeet" Curtis showing up just in time to be Funkadelic's bass player.

DAWN SILVA Mallia and I developed a close friendship quickly because of our days at Marvin and Anna Gaye's house. She had an incredible voice, one of the best. Mal was strong . . . on par with singers like Glenn Goins. I liked that she was so confident, outspoken, and fearless. I don't think that she had a nervous bone in her body. We respected each other and got along really well. Mallia was added to the fold, and we weren't sure of George's plan. He always talked to Lynn and me about a girl group. I thought that Debbie and Jeanette would just continue as members of Parliament.

I would go by the Backstage Management offices in LA to hang out with one of the owners, Ron Strasner. Ron and I had formed a friendship. He always ensured that he had some Acapulco Gold marijuana for me. Ron didn't mess with hardcore drugs, but he always had my little weed sack and never charged me. We talked about the "P-Funk girl group," and Ron said George and Backstage were excited. He then said that Lynn, me, and Mallia were the girls he was speaking of. We liked Mallia, and she liked us. We didn't have issues with her like we did with Debbie and Jeanette. We had our own looks and style, different complexions, with different vocal styles. It would have been powerful. The plan was for us to be the trio. The three of us were supposed to be The Brides of Funkenstein.

LYNN MABRY Mallia Franklin . . . what a voice. I don't recall where I first heard her, but it was a little overwhelming when I heard her sing. I was a bit intimidated. I mean, *I* was a singer . . . but Mallia was a *sanger, sanger.* I felt she was one of the best singers I had ever heard with George. She so overshadowed the rest of us girls. I thought, "This could be a one-girl operation with just her." Once I got to know her and she got to know me, she was so cool that that's all that mattered.

What was very interesting was, for whatever reason, George kind of kept her and me apart. I don't know if he did that on purpose so we wouldn't be so close? We never really shared heart-to-heart talks. It was usually about a gig, traveling, or someone she met. She was funny, goofy, and all about the funk. She wasn't caught up in the *girl* stuff. We got along without a problem, and she had no hang-ups with Dawn and me. Mallia didn't care about what group she would be in, what she sang, or who she sang with. She was always down for *anything*; that's what I remember most about her.

The day came when George finally revealed his big plan. He said, "I want you and Dawn to be The Brides of Funkenstein and the other girls to be Parlet." George explained that he wanted Parlet to be more of the funky, roughter-edged side and The Brides to be more on the softer side. Honestly, that's who we were in real life. When Dawn and I came into Parliament-Funkadelic, we weren't Funkateers by any means. We were straight off the Sly Stone boat with our long gowns and rhinestones. I was cool with being a Bride, but it was not a great gift initially. Jeanette and Debbie felt like *they* should be The Brides because they had been in P-Funk longer than Dawn and I. To them, it was a statement about their relationship with George. I remember Mallia not caring one way or the other.

GEORGE CLINTON Neil Bogart at Casablanca was a serious concept guy, and I took him The Brides of Funkenstein first. Neil didn't like the name. He said it was *too* dark. But I loved the name and knew we had to use it somewhere. He wanted a girl group with a name closer to Parliament, which was on his label. He wanted some "Par-lets." In 1965, we used the name, the Parlettes, on a record for Roy Handy called "Accidental Love," but it wasn't a *real* group. I didn't want the name to sound too much like an old-school Motown act, so we dropped some letters and changed it from the Parlettes to Parlet. Debbie and Jeanette were the first girls in Parliament, and I had already started recording them. Neil was sold on Mallia, so giving Casablanca Debbie, Jeanette, and Mallia made sense.

I knew immediately that I wanted Lynn and Dawn to be The Brides of Funkenstein. They looked like Brides to me. I started seeing them as a group when they came into the studio for their first sessions on Eddie Hazel and the Horny Horns albums. I liked Lynn and Dawn because, as a duo, it looked weird but in a good way. They weren't really Funkadelic, but they had a funk thing about them. Most of us looked strange, but they looked like a different kind of strange. It was beautiful and appealing. I like weird and different, so I dug the whole Brides concept and became more involved with the project. That began to cause a hassle between Bootsy and me because he always wanted me to be right there for *everything* he did.

LYNN MABRY After George made his decision, he would do things that made waves with the girls. We would all be in the studio, and George would play a great song each wanted for our album.

We would ask excitedly, "Whose song is that, George?"

He would grin and casually say, "I don't know whose song that's going to be yet."

Little things like that created more jealousy and tension. George then tried to separate us onstage when we performed with P-Funk. He now wanted Parlet—Mallia, Debbie, and Jeanette—on one side of the stage and The Brides—Dawn and I—on the other. That part was the most strenuous for me because I didn't want us to be separated. It didn't make me feel good.

Was it so we could have our own identities as separate groups?

Was it to elevate our performances onstage?

Was it to manipulate the whole situation?

I wasn't sure. But in hindsight, looking back at how it turned out, I believe it was all a part of George's master plan. In general, there was a lot of jealousy in P-Funk. Like most groups of women working together for any length of time, there is always an underlying envy, resentment, or fear of the unknown. We were all young. We weren't mature and cultivated. It was damaging to us for George not to be as responsible as he should have been. Partly because *he* wasn't mature himself. I also think he created division and competition. I often felt we were all enslaved to the master . . . male and female members alike.

MALLIA FRANKLIN George asked me to meet him and Neil Bogart at Casablanca's offices on Sunset Boulevard in West Hollywood. Parlet would be one of the first girl groups, if not the first, on Casablanca. We came from Parliament, which was a big deal to the record company.

As we sat in Neil's office, George said, "You can do this girl group thing for a while, and then we will break you off like we did with Bootsy." Neil agreed. That plan sounded good to me. He asked George if the contract had been signed yet. George replied, "We're having the contract drawn up as we speak."

DONNIE STERLING (PARLET'S BASSIST) I remember Mallia and me going to Liebert-Krebs Agency in Hollywood. David Liebert was George's agent at the time. Lynn and Dawn were there working out their contracts with David for The Brides. Parlet didn't have a record deal yet; the guys were still trying to get them signed to Casablanca.

David Liebert and Cholly Bassoline, George's manager, wanted a crossover look. Neil Bogart told them he wanted Mallia to do the "Diana Ross"... do a couple albums with Parlet, then go solo. She could sing *most* females under the table and had *the look* . . . that "white-Italian" look that could get them in the pop world, and David and Cholly were adamant about her signing the contract.

MALLIA FRANKLIN George asked me to meet him at Backstage Management a couple of weeks later. When I walked in, Lynn and Dawn were already there. My first thought was, "Where are Debbie and Jeanette?"

Lynn, Dawn, and I sat at a conference table across from George, Ron Strasner, Cholly Bassoline, and David Liebert. We were all handed identical contracts with George's new production company, Thang Incorporated. The only difference was that mine was exclusively for Parlet, and theirs was for Brides of Funkenstein.

I signed the contract about a week later, and was given a check for fifteen hundred dollars toward a five-thousand-dollar advance. Because I was popular in the LA music scene, I had friends in the record business, including Casablanca. I was told later by Cecil Holmes, an executive at Casablanca, that I was the *only* girl signed as a Parlet because of Neil's interest in me as a solo artist. He told me that my deal with George matched his deal with Casablanca—three albums for Parlet.

I had to move back to Detroit to record because that was home base for P-Funk. I called my parents and told them I was coming home.

GARRY SHIDER There were a few P-Funk members that George locked up with paperwork. He locked you down with a contract if he felt you were a moneymaker or needed you to make some shit happen. Most of the guys in P-Funk didn't have contracts, only a few. It created problems for some people in the organization, with jealousy and shit like that. It suggested to the other band members, "This person is important, and you aren't." It's that *competition* thing, and George was all about competition. That's the reason we had so many damn people in the group. "If you don't act right, I can replace you. As a matter of fact, your replacement is already here." That was the kind of shit that kept people *paranoid* about their gig. That's why we had three drummers, four bass players, ten singers, and all the extra people. You were in constant competition. It was a control tactic, and it worked.

CHAPTER 10

FLASH LIGHT

Parliament reached a new career high in 1978 with the release of their funk anthem "Flash Light," the group's first number-one song on the Billboard Soul charts. Their album *Funkentelechy vs. the Placebo Syndrome* was the group's highest-charting to date, reaching the number-two spot. In his autobiography, Clinton said, "If I had to pick one P-Funk record to take to the moon, I'd take *Funkentelechy vs. the Placebo Syndrome*."

Bootsy Collins's success as a spin-off act, with a number-one album, *Ahh . . . The Name Is Bootsy, Baby!*, opened the door for more offshoots from the P-Funk camp to hit the market. New releases from Fred Wesley and the Horny Horns and guitarist Eddie Hazel were already on record store racks.

Clinton contacted Ron Dunbar, the A&R executive of his former label, Invictus Records. Dunbar had a track record as an accomplished songwriter. He wrote Freda Payne's hit "Band of Gold," won a Grammy in 1971 for writing the song "Patches" for Clarence Carter, and penned multiple songs for other artists during his time at the label.

RON DUNBAR (PRODUCER) I had just left Invictus Records, and Jim Vitti, one of P-Funk's sound engineers, suggested that George call me. P-Funk

Dr. Funkenstein: George Clinton on the Flash Light Tour in 1978.

had become a phenomenon with the Mothership. George called me up, and I went to the studio to sit down and talk to him about what he wanted to do. He described a concept to me about starting a record company like Motown. He said he had two girl groups in the works. George made me an offer to partner with him.

He said, "I want you to run this company with me."

His next statement shocked me. He said, "Money is no object!"

I thought about it for a few days, called him back, and accepted. The next thing I knew, George gave me about seven hundred thousand dollars to get the company [Thang Incorporated] up and running. I didn't know what to do with that kind of money. I had a good friend named Ken Doshi, a certified public accountant. I called him, and he helped us start the production company legitimately. After putting it all in order, George gave me my first writing and production tasks. At first, I had my reservations.

He said, "You have a lot of success with female singers and groups. I want you to formulate the girl groups, produce and write on them, and handle the artist relations part."

I said, "George, I don't know if I can write this kind of music. Everything you are dealing with musically is *funk*, and everything I do is *pop* oriented."

He replied, "I want something different than just the *funk* for the girls. I want to incorporate that pop aspect so they can cross over to the pop charts."

George knew I had a background with Holland-Dozier-Holland and could write pop music well, so he put Parlet and The Brides in my hands. He wanted Parlet to be the funkier of the two groups and The Brides to be more mainstream. Based on what George told me he wanted, I tried to project the music and lyrics as I heard them.

He gave me my first music track, and I wrote "Amorous" for The Brides. He listened to it and loved it. I was relieved. Now I had a concept of dealing with the females. All five girls were background singers for Parliament-Funkadelic at the time. I got to know them while writing the songs, and, as a producer, I started listening for *lead* voices. I had to find out who would be the best fit from a lead vocalist's perspective. Mallia had the vocal attitude and disposition George told me he wanted for Parlet. She vocally projected the *power* of the funk. I looked at Mallia as the group's focal point and the other two girls more as background, but they were good singers, too.

I took a much sweeter approach with The Brides, Lynn and Dawn. I toned their songs down a bit. I was looking to get a balance of funk *and* sweetness. I wrote and produced songs for them, like the ballad "When You're Gone." We had them doing a lot of ballads in the beginning. "Just Like You" was one that Lynn was featured on, and "Ice Melting in My Heart" featured Dawn. They were both good vocalists individually, but I loved their blend when they sang together.

After "Amorous," we concentrated on Parlet. They were going to be the first girl group out. I wrote a ballad with Gary "Mudbone" Cooper [vocalist for Bootsy's Rubber Band] called "Mr. Melody Man." Debbie Wright sang lead, and she did a wonderful job. Mallia was still living in Los Angeles, so I brought a group called Brandye [Cynthia Douglas, Pam Vincent, and Donna Davis] to fatten up the background vocals.

We started working on the funkier songs, like "Love Amnesia" and "Cookie Jar," when Mallia returned to Detroit. That's when the group's vocal direction really started to take shape. Neil [Bogart] and Casablanca put real money into the first album. We sent the tapes to David Van dePitte in New York, where he would do the string arrangements over the tracks cut by the P-Funk musicians. David did strings for The Temptations and many of the Invictus artists. George hired the Detroit Symphony Orchestra string section to play on some Parlet songs and a couple of Bride songs with some of that money.

MALLIA FRANKLIN By the fall of 1977, I was back in Detroit and joined Debbie and Jeanette at United Sound Systems. They already had a couple of songs cut when I joined the group. I think they thought that Parlet would be just the two of them and that I would be a Bride of Funkenstein with Lynn and Dawn. The Brides were supposed to be the trio.

My first day on a Parlet session was just Gary "Mudbone" Cooper and me. Mudbone is one of my best friends and one of the most amazing singers. We have done so much together vocally on Parlet, Bootsy, P-Funk, and other artists. Too many to count. He helped me tap into those character voices that I do. He taught all of us girls so much vocally.

He called me down to United, and we did background vocals on "Mr. Melody Man," which was pretty much complete. There's a background track with the group Brandye and a background track with just Mudbone and me. We stacked harmonies on top of Brandye and did background parts that they didn't do. Our blend is and always has been absolutely amazing.

We were recording Parlet and Parliament's *Funkentelechy . . .* simultaneously. We would be recording "Love Amnesia" in Studio A, and George would call us into Studio B to put vocals on songs like "Flash Light" or "Bop Gun" for Parliament with Lynn and Dawn. I remember George saying that *Funkentelechy* . . . was a perfect album. He had Glenn Goins, the original Parlet and Brides, and Bassist Rodney "Skeet" Curtis, who had just joined. He just really loved everything about that album. I think this period in time was George's most creative and important.

RON FORD (PRODUCER) When I started musically, I wasn't a musician, I wasn't a writer. . . I came from the streets. I would work on a song then catch a musician, and he would interpret it with instruments. It was a learning process. P-Funk was a family situation; it was competitive also. When I got my first chance to produce something, it was on Parlet's first album. By the time we got to "Misunderstanding" with Parlet, I really understood who I was dealing with. When I heard them sing, Debbie and Mallia . . . it was frightening.

They were all some singin' women . . . Mallia, Debbie, and Jeanette . . . all of them, Dawn and Lynn too. I'm talking about magnificent artists in terms of vocal ability. All the girls were very at ease working with me, even though I wasn't a real musician. They trusted my ability to try whatever came out of my mind. And that was a blessing.

GARY "MUDBONE" COOPER (VOCALIST, BOOTSY'S RUBBER BAND) In my cowriting with Bootsy and Clinton on "I'd Rather Be with You" for Bootsy's Rubber Band, I was extended writing and coproduction offers to make music with Ron Dunbar for the various artists signed to Thang Incorporated. I loved Parlet and The Brides and was responsible for coaching them vocally. Parlet had that Detroit mix with the funk. The Brides had a funky West Coast thang, giving both acts a distinct sound. We were all working for the same purpose: to represent the funkiest music entity on the planet.

Mallia got lots of attention in the studio because of her powerful vocal style. The Brides were also getting a lot of attention, which somewhat took the spotlight off Debbie and Jeanette. Still, it wasn't intended to belittle them. Debbie showed her vocal chops and soul when she performed "Mr. Melody Man."

FRANKIE "KASH" WADDY It took a minute to develop Debbie and Jeanette into a separate unit away from the guys. They were so ingrained into Parliament that they needed direction to become their own entity as Parlet.

Mallia came in the only way she could . . . as a lead singer. It put Debbie and Jeanette off, but Mallia had that "takeover" spirit. She was more seasoned. She had a direction of who she was and knew her capabilities away from P-Funk. Mal was glamorous and well spoken, and she could really sing. She had what Parlet needed to be a success. That was one of George's greatest gifts; he knew the people to put together to make a project successful.

MALLIA FRANKLIN I got a call from Liz Bishop in the fall of '77. Although she and George were now separated, my sister Jenifer and I were still extremely close to her. Liz called me and suggested that I hire her cousin from Buffalo, New York, for Parlet's band. She said that George had been promising him a spot in Parliament for years but would never hire him.

Liz said, "Mallia, he's bad! He can sing, write, and play a mean bass."

I told Liz that my man, Donnie [Sterling], was going to be Parlet's bass player. She then said that her cousin was in LA trying to get his demos to Berry Gordy at Motown. I told Liz to call Jenifer and her fiancé, Jeffrey Bowen. As Bowen was a producer for Berry, it would be no problem. Liz called Jenifer, and she pushed Jeffrey to listen to the demos. He took the demos to Suzanne DePasse at Motown. A month or so later, I got a call from Jeffrey.

In the most arrogant tone, he said, "Tell Bootsy that I got something for his ass . . . his name is Rick James! I told y'all to stick with me, but y'all wanted to run behind George!" The next thing I knew, Liz's cousin, Rick James, had a deal on Motown Records. Rick always says in interviews that he just *ran in* to Jeffrey. But that's not how it happened. Liz and Jenifer hooked that up.

By the winter of '77, Jenifer was back home in Detroit with me and our parents. Things got bad between Jenifer and Jeffrey because of his excessive drug use, and finding out that he was having an affair with Bonnie Pointer of the Pointer Sisters. Jeffrey convinced Bonnie to leave her sisters to be a solo artist and got her a record deal on Motown. Bonnie had a hit or two, but her sisters [Anita, Ruth, and June] had multiple hits in the seventies and eighties. After severe physical and mental abuse on Jeffrey's part, Jenifer left Jeffrey, Hollywood, and the Berry Gordy house on the hill.

JENIFER FRANKLIN As soon as I heard Rick, I thought there was something special about him. I told Jeffrey, "I think you need to listen to him. He's really good." Jeffrey was arrogant, and misused people, including me. I was young; he was much older and very controlling. But he knew that there was something about me that was magic for him and inspired him to write hit songs.

We ran into Rick hanging out in the parking garage at Motown's offices in Hollywood. A lot of people hung out there, waiting to be discovered. Jeffrey ignored Rick and kept walking, but I stopped. When he came back for me, I made him listen to Rick. They exchanged numbers, and Jeffrey got him the record deal. They wrote "You and I" together... Rick's first hit record.

LIZ BISHOP (GEORGE CLINTON'S EX-FIANCÉE) I took Rick James to George first, and he wanted no part of him. Then I called Mallia and Jenifer. That's exactly how that happened. Rick was my family. He called me "Queen Mother over the bullshit." He said that I knew bullshit when I heard or saw it. When I took him to Jenifer and Jeffrey, Rick said that he would give me 10 percent of what he earned. I love George to this day, but I know that he wanted to control me financially. I came up with the name the Horny Horns, and he never gave me credit for that.

When Rick got his record deal with Motown, he said, "Liz... tell your man George that I'm coming for him!"

I said, "George already knows *all* about you."

It's a shame that I wasn't allowed to have a part financially in Rick James's success, but George's ego wasn't going to stand for that.

CHAPTER 11

PLEASURE PRINCIPLE

Parlet's debut album, *Pleasure Principle*, was released in February 1978. It was intended to catalyze Dr. Funkenstein's new brand of female funk. Parliament laid the foundation in the song "Sir Nose D'Voidoffunk (Pay Attention)," with Clinton proclaiming that his newest alter ego, "Star Child," was the protector of the Pleasure Principle. Every promotional piece for the Parlet album talked of sensual gratification, satisfaction, or various ways the group would musically get you off.

Neil Bogart at Casablanca firmly believed that colorful, sexy cover art sold albums. The label commissioned Shusei Nagaoka, a Japanese artist known for his Egyptian pyramids for Earth, Wind & Fire, spaceships for ELO, and incredible sci-fi art for *Omni* magazine's pages, to illustrate the women on the album. The 1981 Japanese coffee-table book *The Works of Shusei Nagaoka* offered a loose translation by the artist himself of the album's concept. He said, "It's a playful album cover. I was asked to draw a brothel in space. Disco + Space + Brothels is like a Las Vegas revue. I had to figure out how to make the image different from Vegas follies. Many of the people in the record industry who make such orders think that as long as it catches people's attention when it goes on sale, that's fine."

The cover depicts the Parlet trio posed on a starship in spacesuits, bare

The art for Parlet's Pleasure Principle*: Artist Shusei Nagaoka's final rendition of Debbie Wright, Mallia Franklin, and Jeanette Washington aboard the Starship Pleasure Principle in 1978.*

at the breasts with silver stars covering their nipples. The ship is cleverly constructed of components mimicking private parts. There's a chair in the shape of a penis, lamps similar to breasts, and a control panel resembling a vulva. A full illustration of the starship on the back reveals that the vessel is a funk-powered intergalactic vagina constructed of steel, glass, and neon lights.

GEORGE CLINTON Parlet was first out the gate. They would have ended up as Neil Bogart's crossover bubblegum-pop group, which they could have easily been. They had the looks and talent, and Neil was a great promotion man. It surprised me that they came off so good and tight on their first album. Mallia had the power . . . that Patti [LaBelle] and Chaka [Khan] power. Debbie sang with such broken-up passion, and Jeanette just surprised the hell out of me.

We released the title single, "Pleasure Principle." It was a great song. It's one of the best songs we've ever done, but it was too slick. It was so jazzy that you really couldn't dance to it. They could have put any other song out on that album, and it would have been a hit. Parlet would have been big right out the gate. They would have been gone.

MALLIA FRANKLIN You must understand that we were coming off the women's lib movement. Women weren't afraid of sexuality. We were burning our bras and declaring our rights to be *whoever* we wanted to be. When we saw the album cover for the first time, we knew it was provocative . . . but space hoes? We weren't thinking about misogyny at that time. We were just glad to have an album out. Casablanca was really a disco label, and "Pleasure Principle," although funky, was a disco song. Neil Bogart wanted a record to play in the discothèques alongside Donna Summer and the Village People. I know that was calculated to cross Parlet over to the pop charts.

Everything was fine while recording the album, but I could feel things start to shift when it was time to release it. Casablanca sent a photographer to United Sound while we were recording to take pictures of us for the artist doing the portrait for the cover. We were posing and taking pictures when the photographer grabbed a piano bench and told me to sit in the middle. I sat down with Jeanette standing on one side and Debbie on the other.

There was a moment when I looked up at Debbie, and she cut her eyes at me in a way that pierced to the bone. That was the first time that I didn't feel welcomed by her. I felt like an outsider to Debbie, which really hurt my feelings. That fleeting glance let me know this was supposed to be Debbie and Jeanette's thing. I was an intruder. This group wasn't about the three of us, and Parlet sure wasn't going to be about *me*.

When the first rendition of the artwork came in that Casablanca ordered, they started promoting it. The artist re-created the picture of Debbie standing on the left, Jeanette on the right, and me sitting in the middle. That caused a problem, and the album cover became a *thing*. After the first image went public, George had it changed to look more "balanced."

Then the press started, and the organization had me speaking on behalf of the group in interviews, like *Rolling Stone* magazine. That was a problem. George was trying to smooth it over and keep everything cool, but that left room for bitch shit to start between us girls. There's all this tension within the group, and the album isn't even out yet.

I remember one night, out of nowhere, Debbie snapped at me and said, "Are you fucking George? You must be fucking him!"

I was stunned. I said, "What? Girl! Hell, no! You know better than that!"

After all these years, Debbie felt I must have fucked George to get the focus on me. That really hurt, especially coming from her. Jealousy was never an issue with Debbie. I didn't understand where this came from.

GEORGE CLINTON I knew the girls had some bickering, but I didn't think they were going through all that. I knew they were probably going through something, but I was too busy trying to keep shit together. I didn't have time for all those kinds of problems.

TOM VICKERS (PUBLICIST) George and I discussed how we would develop the publicity aspects for the girls. Promoting The Brides of Funkenstein was unique because they were a duo. They were two distinct female voices. Both could lead vocally and had a presence onstage. George played more on the sex appeal and beauty of Lynn and Dawn, not as much of the futuristic vibe as Parlet in their costuming, but they also had the vocal ability and stagecraft. They knew how to be frontwomen as well as background singers. Either one could easily be the lead because they were *both* leaders.

George saw Parlet as the space-age girl group. He kept the trio dynamic that started at Motown with groups like the Marvelettes and the Supremes and thrust that whole mindset into the future. He wanted to give them a very futuristic image, borrowing the whole Labelle vibe in costuming and taking it one step further. There was a lot of trading off of lead vocals on the first album [*Pleasure Principle*], but when we launched Parlet, we were selling Mallia from George's and my perspectives. No disrespect, but Debbie and Jeanette were considered backup . . . more or less.

BRUCE PETERSON (MARKETING/MANAGEMENT) I worked on the marketing strategies for Brides and Parlet. I think that Dawn and Lynn, just being called The Brides of Funkenstein, had the upper hand of sorts with the press. Jeanette and Debbie were fun and great singers, but similar. Mallia stood out. If we needed someone from the group to do interviews or to come to industry events, we wanted Mallia there. She had the personality and was a natural spokesperson. What I liked was that she promoted *all* the women. She wanted all the girls to win. She didn't believe in "a woman's place." Mal wanted to be in the room with the guys. She wasn't going to let anyone close the door on her. "If y'all are in the meeting, I'm in here too!" That's how she was.

After the massive success of Parliament's album *Funkentelechy vs. the Placebo Syndrome* and their first number-one hit, "Flash Light," P-Funk hit the road on the Flash Light Tour in January 1978. Early Casablanca press releases stated that Parlet would debut as an opening act on the Flash Light Tour and return on a summer tour with Bootsy's Rubber Band, who had a number-one album, *Player of the Year*, and number-one single, "Bootzilla," on the charts.

MALLIA FRANKLIN Debbie's brother, Jim Wright, played on the *Pleasure Principle* album and started recruiting Parlet's band. He got Ernestro Wilson [keyboards], Manon Saulsby [keyboards], Gordon Carlton [guitar], and his sister Janice [percussions]. He also brought in Jerome Ali [guitar]; my fiancé, Donnie [Sterling] would be on bass. Casablanca had given us something like thirty thousand dollars to buy new instruments. Johnny Parent and Joey Zaloback [P-Funk's main roadie] purchased a laundry list of instruments for our band. Dunbar said LeGaspi, who designed for KISS and Grace Jones, was making our costumes.

One of the first Flash Light shows, if not *the* first, was in Detroit at Cobo Arena. We were staying at the Michigan Inn Hotel in Southfield, a beautiful suburb of Detroit. After the show, there was a party in one of the hotel's banquet rooms to celebrate the success of "Flash Light" and the upcoming release of the Parlet album in February. The Parliament and Parlet albums played over the speakers, and the waiters passed champagne

Bootsy Collins, Mallia Franklin, and "Friend to the Funk" Lee Rosenbloom in 1978 at a party to celebrate P-Funk's first number-one record, "Flash Light."

around the room. There was a small stage with a podium and long black velvet curtains.

What made this party special was the unveiling of the *Pleasure Principle* album for the first time. The P-Funk staff passed the guests promotional copies of the Parlet album. We signed some for record-store owners and disc jockeys. It was our first taste of success as a group.

Toward the end of the night, George rounded Debbie, Jeanette, and me up and told us that he wanted us to say a few words to the guests . . . a room that included record execs, radio people, and press.

George said, "I'll say a few words, then introduce y'all. Jeanette, go up and do your thing. Debbie, you go up and do your thing. Mal, you go up last, do your thang, and thank everyone on behalf of the group. I need you to thank Casablanca, Neil [Bogart], and all the radio stations."

So we made our speeches as George directed and turned stage right to exit. Jeanette was in front, Debbie in the middle, and I walked in the back.

As we walked off the stage, Debbie grabbed the velvet curtain and furiously whipped it in front of me. When my platform shoe stepped on the velvet, I felt my foot slip and my left ankle roll sideways. I hit the floor on my hands and knees. Razor and Frankie "Kash" from Bootsy's Rubber

Band ran over and helped me up. They carried me to my room with torn stockings, a bruised ego, and a twisted ankle.

The first half of the Flash Light Tour was a wrap for me. I missed the whole East Coast. I didn't want to believe that Debbie did that on purpose. I never thought, and still don't think, that she would ever hurt me. But I also knew there were times when Debbie was angry at everybody . . . everyone except George.

Money was already getting funny with the organization. My mom was my business manager, and I had an attorney, Dan Levit. They contacted George and his lawyer, Jay Kramer, at Weiss & Meibach, about money I was owed from recording the Parlet album that was months overdue. My lawyer had advised me not to go on the road until George paid me the rest of my five-thousand-dollar advance. So they weren't really upset that I wasn't touring. Debbie, Jeanette, Lynn, and Dawn went out with George and the guys to start the Flash Light Tour. I stayed home to heal.

LYNN MABRY As my short-lived relationship with George fizzled out, before I knew it, there I was, falling for lead singer and guitarist Glenn Goins. However unexpected, he became one of the loves of my life. When I first saw him onstage, he was the second-strangest-looking guy besides George. He wore a beanie, a big black spot painted on his eye, leotards with holey fishnet stockings, and stringless tennis shoes. It wasn't his looks that got my attention, but when he opened his mouth and sang, "The Mothership's coming! Can you see the Mothership coming?" I was floored. I found myself being drawn to him often. I connected with him and his voice while onstage. His sound was so pure and captivating. He sang all his life and always knew singing would be his profession. He was a Christian and had a spiritual connection with the gift that God gave him. I realized I had a gift, too, but maybe [I was] not appreciative of it yet. Glenn was one of the first people to listen and critique my voice from a creative standpoint, not just a professional one.

We started out as friends, and, in caring for him, I would style his hair every night before he went onstage. That was something he loved and eventually expected. The romance came very unexpectedly. Glenn opened a creative, loving side in me that I had never experienced. After we dated for a while, he told me he had a wife and a baby on the way. I was young and not as sensitive because I was still immature and self-serving. I felt guilty knowing he was married, but I was sprung. We used drugs excessively and

(Top) *Brides (Dawn Silva and Lynn Mabry) and* (bottom) *Parlets (Jeanette Washington and Debbie Wright) onstage for the Flash Light Tour in 1978.*

drank like everyone else on the road, yet I felt incredibly safe with him. I would've given it all up if things were different just to be with him.

Most of the tension in the organization for Glenn . . . [and for] all of us, was about money. The money got unstable, which was strange because the tours were getting larger, and the albums were selling more. We would see magazine articles about the millions of dollars P-Funk was making, but we barely scraped by.

We went to George and said, "We've been making the same amount of money for a while now. Your money is getting larger by the minute, and it doesn't seem fair because we are all doing the work for you."

He replied, "Don't worry, it's coming."

That was always his response when I questioned him about money. I think George looked at this P-Funk world like a chess game. I don't believe he realized that his pawns had real lives. We were at the peak of success, playing in stadiums all across the country. We needed to work, and the funds were not coming in steadily. The lack of funds was controlling us. Nothing ever changed, and eventually, Glenn got fed up. He did some of the first shows on the Flash Light Tour. Then he left P-Funk for good in early 1978 . . . and I was devastated.

MALLIA FRANKLIN By March 1978, I joined the Flash Light Tour when it was headed down south. Debbie and Jeanette were still at odds with Lynn and Dawn when I got on the road. I tried to stay out of it, but I felt like I was in the middle of a bunch of bitch shit that had nothing to do with me. Debbie was my friend, and we had a history. I was still trying to build a friendship with Jeanette, and I was friends with Lynn and Dawn.

I saw something deeply disturbing in Debbie when I got out on the road. She had changed. She was angry a lot of the time and was just not acting like herself. She was so hostile. Jeanette was even staying away from her. She didn't want to room with her anymore, so George made me her roommate. I knew that Debbie had done drugs. We all did drugs. But I wasn't certain that her behavior was all about drugs. She had an adoration for George at that time that was obsessive.

I didn't know how heavy her issues were until we were at a truck stop down south. Everyone got off the tour bus to eat at a little roadside diner. Afterward, Frankie "Kash," Dawn, and I were walking back to the tour bus. Debbie walked up to Frankie with a scowl on her face. I'll never forget it. He was wearing a beautiful, brand-new tan leather jacket. She said something crazy to him and threw a cup of hot coffee in his face. Frankie remained

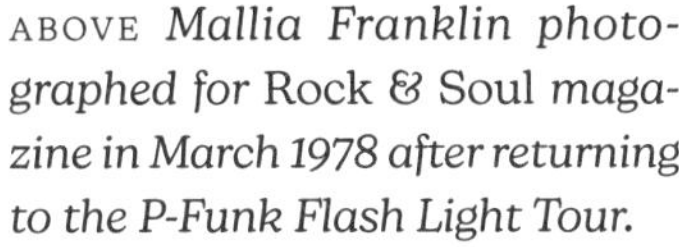

ABOVE *Mallia Franklin photographed for* Rock & Soul *magazine in March 1978 after returning to the P-Funk Flash Light Tour.*

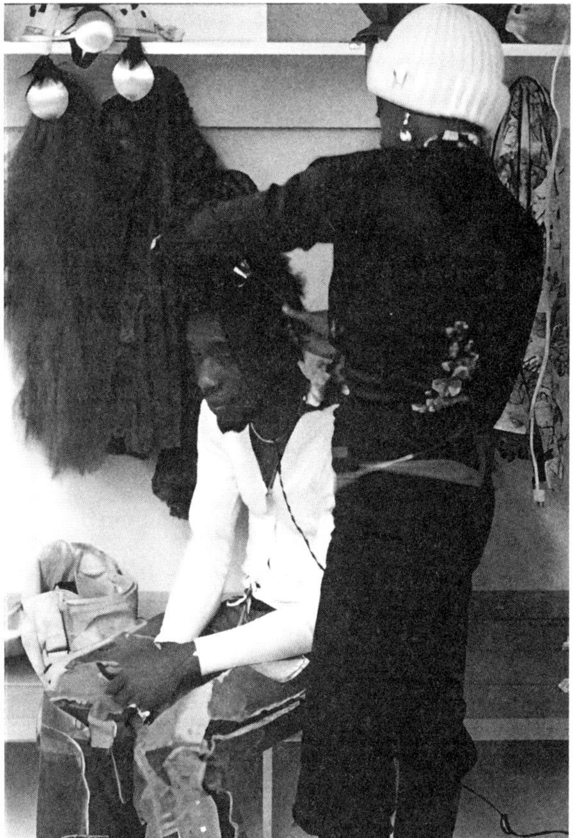

RIGHT *Lynn Mabry curls and styles Glenn Goins's hair backstage before showtime in 1977.*

calm, but Dawn and I were stunned. That was the first time I knew, "This isn't just drugs."

Later that night, I was trying to sleep, but I could hear the water from the shower running. I heard a blood-curdling scream. I was startled but leaped out of bed toward the bathroom door. I opened the door, and Debbie was backed up in the corner of the shower, and she was terrified.

She was screaming, "Get away from me!"

I pleaded with her, "Debbie, it's me . . . it's Mal."

After about thirty seconds of trying to reason with her, she snapped out of it. I helped her out of the shower, and she collapsed.

"I don't know what's going on, Mal. I don't know what's wrong with me," she tearfully said.

Soaking wet, I just held her. At that moment, that was all I could do. Debbie would talk to me about how much pressure she was under.

She said, "Mal, everybody's taking little pieces of me, and I don't know how much more I have left." That broke my heart.

A couple of nights later, I heard her beating on the doors and walls in the hotel hallway. She screamed at the top of her lungs, calling George's name. Now I was convinced that this was *deeper* than drugs.

Some days Debbie was cool, and then she wasn't. I had known her long enough to see when she got edgy. Sometimes I could calm her down and bring her back. But even *I* was becoming afraid of her because her violent behavior increased. It was like watching a volcano and waiting for it to blow. George was saying that Debbie needed some rest. "She needs to go home and take a break." It was deeper than that, and she was still smoking angel dust on top of it.

It got to a point where other bands we were touring with, like the Bar-Kays and Cameo, noticed her erratic behavior. They'd approach Jeanette and me and say, "What's wrong with her?! Is she alright?" It was becoming obvious that Debbie was going through something serious.

DAWN SILVA At the time, angel dust and heroin were taboo in P-Funk. You can snort up all the cocaine in Peru and smoke as much weed as you want, but you can't get caught with those two drugs. Lynn and I would sit at the front of the stage, sing, and smoke weed given to us by fans in the audience. I would take the joint and blow hits to all the band members. One night I grabbed a joint from a fan and took a hit. As soon as I inhaled, I could taste the chemical. A few seconds later, everything started going in slow motion. I could see the fan saying, "You've been dusted." Two security guards had to pick me up and carry me backstage. I stopped smoking weed with the audience after that night.

A crop of angel dust going around at that time was toxic in some way, and I think that Debbie got a hold of some of that dust, and it sent her into a downward spiral, and she snapped. She was losing control and doing bizarre things. Once, Debbie got a big block of cheese from a grocery store and brought it to the tour bus. She stabbed it with a knife repeatedly and called George's name. It was eerie. You thought she was going to turn around and stab *you* next. Everybody was becoming afraid of Debbie.

We had an incident with her on tour in Nevada. The tour bus pulled into a desert gas station in the morning's wee hours. I saw Debbie take off her shoes. She got off the bus and started screaming her head off, "Help! They're raping me! They're trying to kill me! Help!" She ran across the highway into the darkness, where there was nothing but desert. You saw this tiny figure, and then she disappeared. Some of the guys ran after her and caught her. She was brought back, kicking and screaming. She was so petite, but it took four or five guys to hold her. She had a super, *unnatural* strength for a female. You almost had to hurt her to calm her down. Her feet were bleeding from all the cacti and sharp rocks she had stepped on. We wrapped them up with clothes.

LINDA SHIDER I believed that different circumstances were going on with Debbie. When they decided to get lasers for the live shows, they hired a laser technician from Los Angeles. He started hanging out with Debbie a lot. He was smoking angel dust, and he was giving it to her. Once we arrived back in LA for a few weeks of recording, Debbie went to this guy's house and stayed with him. I guess he gave her some dust that was too strong for her to handle.

She returned to the hotel a few days later and was out of it. We started heading back to Detroit on the tour bus, and the bus was continuously having engine problems. Debbie had gone into a twilight zone. The trip took about three days, and Debbie would try to run off every time the driver stopped the bus. She was attacking people and talking crazy. We had to drive back to Detroit with her in that state, which was really scary. We tried to hug her, love her, and bring her down, but nothing worked. That was heartbreaking.

GEORGE CLINTON We had been introduced to angel dust in the sixties. I didn't know it had come back on the scene during the *Mothership Connection* period. That one caught me way off guard. We got past the era of acid. Heroin was so far for me that I couldn't imagine anything worse. Angel dust got me bad one time at the 20 Grand in Detroit. I fell out on the stage during a show, and when I woke up, I was in the middle of the floor. That's when I knew that dust wasn't my thing.

I saw Debbie doing dust with Eddie Hazel and Ray Davis. That was the only time that I noticed she was getting into it. I knew Debbie needed a break from the whole situation from her actions. I think that she was out there too fast. It exceeded our expectations when we hit the road in '76 on the P-Funk Earth Tour. We went from rehearsals to massive venues and tons of press and publicity. We were in front of twenty thousand seats at the first show. Debbie had no comprehension of that kind of success. Hell, I had no understanding of it myself.

I knew that Debbie losing control really affected Jeanette. When Debbie started throwing money out of the tour bus window, there was no mistaking that she needed some time off. She didn't have money like that to throw five hundred dollars out of the window. Angel dust did a number on her. She said she was going to kill me lots of times, but I didn't pay attention to that. When she started doing stuff like stabbing the cheese and laughing, it reminded me of one of our former guitarists, Tawl Ross, when he had a nervous breakdown from LSD in 1971.

Debbie would leave the road and take a break for a little while. But then she would come to the studio and see everybody, which seemed to freak her out. Everything just got worse with her.

WILLIAM "BOOTSY" COLLINS That whole situation with Debbie was sad. To know a person and then to find out that they are tweaking? You're talking to them, and they are talking about something else. That was scary, and I don't think it was a good thing. Debbie was family, and we didn't like to see anybody go through anything deep like that. Then we couldn't do anything about it. It was new to us. It was a shock. It was like, "How do we handle this? What do we do?"

CHAPTER 12

PLACEBO SYNDROME

In the seventies, artists' involvement in promoting their albums and singles was necessary. This wasn't the era of music videos and social media. Recording artists had to be at record stores and radio stations pushing their products, signing autographs, and interviewing for magazines and newspapers. By February 1978, Parlet's debut album hit record-store shelves while Debbie Wright was in the throes of an emotional meltdown. The lack of promotion for the Parlet album was detrimental to its sales. The lead single, "Pleasure Principle," stalled. It didn't do as well as hoped, only reaching number sixty-six on the Billboard Soul charts and then dropping out completely.

LYNN MABRY We were in Atlanta, and everything with Debbie got bizarre. My relationship with George had ended several months prior, but Debbie was still extremely hostile toward me. It was evident that something was going on with her mentally. I remember us being in the locker room at the arena, getting ready to go onstage. There was a giant chalkboard on the wall, usually used by coaches to discuss their strategy. Debbie grabbed a big piece of chalk and started drawing pictures and writing words that meant absolutely nothing. Then she started striking the chalkboard violently. Shards of chalk and dust flew in the air around her until there was no chalk left. Just a cloud of white dust. Then she started nervously pacing the floor back and forth and mumbling. She looked at me and grimaced, walked over, and stomped on my foot. But this time, I didn't take it personally because this wasn't a little catfight. I knew that she was in trouble. She was going through something emotionally too heavy to deal with.

Eventually, George couldn't even control her. Honestly, I think part of him felt responsible for what Debbie was going through, and he didn't know how to deal with it. He was powerless to handle her. We all were.

DAWN SILVA It was showtime. The drummer counted the band off, and we took our places at the microphones, draped in long silver capes. The lights came up, and George's puffy silver car rolled out as it did many nights before. George had a microphone to do his Dr. Funkenstein rhetoric while the car came out onstage. Debbie always rode in the car with him as his chauffeur. George was talking on the microphone, and suddenly we heard, "Motherfucker! I'll kill you!" It sounded like they were tussling. The car stopped, and George leaped out. Debbie came out, and we saw a small knife in her hand. She started stabbing the pillows of the puffy car. George got as far away from her as he could. We were trying to keep her away from him because we didn't know what she would do. Mallia ran to the side of the stage and got two roadies. They grabbed the knife out of her hand. One roadie grabbed her arms, one held her legs, and they picked her up. Kicking and screaming, they took her off the stage. That *scared* George! He had a definite change of heart about Debbie being out on the road after that night. Now her behavior was directly affecting him . . . up close and personal.

MALLIA FRANKLIN After the show, we returned to the hotel, and the phone rang in my room. One of the road managers, Johnny Parent, asked me to come to George's suite. I got there, and Jeanette, Garry Shider, Archie Ivy, and a couple of the guys were waiting. Jeanette and I sat in large wingback chairs across from Johnny, Archie, and George. I knew this meeting had *everything* to do with Debbie's behavior at the show. Johnny leaned toward us, looked us dead in the eyes, and said, "Do you two know what's going on with Debbie?"

"What do you mean?!" Jeanette snapped.

He looked at me and asked, "Is that the same Debbie Wright that you know?"

I paused, looked at him with tears welling up in my eyes, and said, "No. I don't know who this is. It's not *my* Debbie."

He said, "We are going to send Parlet home. Y'all probably gonna have to replace her."

Jeanette broke down in tears. George didn't say much. I know he was really hurt by the whole thing. We knew Debbie could not stay out on the road in the state that she was in, but we didn't want to give up on her so fast. George asked me to chaperone Debbie back to Detroit. We left the tour the next day. I didn't want to leave the tour, but I had no say in the matter.

Jeanette was having her share of issues on the road too. She had been seeing one of P-Funk's bass players. They started having big problems, and a major blowup between them happened one night after a show in Memphis. We were leaving to go to the next city. Jeanette and I were standing by the elevator. She was holding a lily plant a fan had given her. She was trembling. The next thing I knew, she dropped to the floor like a bag of rocks. She was out cold. I slapped her face, trying to revive her, but I couldn't. Some of the guys were coming down the hall and saw us. They picked her up off the floor, and I picked up her purse and the plant. One of the managers called an ambulance, and she was taken to the emergency room. Between her issues with her boyfriend and watching Debbie lose it, she just couldn't handle it, which took a toll on her physically. Everything was falling apart with Parlet before it even got started. I thought, "What kind of shit has George talked me into?"

A few weeks later, the Flash Light Tour returned to Detroit. *Pleasure Principle* was just released, and Parlet sang background with The Brides on the show at Olympia Stadium because we were still trying to promote it. I remember vividly the album playing over the sound system during intermissions. Debbie was still not doing well. I believe that George had hoped that with a break, Debbie could get herself together. Later that month, our first show as Parlet was scheduled in Washington, DC, and Debbie was coming unglued. We tried hanging in there with her during rehearsals, but we knew she might not make it. I know that George wanted to believe that Debbie would be OK. We all did.

DONNIE STERLING (PARLET BASSIST) When George was ready to get Parlet's band up and running, I was in Japan with my band Above & Beyond. George said he wanted me to work with the drummer, Debbie's brother, Jim Wright, to prepare Parlet's band to tour. So that's what I did. I flew back to the USA, and Mallia's father, Godfrey, who was heavily connected politically, went through immigration to get me back into the country quickly without any problems, and we started learning the songs.

When the girls came off the road, we got into rehearsals heavily because we had a deadline. Parlet was supposed to return on the road as an opening act for Parliament in a month. Then we had another tour scheduled with Bootsy. We rehearsed at Debbie and Jim's house in their basement. After about a week into rehearsal, it was apparent that something was *seriously* wrong with Debbie. She was manic. She would run up and down the stairs in a cold sweat, running back and forth all over the house as we tried to rehearse.

MALLIA FRANKLIN A few days after the Olympia Stadium gig, Ron Dunbar brought George to his first Parlet rehearsal. We were all nervously waiting for Debbie to come down the basement stairs so we could begin. After about twenty minutes, we started without her. She heard the music and finally came down with large dark glasses on. Vaseline greased her arms and face so heavily that her skin looked like an oil slick. She didn't make eye contact with anyone; she just went to her microphone. When she started singing, it was with panicky energy. She would mumble to herself between songs and tell everyone that she was "The Shining." She accused us all of being shallow. She said that only she and George were deep and on another level that we would never understand.

Debbie approached me after we struggled through the first couple of songs. She looked at me with all sincerity and the softest voice and said, "Mal . . . these will be my last days with Parlet. Do you know that one of the girls in Labelle had a nervous breakdown and went solo? Well, I plan to do the same thing."

I was trying to keep her calm and listen. I didn't want her to go off. Inside, my heart was breaking. We had been friends since we were teenagers, and I was watching her mentally disintegrate right before me.

After George witnessed her behavior, he realized she was not getting any better, only worse. He and Ron Dunbar pulled me, Donnie, Jeanette, and Debbie's brother Jim to the side to discuss the situation. After we attempted to do one more song, George came to Jeanette and me and said, "We're going to have to make a change with Debbie. She's not gonna make it." As painful as it was, we had no choice. That was the hardest decision for us to make.

DEBBIE WRIGHT Things were going so fast that I don't remember much about that period. My issues stemmed from the mental stuff I was going through and my guilty conscience about being so in love with George and wanting to be with him. I was so blinded by love that I forgot about one of my best friends, Liz Bishop. I had a lot of guilt. "Oh, my God! He was Liz's man!" Since I was a teenager, she had been my friend, and although she wasn't with George anymore, I cherished the ground she walked on. Then Stephanie, one of my best friends on tour and a girl I had introduced to George, was now his girlfriend. It was a constant internal battle that tripped me out. I was also worried about Jeanette. Seeing her living that fast life on the road reminded me of myself when I was younger, and I felt really guilty. All I could hear was her momma's words, "Take care of my baby."

Then the mental symptoms started. Jeanette noticed my behavior first and got scared. She eventually told George. Everyone called my momma and told her that something was wrong with me. I had one of my first "episodes" after a gig in California. Bernie Worrell's wife, Judie, took me to the hospital. But the hospital didn't keep me. They told me that I was just exhausted and gave me some pills. The doctor said that I needed to rest. I *knew* it was the drugs. I tried to kick the angel dust and drugs cold turkey, but I started having terrible withdrawals. It caused me to start hallucinating, and I got sick and was spitting up poison. The group wanted me to go home, and I knew they were worried about me. But I didn't want to go back to Detroit.

My whole life then was in the recording studio and on the road. I didn't have time for anything else. I had a son I wasn't seeing, and I was missing him something terrible. I had a man I lived with back in Detroit, and I knew I wasn't doing right by him while I was on tour. I got pregnant. I knew I couldn't be pregnant and have a career. So I had an abortion. I had no control over what I was doing. Drugs were rampant in the organization, and I felt the other girls were all acting like shit! It was everything. It was a combination of stress, pressure, a hectic schedule, and drugs.

I have memories of when my mother took me to the hospital. She told me she had scheduled a physical for me and wanted to ensure I was healthy before returning to the road. My brother Jap, my mom, and I went to the hospital. I went into an examination room, and the doctor asked me to remove my clothes and put on the hospital gown. He told me to lay back. The next thing I remember was the doctor strapping me to the gurney. I tried to squirm my way out of the restraints. When I realized what was happening, I could only look at my mother and brother standing in the doorway with tears rolling down my face. All I could ask was, "Why?" The doctor injected me with something. They were visibly upset as the orderlies wheeled the gurney past them. I faded off. I don't remember much else after that. I was placed in the hospital's mental ward for the first time and was diagnosed as paranoid schizophrenic.

You don't even realize when you're having a nervous breakdown and losing it mentally. You do things . . . unbelievable things, and you don't remember any of it. Even today, when people tell me stories of things I did or said, I'm shocked. I can't believe it. Angel dust will mess you up. It didn't affect me immediately, but it haunted me daily. In a way, I'm happy I don't remember much of the bad and crazy stuff. It wasn't a happy time for me. But this is show business, and the show must go on . . . even if it had to go on *without* me. They could hire another girl in Parlet, but she wouldn't be my replacement because I could *never* be replaced . . . there is only one Debbie Wright.

RON DUNBAR Debbie had been loyal to George, and she felt that she should be the one who would lead Parlet. That never materialized. When Mallia came into the group, she became the focal point, and Debbie didn't want to accept her *new* role . . . she resented it. That's when Debbie started becoming disruptive, and her mental state became a big problem. I remember conversations with George that she was having issues with Mallia being in Parlet. The narcotics just magnified her paranoia and all her feelings.

As the A&R guy and a producer, I knew we had to do what was best for the group from a business perspective. We knew that Debbie had to be replaced. Nobody ever wants to make that call. George didn't want to have to make that call. But when we saw what was happening, we had to. That was one thing that George always believed in, "You keep it going, no matter what." It was early enough to not impact the group's success. Debbie was a great singer, but we looked at her and Jeanette more as background. Our focus was still on Mallia and what she was bringing to the table. We invested in Parlet, Casablanca invested in them, and we couldn't stop moving forward.

After losing Debbie Wright, the group scrambled to pick up the pieces. Parlet's debut album, *Pleasure Principle*, continued its lazy climb up the Billboard Soul charts, peaking at number fifty-five in the first week of May 1978.

With two girl groups now a part of the P-Funk roster, George Clinton hired his first female road manager to handle his feminine creations, Detroit native Cheryl James.

Cheryl James and P-Funk guitarist Eddie Hazel in 1970.

CHERYL JAMES (ROAD MANAGER) I had a relationship with P-Funk that dates back to the sixties. I traveled to New York with an associate of mine. The Parliaments were performing at the Apollo Theater in Harlem. We were transporting four pounds of marijuana back to Detroit, and P-Funk guitarist Eddie Hazel was our contact. We stayed in touch, and friendships grew with the band members over the years.

I was hired by Dennis Edwards of The Temptations as his personal driver in 1969; that was my first job in the entertainment business. In the early seventies, I moved from Detroit to LA and worked for actress Janet Leigh as her assistant. I coordinated all her functions and private parties with actors like Sammy Davis Jr. and Lucille Ball on the guest list. In fact, Lucy came over and played tennis with Janet every day. Eventually, that job ended, and I moved on. I started working for American International Films. They became famous for distributing horror movies and Black exploitation films like *Blacula*, *Foxy Brown*, and *Coffy*. That job led to me performing in theater and television gigs around LA. After a few years, I grew tired of the West Coast lifestyle and moved back home to Detroit.

At the beginning of 1978, George heard that I was back in town, and he found me. He called and told me he wanted to replace one of his road managers, Johnny Parent. During that initial conversation, George also told me about the girl groups Parlet and The Brides. The industry back then anticipated problems with female groups, and no one wanted to spend time dealing with them. Women were always involved in relationships, pregnancies, and other things that interfered with business. George *clearly* said he didn't want to deal with women's issues. He wanted me to manage Parlet immediately because they had a tour pending. Then, go out with The Brides when they were ready to tour.

LYNN MABRY Cheryl James . . . wow! Cheryl was [our] momma. She was everything. She was our psychiatrist, our rabbi. She was the first to look out for the girls' best interests. We knew that she would take care of us, no matter what. If we had a gig, she would ensure we got paid, the proper dressing room, and anything we needed. I was green in the music industry, but I always felt safe when she was around. She was more mature than us and had been in the industry for a while. She made me feel confident. She always said, "You're a great singer. You've got what it takes." She gave me personal advice about my relationships. If she was concerned about me, she was very vocal about it, and all her advice was right on the money.

CHERYL JAMES George sent me out with the guys first to train. My first day with P-Funk was crazy! They flew me to Houston, Texas, to join the Flash Light Tour. As soon as I got out of the cab from the airport, George came running out of the hotel toward me and said, "You gotta go with Michael Hampton to the hospital!" I panicked and handed my suitcases off to one of the roadies. They rushed Michael past me on a stretcher and loaded him into the ambulance's rear. I climbed in behind the paramedics. I didn't know what was happening; I just knew Michael was in horrible shape.

LYNN MABRY We were on our way to sound check and couldn't find Michael anywhere. We went to his door and knocked. There was no answer. Michael's room was on the ground floor, so I went around and looked through the window. That's when I saw him on the floor beside the bed. I was knocking on the window frantically, but he didn't move. I ran to the front desk and got the hotel manager. He opened the door. When we entered the room, Michael's body was curled up in a fetal position. His hands and feet were contorted. It was really bad.

CHERYL JAMES The doctors pumped Michael's stomach. After a few hours, I discovered Michael had swallowed a handful of quaaludes. All but three had dissolved. That was the only reason he didn't die. I left him safe at the hospital and went back to the hotel. I quickly learned that one of my tasks was to keep people from asking questions and keep incidents like *that* one as quiet as possible. Usually, George would have people around like Archie Ivy or me to deal with band members' situations and conflicts because he didn't want to deal with them at all. His outlook was, "They can take all that drama to the stage if they want to."

Before I got to my hotel room, I started hearing the lurid details of Michael's overdose. I was filled in about his volatile relationship with Dawn Silva that had been going on for the past year. There was a lot of physical violence. Dawn had broken up with him after she caught him with a groupie. I guess Michael couldn't handle the breakup and decided to jump off a bridge in the back of the hotel. He was unsuccessful because the bridge was only about seven feet high, and the ground underneath was soft mud. When that didn't work, he swallowed the quaaludes. This episode was the first of many dramas with Michael and Dawn I would witness over the years. That was on my *first* day as a road manager for P-Funk. I stayed out with the guys for a few weeks, and then I was sent back to Detroit to meet with Ron Dunbar, Mallia, and Jeanette.

Parlet was trying to regroup and looking for someone to replace Debbie, and I was involved in finding the new girl. I remember meeting Mallia and Jeanette at United Sound Systems soon after returning. Jeanette Washington and I forged a friendship quickly. As I got to know her, I learned that Jeanette came into the P-Funk situation with her own baggage. She was young, and her relationship with her family was so dysfunctional that Jeanette didn't trust anyone. They were abusive toward her. Her mother even stole money from [Jeanette] while she was on the road. Jeanette had been let down by so many people that I think she *expected* people to let her down. She already had a lot on her, and she had just lost Debbie to her mental breakdown. I was one of the only people that Jeanette trusted and listened to. I was very much like a big sister to her.

MALLIA FRANKLIN Parlet's rehearsals were moved to my parents' house after we lost Debbie, and the search was on for her replacement. A lot of money was on the table for Parlet from the label, and no damage control was done when Debbie left. *Pleasure Principle* had been out a few months without promotion because there was no third girl. The organization could've sent Jeanette and me to do press until we got a replacement. Two is better than *none*.

We missed our slot on the Flash Light Tour but were still booked on a summer tour with Bootsy's Rubber Band that started in June. I knew we would lose our window of opportunity if we didn't act fast. Originally, I wanted to bring in a singer named Nidra Beard from LA to take Debbie's spot. She was a pro, learned fast, had a great voice, and kind of looked like Debbie. I was told by Archie Ivy that it would be too expensive to bring her to Detroit. She married producer Leon Sylvers and ended up in a group called Dynasty. One thing that I was sure of, everything would be over for Parlet if we didn't find a third girl *fast*.

CHAPTER 13

ARE YOU DREAMING?

Parlet's first live performance took place on a blistering June day in 1978. As the opening act for Bootsy's Rubber Band's Player of the Year Tour, Parlet took the stage at the Charlotte, North Carolina, American Legion Memorial Stadium, ready to dazzle a crowd of 20,000 funk fans. As the band hit the show's intro, the girls entered the stage one after the other. Mallia Franklin entered first, wearing a massive crown embellished with sequins, rhinestones, emeralds, and rubies. She was compressed into a tight black costume littered with multicolored jewels and wore a cape with layers of nylon wings draped to the floor. She spread her psychedelic butterfly wings and let out a humongous "What's happenin'!" to the roaring coliseum.

Jeanette Washington entered next. Her provocative gold lamé costume included a bikini top with small mirrors on her prominent breasts that emoted beams of light across the crowd. It was paired with tight pants open down the sides, with large flaming hearts made of numerous chiffon colors. Her hair, now cut very short, was packed with gold glitter. Rhinestones and stars were scattered across her face like a solar system.

A new singer entered last. She was sultry, wrapped in a white bodysuit with a neckline shaped like a lightning bolt that plunged to her navel. A

Shirley Hayden takes the stage with Parlet at the Masonic Temple Detroit auditorium in 1978.

shiny gold harness with multicolored feathers was strapped across her pelvis and thighs. Her hair was long and wild, with stray feather plumes peeking from the untamed mane. Her name was Shirley Hayden, and most fans were unaware she'd replaced Debbie Wright within sixty days of Parlet's debut release.

The trio looked like three space goddesses strutting to the stage's edge. They threw up their hands, giving the sea of people the P-Funk sign, with thousands of hands returning the gesture. To the delight of screaming fans, they unzipped small sachets, sprinkling handfuls of glitter all over the front row. Jeanette and Mallia felt good about the addition of Shirley. They had high hopes to bring their specialized female funk to the masses and compensate for the lost time in promoting their album. Other big shows would follow, including the Chocolate Jam at RFK Stadium in Washington, DC, and the summer's largest show in August at Chicago's Soldier Field stadium.

SHIRLEY HAYDEN We did our first Parlet show, and it was wild. We took the tour bus (the Mothership) to North Carolina. We were running late, and as soon as we got off the bus, we were whisked into a tent full of groupies, dope men, and hangers-on. It was hot and muggy. We hadn't had anything to eat, and the scraps of food on the craft table set up for talent were now swarming with flies.

"Where's the dressing room?!" Cheryl James yelled.

"You're in it," someone responded.

"Where the hell is the bathroom? We need towels for the girls to get ready."

"Ain't none!" was the response.

Mallia looked at Jeanette and me and said, "Fuck this!"

She went up to the craft service table and ripped the tablecloth from under the half-eaten food. She tore it into three pieces, one for each of us. We grabbed our brand-new costumes and went into the public bathroom. About five minutes passed, and Cheryl knocked on the door for us to hurry. Mallia was cursing as we tried to wiggle into our skintight costumes. The band hit the first lick, and we flew out the bathroom door, passing through the crowd of fans, crew, and other groups to the ramp leading to the back of the stage. We were about to perform in front of twenty thousand people on our first show. My knees were shaking, and I could feel my heartbeat in my throat. We sang so hard that day that I don't even know how we still had voices.

MALLIA FRANKLIN Debbie's brother Jim brought Shirley to the table. She was his girlfriend at the time. We knew that she had the voice . . . a big voice. She was new to singing on such a professional level, so we worked on control. I knew she could sing Debbie's parts. That was something that I was sure of.

Shirley brought a sense of elegance. She looked like an *Ebony* model, very statuesque and pretty. Eventually, she was destined to be a jazz singer because she had that air of sophistication and maturity in her voice and style. Even in her funk, she was sophisticated. Shirley was willing to learn, and that's all that mattered.

I was still waiting for the money I was owed for *Pleasure Principle*. Management told my mom I didn't need to worry about getting my money; I just needed to get the new Parlet trained to be ready to go on the road. Ron Dunbar told us that we would start personal appearances in May. Then we got word from Archie Ivy that the album wasn't selling, so we weren't going anywhere. The album's not selling because we aren't out there promoting it. It was a lot of promises made and broken.

SHIRLEY HAYDEN I had been dating Jim Wright for a while. My best friend, Ping Spells, and I joined his group Stiheem in 1977, and, eventually, a relationship developed. We were dating when everything was going down with Debbie's sickness. Jim was very angry with George. He felt George did not do all he could to help Debbie, and the family was not getting much assistance from the organization. Jim fought hard for his sister, and that dedication was beautiful to see. I visited Debbie in the hospital with Jim. She was heavily medicated and muttering. She shuffled toward us and wrapped her arms around Jim. She walked us over to her bed, and we visited her for a while. I was a fan of Debbie's; seeing her in that condition was hard for me.

About a month after Debbie's absence from Parlet, I heard Mallia and Jim discussing their displeasure with the girls they auditioned to replace her. As the conversation continued, Mallia heard me singing the Parlet songs over their LP playing in the background.

"Who is that singing?" she asked Jim.

His nonchalant response was, "Oh, that's just Shirley."

"That's the voice right there! Why hasn't she auditioned?" Mallia said.

The next thing I knew, I was set up to audition for Ron Dunbar at Mallia's house. Jim brought me over, and I was a nervous wreck, but Mallia assured me everything would be fine. Mal was pretty and had a very amorous nature about her. We became fast friends. I loved her right off the bat, and Jeanette was lovely initially.

Mallia said, "Girl, calm down. It's all going to work out. Here, take this."

She gave me some kind of pill. It was either a muscle relaxer or a quaalude. I wasn't sure. I just swallowed it, and the band struck up. I started singing, but the medicine began to take effect. It hit me hard, and I felt like I was moving in slow motion. It had relaxed me to the point where my tongue felt fat and lazy. After it was over, Ron Dunbar gave me a wink and said, "I'll see you later at the studio." That was his way of letting me know I was *in*.

A few days later, I attended my first session to record Funkadelic's song "One Nation Under a Groove." That was my first time meeting George. He was happy but didn't say much; he just observed how I fit in. That session was also the first time I saw a Ziploc bag full of cocaine. He was snorting it from his long pinky fingernail. He then went around the studio, wanting everyone to snort cocaine from that same stinky fingernail. This was an initiation.

I was elated for the opportunity to be a part of a group that was so huge. But my decision to join Parlet and Parliament-Funkadelic did not make my mother happy. I was not getting any support from her, and, as far as she was concerned, this career choice was the worst decision I could make.

I was the firstborn of four children, born on April 9, 1952, to parents Minnie and Leon McWilliams. My parents were born and raised in rural Lauderdale County, in Meridian, Mississippi. Momma was raised in the fields, and by the time she was twelve or thirteen, she'd done her share of chopping cotton and shucking corn. Mother was raised by her grandmother. She was a tough, fiercely strict woman who didn't allow her or her sister any freedom as a young teenager. Mom wanted to leave Mississippi for Chicago to live with her mother, a woman with four children by four different fathers. During summer vacations, she would go to her aunt and uncle's farm to make "a few pennies" for herself, dropping out of high school in the ninth grade at sixteen, the same year she met my father, who was five years her senior.

Mom was seventeen when she became pregnant with me, and my father asked for her hand in marriage. She didn't want to marry him but saw him as a way out of Meridian, so she agreed. They married on the seventh day of July 1951. Shortly after, Dad left Meridian for Detroit. He was a part of the southern migration seeking permanent work in the car industry. Once he landed a job, he sent for my mother. I was born shortly after. Over time, Daddy had all sorts of jobs. He was a sanitation worker, a cook, and a carpenter. He was also a hell of a vocalist, and his brother, my uncle Bobby, was the key pianist for the Mississippi Mass Choir. Daddy struggled heavily with the demon of alcohol, but he was a great provider when he was sober. He didn't make much money, but we always had what we needed.

Dad was the breadwinner and enjoyed shopping for beautiful clothing for his daughters at Mom's favorite department store, Kresge's. Mom was the caregiver and disciplinarian. She was also the one who taught us how to dream. Mom found joy in cooking big holiday meals and keeping her children beautifully clothed, with hair in place, ribbons, and starched pleated skirts. She also made sure that we had a spiritual foundation to stand on. We had to attend Sunday school and summer Bible classes.

My parents' relationship was strained as far back as I can remember. Around the age of five, I began to see signs of abuse. I never witnessed the fights, only heard them. I remember the aftermath . . . Momma's lip and face swollen, crying, blood, gathering the children up and getting into a cab in the dead of winter. Weekends were always very stressful for me because that's when my father liked to drink. And I knew that he would beat my mother. He never hit the children; it was always directed toward Momma. She was a light-skinned beauty with green eyes; long, sandy brown hair; and a strong personality. She was not a subservient woman, and I think he beat her to make her submissive and break her spirit. Coming from that kind of environment, I was very timid as a child. My grandma would always say that we [the children] were trained like little puppies . . . to be seen and not heard.

I really started finding myself, my singing voice, and my acting skills in junior high. Because I was raised in the church, I sang my first solo, "His Eye Is on the Sparrow," in the junior choir. I still remember the feelings; I was nervous, but I always knew I wanted to sing professionally. My best friend, Ping, and I had a grand idea to have my mother take us to Motown's Hitsville, USA, right down the street from our house. My mom looked at me and laughed hysterically. It took the wind right out of my sails. That was the first time my aspirations were deflated by my mother. After all, she was the woman who taught me how to dream in the first place. Being raised by her incredibly strict grandmother, she couldn't wrap her mind around singing as a career. Her biggest dream was for me to go to college and further my education, and I admired that. But I knew what my goals were, and I was determined to work toward them. But now, she had been through so much that she had a pessimistic attitude about life. "Dreams are for dreamers. Get a job!"

Bri'an and Shirley Hayden on their wedding day in February 1971.

Once I entered high school in the fall of '67, I realized I didn't like my family situation and wanted to change it. When I was seventeen years old, I started dating my high school sweetheart, a young man named Bri'an Victor Hayden. Bri'an came from a highly educated, physically attractive family, but his older siblings were deeply involved in street life . . . drugs, pimping, and prostitution. He was *also* experimenting with that life at a young age. I became pregnant with my daughter, Shelly, and Bri'an and I married four months later.

After Shelly was born, I worked as a waitress at a local diner to make ends meet. One night, after working a long shift, I waited for Bri'an to pick me up, as he always did. He was a no-show. I caught a ride home with a coworker who lived on my block. Upon entering our apartment, I discovered my baby in the corner of the living room, her face flushed from crying. I looked around and found my husband, who had fallen from the toilet to the bathroom floor. He was dead from an overdose of heroin. I was totally devastated. I was married at eighteen in February 1971 and widowed within a year. Years later, I spoke to my husband's sister about my life with her brother. She lamented how drugs devoured her family. My late husband, Bri'an, would only be the first.

After my husband's death, Momma said, "Come back home." My daughter and I moved back in with my parents. This time, I was different; I was confident. I tasted freedom and was tired of my father's drunken antics. He was hardly going to work by now. He was fucking up his money and was a womanizer. He had a girlfriend who lived a block from our house for over twenty years. She was also married. My father was brazen about her and regularly threw it up in my mother's face.

One day, he had gone too far. I wasn't a witness, but, allegedly, a fatal stabbing by my mother's hand ended my father's life. He was drunk when it happened and didn't seek medical care. Instead, he drowned in his own blood on the bathroom floor. After a lengthy trial, my mother was acquitted because of their abusive past. But that event still resonates in my family to *this* day.

I continued to work odd jobs and attended college intermittently while raising my daughter. Eventually, I began gigging with local bands in the city to get my singing career underway. I joined Stiheem, a band started by Debbie Wright's brother Jim and brothers Kevin and Robert Carter, in 1977. I came in after Jeanette Washington left the group to join P-Funk with Debbie. Stiheem was a dynamic and popular band. It was a musical force to be reckoned with, performing at many nightclubs around the city, such as Kings Row and Little Egypt. I left Stiheem to join Parlet, and the opportunity was thrilling.

After I was hired, rehearsals with Parlet started immediately. We were rehearsing five days a week at Mallia's house. Everything was rushed, like being in a whirlwind. We were learning steps, working with the band, and were measured for costumes between songs. George was very image-conscious and visual. He liked his girls to look a certain way. You had to be very *sexy* and *hot* to be a P-Funk girl. The outfits were so risqué; I had never dressed like that before. To me, it was like wearing nothing at all.

JEROME ALI (PARLET GUITARIST) Shirley came in fast. It wasn't a long wait to find someone. If I recall correctly, Shirley was at some of the first Parlet rehearsals with Jim and the band while the girls were still on the road with P-Funk. Shirley worked out fine because she was open-minded, a sweetheart, and a great vocalist. Mallia was a strong vocalist, strong-minded, with a strong personality. Jeanette was also. It was a rocky start because Mallia and Jeanette started bumping heads immediately. We were the musicians backing the girls up; we weren't trying to get involved in the bickering aspect of who was going to *run* Parlet.

MALLIA FRANKLIN Things changed with Jeanette as soon as Debbie left. She didn't want me in the group; she tolerated me. The *Pleasure Principle* album was a "Debbie and Mallia" album. We did the majority of lead vocals. Jeanette was now determined to be the center of attention. When Debbie left, Jeanette insisted on singing the song that was Debbie's signature, "Mr. Melody Man." I wanted to split it between the three of us. We could all sing parts that fit vocally. She wasn't having it. She didn't have Debbie's vocal chops, and the song fell flat *most* nights.

George told me early on, "You know what to do with this group and *how* to do it . . . handle it." Shirley and the band members followed *my* lead musically, which pissed Jeanette off. Singing was *my* strength; there was nothing she could teach me about singing. Jeanette wasn't always willing and [was] usually resentful.

SHIRLEY HAYDEN I learned early on that George had his "favorites." I felt The Brides, Lynn and Dawn, were the chosen ones when it came to George. I thought, "What's so special about The Brides?" I was hearing rumors that they were sleeping with him and all sorts of other things. I didn't know what was real and what wasn't.

I liked Lynn. She was a sweetie pie, a free spirit, and had that California Valley girl thing on her. She seemed a little *dingy* sometimes, but she had a good heart and never had ill intent. Lynn would always bounce in the studio, happy and jovial, and Dawn would *slither* in behind her like a viper. Dawn and I were cordial, but no love was lost between us. I always thought that she was sneaky, manipulative, and conniving. You never knew what you were going to get with her. She never said much to me but continually sized me up.

Eventually, she asked me, "How old are you?"

"Twenty-six," I replied.

She said, "You'll be through in the music industry by thirty."

For her to say that to me was shocking. She was definitely a queen bee . . . a bitch.

DAWN SILVA I tried to be nice to Shirley on more than one occasion. I never got to know her because her loyalties to Parlet made it difficult. She appeared to be in another zone. She was at odds, as if the Mothership beamed her down without instructions. Ultimately, her royalty would emerge, dismissing me with the wave of a hand. She would look down on me as if to say, "How dare you even speak to me. You're the enemy!" We didn't get along when Shirley first arrived, and I wasn't broken up about it either.

The ladies of Parlet and their band onstage at the Chocolate Jam *show at RFK Stadium on July 1, 1978.* (Left to right) *Janice Carlton, Shirley Hayden, Jeanette Washington, Donnie Sterling, and Mallia Franklin.*

LYNN MABRY My first impression of Shirley Hayden was that she was snooty. Personally, we had no issues with each other. I thought she was sweet, but she could come off as pretentious. Everything had to be perfect. Her makeup had to be flawless. Her lipstick had to be just right. Her hair had to be pinned up in a certain way. Everything about her was just *so* perfect, and *so* put together. That's what I remember most . . . she was perfect, put-together Shirley.

SHIRLEY HAYDEN My relationship with Jim Wright began to change after our first Parlet show. Ron Dunbar, who was handling Parlet for the most part, would tell me things. Ron was having a problem with Jim's attitude. He thought Jim was cocky and talked too much. He fed me information, hoping I could rein in his ego because he was my boyfriend. After many attempts, George instructed Ron to fire him from the band . . . a band that Jim put together. Of course, Jim wanted me to leave when he was fired. I didn't want to leave. I wanted to go on with the group, and my decision to stay in Parlet ended my relationship with Jim Wright for good.

RON DUNBAR I fired Jim Wright because his disposition was not helping an already tense situation. When Jim's sister Debbie was involved, Jim thought the group should have been directed differently than what he saw. I think that Jim, like Debbie, thought Parlet was *her* group. It was George's group, and he would run it how he saw fit. When Debbie left and Shirley came in, Jim started bringing more negativity into the situation because of Debbie's relationship as his sister and Shirley as his girlfriend. Jim thought he had control of the group. It was causing too many issues, and George decided to let Jim go. A person was gone if George told me to get rid of them. He was notorious for having the disposition "if it [isn't] working anymore, change it and move on." That was always George's thought process.

MALLIA FRANKLIN I didn't want Jim to go. I, as well as Donnie, was against it. We had already lost Debbie. I talked to Dunbar, but he said that Jim's attitude was causing more problems for us. I worked well with Jim because we had love, friendship, and respect for each other. I had known Jim almost as long as I had known Debbie . . . and Jim and Donnie worked well together as musicians. They had Parlet's band super tight.

Jim and Jeanette were not getting along at all. Jim didn't like Jeanette's attitude after Debbie left. In Jim's mind, Jeanette was conspiring to take over Parlet with assistance from Cheryl James. He believed that she did whatever she could to get rid of him. When Dunbar fired Jim, he was under the impression that Shirley would leave.

"That's my girl. If I go, she goes!"

That wasn't the case. Shirley wanted to keep going with Parlet. I was sad that Debbie *and* Jim were gone, but I was happy Shirley continued because we became best friends through the process. I lost two people I loved but gained someone new that I loved as well . . . Shirley.

CHAPTER 14

MISUNDERSTANDING

On August 26, 1978, Parlet was on the bill with Bootsy's Rubber Band and Parliament-Funkadelic at the epic first annual Chicago Funk Festival at Soldier Field. An array of opening acts, such as Con Funk Shun, the Bar-Kays, and A Taste of Honey, were in place to raise the momentum throughout the day until Parliament-Funkadelic took the stage. Sixty-seven thousand loyal funk fans braved the hot sun to see the landing of the Mothership. This show would become one of the largest funk festivals in the world. It would also be the first gig without the founding member of Parlet's band, Jim Wright, after his dismissal via Ron Dunbar. A new drummer named Kenny Colton, the cousin of Parlet band members Gordon and Janice Carlton, now sat in Jim's place.

SHIRLEY HAYDEN We went to Chicago to perform at Soldier Field, and I got a knock on my hotel room door early in the morning. I crawled out of bed, assuming it was one of the other girls. I looked through the peephole and got a sinking feeling in my stomach. "What is he doing here?" Standing on the other side of the door was Jim Wright. We hadn't really talked since he was fired by Ron Dunbar. I reluctantly opened the door. Jim's demeanor was humble, so I invited him in. We talked, and I understood his frustrations. His sister had to drop out. His girlfriend came in to replace her, and then *he* was fired. That's a lot to handle, and I empathized with him. It seemed like our discussion was making progress. After thirty minutes or so, I ordered two strawberry daiquiris from room service.

Jim started trying to woo me again. He wanted to stay in Chicago with me, but that would not happen. His motives for coming seemed to shift, and the conversation took a different tone. It wasn't about us fixing our relationship anymore. Parlet wasn't the first indication of trouble. I'd doubted Jim's fidelity, and there were other issues between us for some time. We started to argue, and in a split second, "BAM!" I flew over the bed and onto the floor from a backhand from Jim. The daiquiri in my hand traveled across the room, smashing against the wall. I was stunned, but I got to my feet.

Jim tried to apologize, but my instincts told me to run. I pushed past him and ran down the hallway to Cheryl James's room. I was knocking frantically when she snatched open her door. She looked at my face and said, "What the fuck happened to you?" I told her that Jim had shown up. Anticipating a fight, Cheryl marched down the hallway to evict him. Jim apologized, said he felt terrible, and reluctantly left the hotel. Our relationship was never the same after that day. I was afraid of Jim from that point on. If I saw him, I felt nervous and queasy. I was shaken up, but I returned to my room, packed my costume, and headed for the bus to take us to the stadium. We got to Soldier Field, and the coliseum was packed to the rafters. We hit that stage, and after all the drama from the day, our show was phenomenal.

Bootsy and his Rubber Band were billed as headliners for the first annual Funk Festival in Chicago. But, unfortunately, Bootsy did not play that night at Soldier Field, canceling abruptly. A spokesman for P-Funk told *Jet* magazine that "he was exhausted from working too much." An internal decision was made to cancel the remainder of the US Bootzilla-Player of the Year Tour in its entirety, leaving Parlet, the scheduled opening act, without a second tour.

FRANKIE "KASH" WADDY By 1978, Bootsy's Rubber Band sold out arenas . . . tens of thousands of seats. We were topping the charts and just came back from a European tour. Soldier Field was around the time that Bootsy needed a "break." He broke out in hives because of his nerves, which scared

Mallia Franklin onstage with Parlet at RFK Stadium in Washington, DC, in July 1978.

Mallia Franklin and Dawn Silva pose for the camera between shows at RFK Stadium in July 1978.

him. We lost the remainder of the Player of the Year Tour when Bootsy left the road . . . definitely our biggest [loss].

Bootsy quit and went back home to Cincinnati. I went to his mom's house to check on him, and he was down in the basement, sitting in the dark. I talked to him, but he didn't want me to *see* him. He came into the light. He had knots all over his face and body. It startled me at first . . . freaked me out a little bit. It took a minute, but, thank God, he eventually got it together and came out of Mom's basement.

George wanted to keep the Rubber Band working, so he hired us to play behind The Brides, who were touring in a few months.

MALLIA FRANKLIN The bigger Bootsy got, the more he had problems being Bootsy "the rock star." He was a musician at his core. He didn't like the responsibility of being up front . . . but Bootsy *was* a star. No one could deny that. He will be one of the greatest bass-playing mugs ever to grace this planet. That will be his legacy. "Rock Star Baby Bobba!" He was always a very humble guy. Fame was not easy for him, and it came so fast when he stepped out front. We talked about some of the problems and pressures he sometimes felt . . . but Bootsy was also very private.

When the single "Bootzilla" became huge and went to number one, it overwhelmed him. When we got to Soldier Field in Chicago, everybody wanted Bootsy. He started canceling shows because he needed a break mentally. He canceled a whole United States tour that we, Parlet, were the opening act [for]. That hurt us because Bootsy was arguably a *bigger* star than George at that moment.

My mother constantly fought with Ron Dunbar regarding getting paid correctly. I still hadn't been paid all my money for recording *Pleasure Principle* . . . we're talking close to a year later. I couldn't get a clear answer from George. We could never get an accounting of anything, and they didn't want to deal with my mother at all. That caused a big strain on my mom's relationship with George. He was like one of her adopted sons; she never thought things would go down like this with all his history with my family. That was a real disappointment for her.

After Soldier Field was such a success for Parlet, Thang Incorporated and I had somewhat agreed to the past monies I was owed since signing my contract. By the end of August, George and Dunbar gave me a deposit and started paying rent for a house on Andover Street on Detroit's east side. It benefited both of us. It got Donnie and me out of my parents' house, and P-Funk members had another crash pad and rehearsal spot in the city.

SHIRLEY HAYDEN After the show in Chicago, Dunbar instructed Parlet to prepare for the One Nation Tour with P-Funk and The Brides. Cheryl James booked us a gig with WAR at the Masonic Temple in Detroit. Parlet and WAR sold out the venue, and we were excited to debut our new show.

While we were dressing at Masonic, Jeanette Washington's mother entered the dressing room. I had never met her. She was a minister and a spiritual prophet or something like that. She was a bit of a strange bird—a little thing with some sort of fur patchwork cape. She was milling around the dressing room, and I saw her eyeing Mallia, but she knew not to fuck with her. So she changed directions and came over to talk to me. We were lining up to go out onstage, and she walked up, closed her eyes, and started prophesizing. Once she was done, she opened her eyes, leaned into me, and softly said, "You will be dead by thirty from cancer."

I was stunned. Why would Jeanette's mother say that to me . . . and at that moment? My legs felt like cement. It took all I had to get myself together. I think it was a tactic to throw me off. It was really an evil thing to do, especially for someone who was supposed to be a woman of God. Jeanette's issues with females clearly stemmed from her relationship with her mother. I didn't let Jeanette's mother's *false* prophecy throw me off. We went out onstage, sprinkled the glitter we called "Lust Dust" all over the front row, and turned it out. Afterward, I received my pay—a *whopping* twelve dollars. I still have the receipt to this day.

That was an early sign that the organization didn't treat Parlet fairly. I do remember Mallia's mother fighting for us. Mrs. Franklin would come up to the studio when she would find out George was there, and the guys would be frightened of that little woman. She would walk into the studio, and everybody would tense up, stating, "Here comes Mallia's momma!" They knew some shit was about to jump off. Mrs. Franklin acted as Mallia's business manager, and, in turn, she looked out for Parlet. She would hem George up in a room, and all you would hear was her screaming at him, trying to make him do right by us. She was tough and fought hard for her daughter.

GARRY SHIDER Mal's momma was a politician and a business owner, and she knew her shit. I always say that Momma Christine played a big part in our success and helped us survive. She didn't take any shit off of George, Dunbar, Johnny Parent . . . none of them, and would get in their asses if she thought they were trying to bullshit her. She wanted to handle it the business way, but sometimes she had to handle it the "ghetto" way. Christine would come to the studio with her big-ass purse and that damn

Parlet's Jeanette Washington performing at Detroit's Masonic Temple in 1978.

Pall Mall cigarette hanging out of her mouth. We thought she had a gun in her bag. It reached the point where George would run and hide in the bathroom when she showed up. She fought the organization for Mallia's money. That became a big problem for Thang Incorporated because they weren't used to someone in the band fighting them . . . especially women. Some guys like . . . Glenn Goins and Jerome [Brailey] had kicked up some dust. But never one of the girls. It affected what Thang would do and *didn't* do for Parlet.

There were several reasons why P-Funk players were not being paid in a timely manner. The increase of cocaine within the organization was becoming a costly expense. Many members and staff of Parliament-Funkadelic would attach that claim to one of Clinton's confidants—Nene Montes.

According to George's 2014 memoir, Clinton met Cuban-born Montes in 1977, when Montes was part of a film crew considering a documentary on the group. Montes began following the tour as a cameraman and quickly inserted himself into the P-Funk realm. Soon, Montes became Clinton's personal "consultant."

Clinton's ex-fiancée, Liz Bishop, cites Montes's involvement in creating dissention between George and the original Parliaments, resulting in their defection, as well as his influence on Clinton, causing the implosion of her personal relationship with George. "George had a lot of ego and pride. He brought in this guy Nene Montes, and Nene played on that. One time I heard Nene call the other guys in Parliament "a bunch of monkeys." I didn't like that at all. I always had George's back, and I loved all the guys. I told George what Nene was saying, which turned out to be one of the biggest mistakes that I could have ever made. George got mad at *me*, and I started seeing less and less of him. When people started getting rid of the original Parliament members, I knew that I would be the next to go."

Even with cocaine penetrating the group, by the fall of 1978, the Parliament-Funkadelic organization had grown so profitable that Thang Incorporated opened offices in Hollywood and their home base of Detroit.

World Funk Headquarters, headed by Archie Ivy, Nene Montes, and office manager Brenda Adams-Pierce, located on the iconic corner of Hollywood Boulevard and Vine Street, handled most business affairs and marketing and publicity aspects.

BRUCE PETERSON Nene Montes was the master and commander of the cocaine trade in Miami. He had ties to Cuban president Fidel Castro. Nene's official title was "The Janitor." Every time George made a mess, it was up to Nene to clean it up. If George had any problems, Nene came in, dusted for prints, and made them disappear. When he came into the organization, everything went to a weird level.

We started getting undermined when a high, intense level of drugs was introduced into the mix. Our business team could handle the organization. We had the skill, but we were now being undermined with large amounts of cocaine, and it didn't take long to start sabotaging ourselves.

Clinton's second office, Funk East in Southfield, Michigan (a Detroit suburb), run by Ron Dunbar and Leslie Vocino, handled everything related to the recordings, artwork, album credits, and finished products released to the marketplace.

LESLIE VOCINO (OFFICE MANAGER, FUNK EAST, DETROIT) I was hired by Ron Dunbar. We didn't even have an office in the beginning. I was put in a corner in the basement lounge of United Sound Systems, next to the soda machine with a mountain of invoices and paperwork. Dunbar pointed at it and told me to get it all in order. Eventually, we moved to the Advance Building in Southfield, which was a block or so from George's townhouse. He could walk to the office because George doesn't drive.

Mallia's mother was always at the office, trying to ensure that Mallia's business was right. She was the only parent that I remember doing that. The more she tried to keep shit in order, the more George got turned off. He and Dunbar were also putting Mallia off because, like her mom, she was aggressive and abrasive. She insisted on getting things done, and she never gave up. George didn't like anybody telling him what to do. He was laid-back and didn't want to be bothered with the "business" part of the music business. He just wanted you to be with him, kick back, get high, stay in the studio, and make music for free. The business aspect was always secondary.

BRENDA ADAMS-PIERCE (OFFICE MANAGER, WORLD FUNK HEADQUARTERS, HOLLYWOOD) I became a part of the P-Funk organization strictly by chance. I met their agent, David Liebert, while working for Black Radio. Through David, I met one of George's managers, Archie Ivy. He told me he was the vice president of Parliament-Funkadelic and needed someone to set up and run a West Coast office. World Funk Headquarters is what they called it. I said to him, "Look no further." I was hired and ran the office with Archie and Raymond Spruell. About a month after being hired, I was at the office, and the door flung open. It was George Clinton. He walked in, looked around, and said, "So this is Parliament-Funkadelic West Coast!" That was the first time that I met George.

Mallia was the only girl in the band that I really talked to in the beginning. We talked a lot about what was happening in the organization. She didn't like the treatment she was receiving and was very outspoken about it. The band was successful, and money flowed in and out of the office. I remember when George was about to receive a massive check. He called me for about a week, asking if anything had come in from Casablanca Records. Each day I had to tell him, "No." Casablanca finally sent a check to the office by messenger for $375,000. It was for tour support for the Casablanca acts—Parliament and Parlet—and payment for the props and costumes for the upcoming Aqua Boogie Tour. I remember the amount because it was the biggest check I had ever seen in my life at that point.

There was constant mismanagement of money in the organization, and I hoped George would start being smarter with P-Funk's money one day.

Siegel & Goldman, one of LA's biggest money management companies, started handling P-Funk's money. They hired a guy named Dwight Smith as our in-house accountant. On his first day, Dwight came to the office to meet me. It was the same day that we received the big Casablanca check. We sat and talked about the organization and how I could help him. I gave him the check, and, in speaking, he told me his plans of what he would like to do to aid and strengthen the P-Funk organization financially. Dwight was very excited at how this money could benefit the company. He talked about pensions, investments, and things companies do to keep the cash flow coming in. I heard him out, chuckled, and said, "Yeah, OK. That would be good if you could get that to happen. It would be a wonderful thing. But I doubt seriously that it's going to happen." He was puzzled by my response.

Dwight called George and told him that the Casablanca check had come in. George replied, "Good! Do what you have to do with it as far as finances. But don't give out monies to anyone unless I OK it first." The next day, Dwight called me and said, "Well, I guess you were right. George told me not to release any money until he said it was OK. Nene Montes called me and asked for a big chunk of the money. He was very vague and sketchy about what he needed it for. I called George and told him that a request was made by Nene Montes for a really large sum of money. George flatly said, 'Give it to him.'"

After Dwight got that call from Nene, I knew most of the tour support money wouldn't be utilized for Parliament, Parlet, or the upcoming tour. Once George said, "Give Nene whatever he wants," I knew that money was gone.

And Dwight, our new financial advisor, was gone just as fast as the money was.

CHAPTER 15

WHEN YOU'RE GONE

Atlantic Records was known for soul music stars like Aretha Franklin, Roberta Flack, Ben E. King, and Otis Redding—not particularly known for funk music. The Brides of Funkenstein were the first female funk group on the label.

In the studio and onstage, Lynn Mabry and Dawn Silva were in synch with each other. Their vocal tones differed—Dawn's more melodic and airy, Lynn's more soulful, gritty, and spontaneous—but when they sang together, they blended as one. George wanted to make The Brides of Funkenstein the most mainstream commodity in the P-Funk portfolio.

GEORGE CLINTON We were gigging in New York at Madison Square Garden on the Mothership Tour in 1977. We were also filming a movie about the group called *The Clones of Dr. Funkenstein*. We shot some stuff in front of the United Nations building. We even took the movie crew and filmed the Mothership landing in Times Square. We shut down about four blocks and got a dude out of a manhole who worked at night. He hooked the ship to a generator, and we filmed the whole thing. But the movie never came out.

During that trip to New York, I was one of the guests of honor at the movie premiere of *Close Encounters of the Third Kind*. At the premiere, I

A rare photo of The Brides of Funkenstein, Lynn Mabry and Dawn Silva, from their first photo session in 1978.

met Julia Phillips. She and her husband, Michael, were the movie's producers. She wanted to talk to me about producing a disco album to go with the film. *Star Wars* had done one, and it was a smash. I accepted her offer and decided to use Lynn and Dawn as the singers for the sessions. We did some songs, including "War Ship Touchante," with a *Close Encounters* feel to it. I sent it to Julia, and she loved it. She negotiated a five-million-dollar record deal for the disco album. But she only wanted to give me one hundred thousand dollars. I refused her offer and kept the material. I took the songs to Atlantic Records and got the record deal for Lynn and Dawn as The Brides of Funkenstein.

GARRY SHIDER George was really into The Brides. They appealed to that melodic side of his musical personality, coming from Sly Stone. There was a polish about The Brides that George got off on. It classed him up because they had such a "classy" way about them. The Brides were his "trophy wives," meaning they were probably too good to marry a guy like him.

All the offspring groups were little pieces of George's mind. He was the creator when it came to concepts. But musically, we all contributed. George's real talent was getting what he needed from *us* to get what he heard in his head. He didn't play an instrument. He wasn't the musical talent; he was the mastermind. A lot of fans don't look at it that way or don't want to accept that. They look at him like he did everything. It was about fifty-fifty, sometimes less, depending on what he was into at the time. We all wrote and produced on Brides, Parlet, and Parliament-Funkadelic. It wasn't just George Clinton, but he would give the thumbs-up and put his name on it.

WILLIAM "BOOTSY" COLLINS George drilled the whole thing in our heads, "If Parliament doesn't have a hit, Bootsy may have one. If Bootsy ain't got one, The Brides or Parlet may have one. Whoever got the hit can carry the load for all of us." As long as a mug is working, that's all that matters. It wasn't like, "We're going to make Funkadelic the best or Bootsy the best." George would say, "Go in the studio and cut tracks." Then he would pick the tracks and give them to whoever he wanted to record them. Whoever needed the hit, he'd take the music and put it on that group. That's the way it worked.

George said that we needed a track for The Brides. When I did the track for "Disco to Go," we took the basic groove of "Ahh . . . The Name Is Bootsy, Baby" and changed a few little things. We changed the guitar lick and added the intro to a groove that Bootsy's Rubber Band was already doing onstage. It was great because we didn't have to do too much to it. The groove was already there, and everybody was digging on it.

DAWN SILVA We recorded our first song, "Love Is Something." It was a song written by one of our engineers, Jim Callen. I thought it was for Eddie Hazel's solo album, but Jim said he wrote it for us. He told me George got the Atlantic record deal with that song. It was one of the better songs, but George dropped it.

GEORGE CLINTON "Love Is Something" was The Brides' first record that we cut on them. The Brides and Eddie Hazel. This was the beginning. Jim Callen wrote it, and we all knew it was one of the best songs we'd ever heard; all the groups said the same thing. We were doing so well, and the Mothership was flying everywhere. One thing I hate to do in records is "pimp" love and that breakup thing. I felt uncomfortable. This record was so good in that direction of being "sad" and making "sad" seem positive. I was scared of it. Everybody was in love and breaking up with everybody, including myself. I didn't want to put out something bittersweet. Let's just fly a Mothership.

DAWN SILVA I didn't like any of the corny Ron Dunbar songs like "When You're Gone," another song I thought was a throwaway track, much like most of the songs George and Ron had us singing in the beginning. "Rat Kissed the Cat" was another horrible song. Lynn and I hated it. Then George played us the Bootsy track. I was very excited when he said he would give the song to us. I knew that song would be our hit.

LYNN MABRY When it was time to put The Brides' record together, George didn't take the time to give it the quality of music he should have. We just went through the motions and accepted George's direction. Ron Dunbar was there in the studio a lot. He was old-school Motown and tried to give us that Supremes vibe, and we didn't want that. I always thought Parlet's songs were much better than ours. But I loved "Disco to Go."

My relationship with Glenn Goins continued after he left Parliament-Funkadelic, and we still saw each other when we could. Dawn and I were in the studio finishing The Brides' album, and he was supposed to come to spend time with me, but he never showed up. I couldn't believe it. He didn't even call. About three weeks passed, and I was fussing to my mom and Dawn, "Glenn hasn't called me, and he's not returning my calls!"

After the recording was done, I returned to my mom's house in Berkeley, and she told me that Glenn called. She said he sounded weird and sad. My first thought was, "He knew that I was in LA. Why would he call my mom's house in Berkeley?" A day or so later, I got a call from Cheryl James.

She said, "Lynn . . . have you heard about Glenn?"

I responded, "No! But I'm so upset with him."

Cheryl tearfully said, "He's gone, baby."

"Gone where? What do you mean he's gone?" I asked.

She said, "He passed away, Lynn."

I dropped the phone and let out a gut-wrenching scream. I was hysterical and felt like my life was over. My mother ran into the room to comfort me. After a few moments, I picked up the receiver. Cheryl told me that he checked himself into the hospital. Glenn had Hodgkin's lymphoma; it came out of remission, and he didn't make it. As I was trying to process that he was gone, I was upset at *myself* for being upset with *him* for not calling me. I was mad at my own selfishness. Why couldn't I think that something was wrong? More importantly, I was sad because I didn't get a chance to say goodbye to one of the true loves of my life.

Dawn and I flew to Glenn's funeral in New Jersey. It was like a surreal, out-of-body experience. I remember walking down the church aisle and seeing the open casket. As I approached, I thought of all the times we sang and wrote songs together, laughed, cried, and played in the snow . . . how many times we lay in bed with each other. Seeing him there in that coffin was too much for me to bear.

On top of that, his wife and the mother of his child, Bobbie, was there, and I didn't want to disrespect her. I got to the casket and placed my hand on his chest. I kissed the corner of his mouth. It was hard and cold. That was the moment I knew it was over. I felt my knees buckle, and I collapsed in sorrow. Dawn grabbed one arm, Ray Davis was on the other, and they carried me out of the church. I never felt the ground underneath me until I was outside.

After the funeral, we went to Glenn and Bobbie's house for his repast. As we ate and told stories about him, a massive storm began. Big booms of thunder shook the ground and knocked the electricity out. We were all saying, "That's Glenn! There he is. He's letting us know that he's still here." We lit candles, continued eating, and reminisced as the rain came down in buckets.

For months after Glenn died, he would come to me in dreams. He would appear, walk over, kiss and hug me, and tell me he was sorry it ended the way it did. He'd say, "I was trying to say goodbye." Whenever I dreamed about him, the bizarre thing was that I would wake up and smell the strong scent of a flower . . . like a Casablanca lily or gardenia. It was always in the same spot. I would call for my mother to come in, and I insisted she smelled the fragrance. She could never smell it. I'm a Christian woman and don't believe in the paranormal, but *that* was real. His visits gave me a sense of peace, allowing me to release him.

DAWN SILVA When we got to Glenn's house, his wife, Bobbie, was sitting on the sofa, still in a state of shock. His family came in and took stuff out of the house, even removing pictures from the walls. They were walking out with his clothes. I kept saying, "Bobbie, they're just taking stuff out of your house." She didn't hear me. She was grieving so hard that she was in another zone. George doesn't do funerals, so he wasn't in attendance.

Someone walked up to Lynn and me and said George sent a car for us, and it was waiting outside. It was there to take us across the harbor to New York City to do our first Brides of Funkenstein photo shoot. We'd cried all day; the last thing we wanted to do was take pictures. I was angry with George. I thought sending a car to Glenn's house to take us away was insensitive and thoughtless. We should have stayed. But we were young and naive, and if George told us to do something, we did it. We may have been confused or concerned but didn't question it.

We went to New York to the photo studio. We walked in, and they had two vintage wedding gowns on hangers for Lynn and me to put on. Our hair was messed up from the rain. We barely had on the makeup we hadn't cried off. We looked terrible, but the photographer liked it. We put the dresses on, and they set the lights up under our faces to make us look ghoulish. At that point, we didn't even care. We just lost our friend, and Lynn lost the love of her life. We took the gowns off and put on black tights and fishnets for the next setup. I thought the pictures were horrible. Some were nice, but George picked the ugliest ones in the bunch.

LYNN MABRY I couldn't understand George's reasons why we had to go through with this photo shoot after such a tragic loss. We were being directed by the photographer, Diem Jones, to look scary, not pretty. That was easy for us since our eyes were swollen like caterpillars from the endless tears we shed after burying my beloved Glenn. I hated the pictures. In hindsight, The Brides always represented George's mood at that time. The Brides' conceptualization appeared dark and disturbing if George's attitude at that time was dark and disturbing.

THE BRIDES OF FUNKENSTEIN

Here come The Brides! Dawn and Lynn pose for photographer Diem Jones in 1978. Atlantic Records promotional picture.

The Brides of Funkenstein were set to blast off into the musical universe with their first single, "Disco to Go," in September 1978, and their debut album, *Funk or Walk*, would follow in November. "Disco to Go" reached number seven on the Billboard Soul Singles charts. The album followed, reaching seventeen on the Soul Album charts and seventy on the Billboard

Hot 100. The Brides' success made up for the lackluster performance of Parlet's *Pleasure Principle*.

As with Parlet, the *Funk or Walk* cover art presented Clinton's sexual concept and imaginative vision to the public. The album cover depicts the vocalists as a team of identical fembots, with breasts at attention. Their welcoming open mouths with curled tongues are in the fashion of inflatable love dolls. Decked out in gloves, platform boots, hot pants, cyclops visors, midriff tops bursting at their cleavage, and wires connected to every limb, the sexual innuendo suggested that The Brides could be controlled for anyone's pleasure.

Clinton chose to play up the bigamous aspect of having two brides, creating the illusion of a ménage-à-trois lifestyle with his beloveds. Some fans thought the members of The Brides were actually married to Clinton. This enhanced the sexual fantasy and popularity of the duo. Unlike their sister group, The Brides' promotional machine was in high gear for the album's release. George was fully aware of the sexual impact of the duo and exploited it mercilessly. The Brides' photos in wedding gowns, with peculiar lighting, made them look more sinister than beautiful. Oddly enough, they added to the group's mystique.

DAWN SILVA I remember Lynn and me driving down Sunset Boulevard in LA. It was early in the morning, and Lynn was flipping through stations on the radio. Several songs later, the announcer said, "We got that new song from The Brides of Funkenstein." We heard the intro for "Disco to Go," and Lynn and I screamed. It wasn't just a fantasy or a dream. It was real. "Wow! We really have a record on the radio. We are now legitimate recording artists."

When Atlantic released "Disco to Go," it quickly catapulted to number seven on the charts. They sold 300,000 units right out the gate, and it played all over every Black radio station in America. The hype about The Brides of Funkenstein was big, and I knew the song would blow up because it was a Bootsy composition. When the song reached the top ten on the charts, executives from Atlantic Records came to United Sound Systems in Detroit to congratulate us and talk to George about pushing the single to number one.

Henry Allan from Atlantic said to me, "Congratulations! Your record is blowing up, and I think it will be number one in a couple of weeks."

He asked George, "When will you drop the new Funkadelic single, 'One

Nation Under a Groove'? If you wait a few weeks, we can push 'Disco to Go' to number one."

George said, "OK. It's cool. We can wait a few weeks."

I was so excited that our record would be number one. It had already gone gold on the hype behind The Brides of Funkenstein. A day or so passed, and George dropped "One Nation Under a Groove" on top of our heads. Our single stopped at number seven and then started sliding down the charts. He knocked The Brides, his own artists, out of the box. Why would he do that? We were confused, as was Atlantic Records, especially since he had given them his word. Funkadelic went number one. Parlet and The Brides were all over "One Nation," but it didn't help us as The Brides; it didn't help Parlet. It helped George. That whole situation saddened me deeply. He was really my funk hero, my funk guru at that time, and I was afraid to ask him, "Why?" It was the "one star per family" concept, and that "star" sure wouldn't be The Brides.

LYNN MABRY Even with our limited knowledge of how songs were promoted, the record company knew we were about to be number one. And what Dawn and I couldn't understand was, with the executives telling him to wait, what would possess him to knock The Brides out of the box? "One Nation" would have been a hit record, regardless. That was one of George's actions that left me dumbfounded. It didn't seem like the right decision for a producer to make if he genuinely wanted his artists to be successful. A handful of circumstances made me start to think it was more of a game to him than a business. I just assumed George wanted us to succeed . . . why wouldn't he?

CHAPTER 16

DISCO TO GO

Funkadelic's *One Nation Under a Groove* album and single stayed at number one on the Billboard Soul charts for the entire month of October and the first two weeks of November 1978.

The One Nation Anti-Tour would be different than the previous. No Mothership would descend from the rafters, and simple army fatigues would replace sparkly costumes. Smaller venues were booked versus the large stadiums to which P-Funk had become accustomed. The Brides of Funkenstein would be the opening act.

George Clinton took to the airwaves of radio station KKTT in Los Angeles on November 16, 1978, to promote the live performance of The Brides of Funkenstein at the Starwood Nightclub in West Hollywood. By showtime, the Starwood was packed to capacity. A duet of robotic female voices called through the darkness, "We are The Brides of Dr. Funkenstein!" The crowd roared as Lynn and Dawn entered from opposite sides of the stage, bathed in diffusions of light. Iridescent white bodysuits hugged their figures. Sizeable white leather belts adorned with silver studs straddled their hips, and powder-white foxtails dripped around their thighs to the stage floor. Matching studded capelets with hanging foxtails completed the outfits.

"Those white fur outfits were the prettiest outfits in the world," George Clinton declared. "I designed those . . . they were a female play on my most expensive Dr. Funkenstein costume."

It is fair to say that many nights, just the vision of The Brides in their sumptuous costumes, with a price tag of five thousand dollars each, stole the show. For nearly an hour, The Brides covered a tapestry of songs from Parliament album cuts "Ride On" to the Bootsy ballad "Vanish in Our Sleep." They closed with their own top ten record, "Disco to Go."

With the remainder of Bootsy's 1978 tour canceled, Clinton hired most of his Rubber Band to accompany The Brides. Drummer Frankie "Kash" Waddy, keyboardist Joel "Razor Sharp" Johnson, and the Horny Horns (Maceo Parker, Fred Wesley, Richard "Kush" Griffith, and Rick Gardner) joined new P-Funk recruits, bassist Jeff "Cherokee" Bunn, and guitar phenom DeWayne "Blackbyrd" McKnight (from Herbie Hancock's band The Headhunters) when The Brides were slated as the opening act on the One Nation Anti-Tour.

LYNN MABRY Dawn and I got with George to put together The Brides show for the tour. George always said he wanted The Brides to be very showy . . . borderline Vegas. He told Dawn and me that he wanted the guy who had done Labelle's costumes, Larry LeGaspi, to do ours. We were excited because having a famous designer make stage clothes, especially for us, took The Brides to a higher level professionally. George showed us some costume sketches, and I was at odds. When I saw them in person, they were a little busy for my taste. Still, I had to take away the California girl in me and incorporate the funk I was *trying* to be.

George also said we needed three background girls, and I think Dawn and I decided to call them the Bridesmaids. He said we needed to find a way to pump up the live performance. It was all a tool to make our show look bigger than it really was. George said, "I want The Brides to be on another level and open a new door." He wanted The Brides to have the background singers, dance steps, and talking between songs. He tried to make our show more versatile and different from Parlet. We had to get close to the audience . . . singing the ballads and touching the fans. I didn't have a problem with that.

In September 1978, P-Funk set up camp at the Bel-Mar Motel, a little place in the heart of downtown Detroit on Jefferson Avenue by the docks of the Detroit River. During recording and rehearsals, the modest dwellings became most of Parliament-Funkadelic's temporary residences. It was a seventy-room exterior corridor motel with a slimy swimming pool and possibly the only palm tree in the city. The Bel-Mar was a spot for transients, hookers, pimps, and drug dealers. Hidden behind the motel's bright orange doors was the biggest Black band in the world, preparing for their largest tour to date.

DAWN SILVA I went to one of the band member's hotel rooms at the Bel-Mar. He opened the door, and I saw a girl wrapped in a sheet in his bed. As soon as I entered the room, she said, "The Brides of Funkenstein! Hi, I'm Val Young."

Val Young was maybe sixteen or seventeen at the time. She was at the Bel-Mar often with the boys in the band and started hanging out with Lynn and me. She was cool, real country, and drove us around Detroit in her grandmother's station wagon. She was eager to show us that she could sing. When it was time to audition for the Bridesmaids, we asked Val if she wanted to audition. She had a good voice; we might have even told her she had the gig. She was so happy.

The next day, I got a knock at my door at the Bel-Mar. I saw a petite girl with a long gray coat and thick glasses.

She said, "Hi . . . I'm Sheila Horne. Can you wave at my boyfriend?"

I said, "Excuse me?"

She said, "I'm a singer for The Brides. Could you wave at my boyfriend so he knows I'm not coming up here to see a man. He doesn't believe P-Funk would stay at a sleazy motel on Jefferson."

The first thing I thought was, "Who are you? I haven't heard you sing."

I reluctantly waved at her boyfriend and watched him drive off.

She said, "Thank you," and then just walked away.

A member of Bootsy's crew, a guy named E-man, brought her to meet George at the studio the day prior. George just hired her.

LYNN MABRY We were running out of time to find background singers. We knew Val was a pick already. We didn't hear a lot of her vocally but felt it was enough to work with whatever girls we hired. Then we were told Sheila had been hired by George. There was one more slot to fill. A friend of my mother's said she knew someone with a nice voice, so we sent for Marion "Babs" Stewart from California. We were then introduced to Jeanette McGruder, a singer and friend of P-Funk cover artist Overton Loyd.

We were told she was also hired. This put Dawn and me in a bad position. We only needed three.

We had to decide . . . and the deciding factor was to hear them sing together.

DAWN SILVA I remember Lynn saying we didn't need Jeanette McGruder, or "Mackie," as we called her, because we had Val. I wasn't too bothered by the whole situation until we got to the first rehearsal later that day. I think everyone was confused. They thought they *all* had the gig. When the four of them started singing together, they didn't blend at all! We didn't accomplish much that day, and my stomach was upset by the end of the first rehearsal. We got back to the Bel-Mar and immediately went to George's room.

I said, "George, we don't have to have background singers. They will just cancel out Lynn's and my unique sound."

George disagreed. He said, "Background singers will enhance your sound, and you always have to look bigger and better than you are. You need the Bridesmaids because you can't sing lead *and* background."

We got to the second rehearsal, and Lynn and I again disagreed on who should leave. Richard "Kush" Griffith, the bandleader and horn player, stepped in and had the girls sing in sections. We both agreed to keep Sheila. She had the best voice and was sweet and soft-spoken. She was willing to do whatever she could to get the job. Mackie had an operatic, almost cabaret voice. It was powerful, but I didn't like that you could hear her tone over the others. I told Lynn I didn't care for Babs's voice, but Lynn wanted her. Lynn didn't really care for Mackie's. And Val, well, she was all out of tune. So it was between Mackie and Val. It didn't matter what note we gave Val; she jumped on someone else's and was loud and flat on top of it.

Mallia Franklin and Jeanette Washington watched everything from the sidelines. Ron Dunbar had them come to our rehearsal and informed them that Parlet was not going out on the One Nation Tour, and they were pissed. I could hear Jeanette's nasty mouth in the corner saying, "I don't know why they takin' these non-singing motherfucking bitches on tour!" She pointed at the potential Bridesmaids.

A few moments later, I walked up to Mallia and asked, "What do you think?" Mallia was usually brutally honest. She said, "Get rid of them all! All them bitches gotta go! They need to blend. Ain't no blend nowhere!" I laughed at Mallia's response but knew she was right.

LYNN MABRY Dawn and I picked Val to be one of the Bridesmaids together. She was technically the first. But when she got to rehearsal, it didn't quite work out as we had hoped. The most crucial factor was her voice wasn't as strong as the other three. She wasn't blending vocally. Val was also more of a party girl, and that concerned us. She was flirting with Bootsy and all his band members. Honestly, we were shocked, and I was personally disappointed. I knew it wouldn't work after that second rehearsal. I was young, so I didn't know how to explain the situation to her and be quite as eloquent, so we looked to Mallia to handle it.

DAWN SILVA We were too chickenshit to tell Val she was fired, so George approached Mallia and asked her to fire Val for us. He knew Mallia was already pissed off because Parlet was being dropped from the tour, so he used that anger. Through the tensions going on with Parlet and The Brides, Mallia and I maintained a close friendship. She had an uncanny way of getting her point across. Biting her tongue was *never* an option. She was blunt, hard as nails, and usually right nine times out of ten. She walked over to Lynn and me.

Mallia said, "Do y'all want me to tell her? I ain't got no problem with it. I'll handle it."

Lynn and I nervously nodded in agreement. Mallia walked over to the four singers, tapped Val on the shoulder, and took her out into the hallway. I don't know what Mallia said, but Val returned to the rehearsal after a few minutes. She ran up to us, crying, "What's that bitch talking about?" Lynn and I couldn't even look Val in the face. Val was our friend, and we gave her the gig, but it wouldn't work out, and we knew it. Lynn and I hugged her, and she walked out of the rehearsal.

We walked up to Mallia, and we asked, "What did you say to her?"

Mallia responded, "I told her the truth. 'You can't keep your note, and you're flat. It's not personal; it's business. This time ain't your time. Maybe next time.'"

MALLIA FRANKLIN Val wasn't ready to "funk," so she had to "walk." She had a decent voice. But she needed to mature vocally and otherwise. Val was nowhere near professional. Donnie wanted to form a band outside of Parlet, and I told him that maybe Val could do some sessions and get experience. That would be a way for her to get into the door. Val was an immature teenage girl, and I gave her valuable advice, as well as deodorant, a razor, a bar of soap, some Topol toothpaste, and a toothbrush.

DAWN SILVA I will always say that hiring the Bridesmaids canceled Lynn's and my unique sound. It didn't enhance anything. It took away from the formula and changed our entire chemistry onstage. We recorded our first album in two-part harmony. We studied how to sing together for years and sound like *one* voice. Our harmonies were tight. Atlantic Records loved us because we had a unique vocal blend that we had established with Sly. We weren't just tight musically but also spiritually, mentally, and emotionally. We were best friends, and that's unique in this industry.

George wanted us to have background singers, and he knew asking Parlet to sing behind us onstage would have been an insult, especially since they were in P-Funk before The Brides were. If he had given them the option to tour with us and get a paycheck or stay home and make nothing, they probably would have chosen to go on the road to make a living. Parlet would have been a better choice if The Brides had to have additional singers. We all knew how to sing together. We knew who was going for what note. We knew the secret to the funk flavor. We knew the chemistry and the magic that created the sound. We sang together in the studio and shared the same stage for the past year and a half. Our vocals were tight.

George never gave Parlet the option to tour, and they were very resentful. Mallia was pissed, but Jeanette Washington was devastated. She gave her whole soul to P-Funk. She felt like Parlet was being replaced by the Bridesmaids; in a sense, they were. George decided to take three new girls on tour instead of Parlet. It was total bullshit. They could have just paid The Brides' band to play behind Parlet too and took them with us. But when you have a lot of talented individuals under one umbrella like P-Funk did, there will *never* be real harmony.

LYNN MABRY Once we went on tour as The Brides, there were only two songs in the show I was excited about performing, "Disco to Go" and a Bootsy song, "Vanish in Our Sleep." We weren't given the creative license to decide where we shined the best. It was like we were singers for hire, performing someone else's songs versus having songs suited for us. Although this was George's creation, he didn't make the best decisions for us regarding the live show. In my opinion, Parlet was more powerful as a live act. They were funkier . . . more of an extension of Parliament-Funkadelic.

We had a great band once we got the Bridesmaids' situation together. P-Funk was generally a free-for-all onstage. That was because George just wanted to jam mostly. The Brides band's difference was that we had a solid group that listened to each other, played well together as a unit, and usually got along.

The Brides and their wedding party (left to right)*: Dawn Silva, Marion "Babs" Stewart, Jeff "Cherokee" Bunn, DeWayne "Blackbyrd" McKnight, Jeanette "Mackie" McGruder, Sheila Horne, Gary Hudgins, and Lynn Mabry.*

Blackbyrd McKnight was an unbelievable guitarist, but he always seemed unhappy to me. He never smiled. He was angry, and I never knew what upset him. I know that we were all stressed out because we were touring. I think he felt he wasn't getting what was due to him.

One night, he decided, "I'll show them!" Dawn and I dressed away from the band, so we didn't see them until they were onstage. We walked out onstage, and Blackbyrd had on a pair of fishnet stockings . . . that was it. His butt was out, and thank God he kept his guitar down in front because he had no underwear on. We were petrified. I think Cheryl James came on the stage and told him that he had to stop playing and put some clothes on . . . now! He wasn't happy about that, but he did it.

DEWAYNE "BLACKBYRD" MCKNIGHT (BRIDES GUITARIST) The Brides were great performers. They both had such stage presence and flow. They had great timing as a team, and we could follow them as a band. Dawn was a pro. Talented, funny, serious when needed, and fine, she always fought

The Brides of Funkenstein onstage in Washington, DC, in 1978.

to keep us together. Lynn was so comical and so badass on vocals. She was good onstage and brought elegance. I know I was the wild child of the band. Lynn was the one to explain to me that we [were] an *elegant* band and reminded me that there were ladies onstage.

GEORGE CLINTON We hated coming on after The Brides on tour. They had the best band of all of us, in my opinion. They had a real show . . . they rehearsed. Their band was serious, young musicians, like a tight jazz, rock, and funk band all in one. They were doing all *our* songs with a good band. They had sense enough to let their musicians take solos. If you do that, then you have a *real* music group. You're just a top forty band if you don't give the musicians solos. Bootsy would wear us out onstage, and his performance was so organized and tight at the height of his thing. If Bootsy had been a little wilder, Parliament would have caught hell. But when The Brides hit the stage, Bootsy had a problem. The Brides did to Bootsy what Bootsy was doing to Parliament. The Brides came out and wore *both* of us out.

Lynn and Dawn were gracious. They let the Bridesmaids come out and sing up front. It's usually the opposite; the star doesn't want others to come out and shine. The Bridesmaids were young and didn't appreciate the gesture. They didn't understand that The Brides were being gracious by letting them come out from behind their shadows. They didn't realize or care that Lynn and Dawn were giving them a break. The Bridesmaids' attitudes toward them were, "They're giving us a break?! We don't need *them* to give *us* a break!"

CHAPTER 17

AMOROUS

In an excerpt from a 1979 article titled "Women in Rock," Dawn Silva revealed to Liz Derringer of *High Times* magazine her love life and the challenges of being a music sex symbol: "It can be very difficult. In fact, I'm going with the guitar player that's in the group. It's kind of hard to really get into men on the road because most of the men are after you for some kind of freaky sexual thing, just to say that they've been with a Bride—"I've been with her," or "I've been with the chick in Parliament"—or it's just because they figure you've got a lot of money. It's a little prestige thing. And it's hard to trust a man unless you've known him before you even got into the business. I have never met a man on the road 'cause I'm really careful about who I get involved with. Like my old man now [Michael Hampton], we've been together for four years. And we've had our ups and downs. If you really loved somebody, it wouldn't matter if you are around five people or five thousand if you were going to be with that person."

As The Brides of Funkenstein enjoyed the road to fame, they traveled a trail of ups and downs in their personal relationships. After Glenn Goins's death, Lynn Mabry found comfort and a sensitive ear in the newest addition to P-Funk, producer Walter "Junie" Morrison. Junie was a significant component in P-Funk's "next level" of success, writing and producing

Bride Lynn Mabry sings to the fans in New York in 1978.

some of their biggest hits, including "One Nation Under a Groove," "Aqua Boogie (A Psychoalphadiscobetabioaquadoloop)" and "(Not Just) Knee Deep" (Funkadelic's second number-one single) from the 1979 album *Uncle Jam Wants You.*

MALLIA FRANKLIN We had a gig in Dayton, Ohio, during the Flash Light Tour in early 1978. I walked into the hotel where we were staying, and Junie Morrison was sitting in the lobby. Our friendship started as teenagers while Junie played gigs at the Pine Grill Lounge. At seventeen, he was already a piano, vocals, and instrumentation virtuoso. We continued our friendship through his early years as a member of the Ohio Players. When my mom owned her specialty advertising business, Program Products, Westbound Records was one of her biggest clients. She did many of the promotional items for the Ohio Players and Funkadelic in the early seventies. I knew Junie knew Bootsy and those guys from the Ohio music circuit, but he didn't hang around with P-Funk a lot, maybe Garry Shider and a couple of others. Anytime I saw Junie, I suggested he work with P-Funk, but I knew that moment in the lobby was *the* moment.

I hugged him, smiled, and said, "What you gonna do, Junie?" or "Scoone," as I called him.

He just gave me a grin of uncertainty.

I grabbed him by the arm and said, "Come on!"

I pulled him into the elevator, taking him to George's door. I marched Junie into George's room, pretty much like I did with Bootsy, pushed him toward George, and said, "Here you go, Bert!" The rest is funk history.

Junie had his own thang. He was eccentric, unique, and really into spirituality of different kinds . . . symbols, energies, vibes, auras . . . that mystical syndrome. He was a musical genius. But with most geniuses, there was that deeper side to him that some people didn't understand, and I think he was very much a loner because of it. It was his Cancer nature. Junie was intelligent and complex and knew how to motivate people. He was like George in that respect.

GEORGE CLINTON Mallia brought everybody around . . . she was always that *one*. She always found the funky folks. She was the best talent scout that the funk ever had. I told Junie to come on up to Detroit. He came, and we recorded the *One Nation Under a Groove* album. When Junie came along, he was a big help because he could finish anything I started and vice versa. I could give him something, and he'd finish it in half an hour. Then he started rehearsing with the band, and I liked how much attention they paid him.

One Nation Under a Groove and *Motor Booty Affair* were so successful that Junie was *it*, as far as I was concerned. He was super-duper when it came to music. I never saw his methods in the studio with the group, only when we worked one-on-one. But whatever it was, it was quick and precise, and the band didn't give him problems.

LYNN MABRY George first introduced Junie to Dawn and me as he observed us at one of our Brides' recording sessions. We could see he had a shyness about him that was somewhat endearing. My knowledge of Junie was limited, besides his voice on the Ohio Players' singles "Funky Worm" and "Pain." I hadn't experienced his musicianship firsthand. Once he started working directly with the organization, specifically The Brides of Funkenstein, as our bandleader, I could hear his creativity and talent. Playing almost every instrument except brass, he knew how to magically bring sounds and rhythms together. He always offered excellent vocalizing advice and showed us weird arrangements while performing them in the studio. Still, when it all came together, it was brilliant . . . he was brilliant.

Junie brought a great new sound and feel to this funk movement overall. I think he escalated George's music to another level. He insisted we gave our all, 100 percent of the time. He provided more attention to melodies and vocal arrangements, which I wholeheartedly welcomed and embraced. He brought a sense of mystique when he performed wearing his signature long velvet capes, accessorized with gold chains and dark sunglasses, yet his musicianship never wavered. He was earnest about music in general. It was indeed his first love. He was somewhat of a spiritual man, which I also believed influenced some of his production arrangements. I was honored to have him guiding our sound until Junie's and my relationship shifted from professional to romantic.

Dawn and others thought Junie was a rebound from the loss of Glenn Goins when we began a romance. Yes, I was young and impressionable. However, I did not need to rebound from a man I loved and lost. When Glenn died, I felt everybody in the organization swept our relationship under the rug. At the time, Dawn was so into Michael Hampton, and so many other relationship dynamics were going on that I did not receive the sympathy or support I needed. I don't recall anyone having the ability or maturity to deal with death in any capacity. Junie was the only one who genuinely seemed to lend me an understanding ear at the time. However, looking back, I can see he was on a mission. He was interested in me, so he used his sensitivity ploy. He opened himself up to me and allowed me to talk about Glenn. I would speak to him about my often confused and roller-coaster feelings, and Junie became a confidant. That's how he got me into a romantic relationship. What I didn't see coming was the closer we became, Junie systematically morphed into the most jealous man I'd ever been with. Every man I came in contact with was now a threat.

There were always love interactions with group members. It's bound to happen when a group of men and women are working together and traveling around the world. Unfortunately, what also happens is segregation. You create your own world once you pair up with a person in the group.

Musician, producer, and Brides musical director Walter "Junie" Morrison onstage in 1978, throwing a "whammy."

Then that world begins to take shape, and you alienate everyone else. I did it. Dawn did it. We'd all done it. As a young girl, I didn't take stock of the ramifications of pairing up with people I worked with or those who had relationships with someone else at home. These careless actions inevitably created segregation within the organization and sacrificed friendships and relationships along the way. As usual, there was a double standard. Women were seen as loose, but it was just "normal" behavior for guys.

DAWN SILVA In the beginning, it was all so very weird. I realized that Junie's sudden appearance in The Brides band was no coincidence; it was calculated. There were no introductions. I just looked up one day, and there he was, sitting onstage during our set behind a stack of keyboards. I questioned, "Who is that?"

Junie was short, maybe 5'6". He had dark, mirrored glasses, wide-legged jeans, a short black leather jacket, and a white commander's hat. He had a superiority complex, and, around the band, he acted like *they* were the newcomers, not him. Onstage, he'd weave in and out of the musical compositions with precise timing, fingering pretty melodic chords that gave the songs a richer feel. By week three, he seemed harmless enough. But I swiftly discovered that his soft-spoken words and shy and flirtatious demeanor were just a method of forcing you to lean in closer to him, and it worked effortlessly. Lynn was still grieving hard over Glenn Goins's death, and she found another way to combat the pain. Morrison became her consoler and, eventually, her controller.

LYNN MABRY One of our first major performances as The Brides was at Madison Square Garden, in New York. We stayed at the Sheraton Hotel in Manhattan. Glenn Goins's brother Kevin called from New Jersey. I was so glad to talk to him, as I hadn't heard from him in a while. Although he was a year older, he was like my little brother. During our conversation, I asked him if he was coming to see the show. Junie was in the other room, eavesdropping. When I got off the phone, he said, "Who was that?" I told him that it was Kevin, Glenn's brother. He got angry and became violent. I was caught off guard as he backhanded me across the face. Stunned by his reaction, I asked, "What did I do?" The more I tried to explain, the more he came after me. While fighting, we lost track of time as people kept calling the room. The band was waiting for us to go to the lobby to head to the Garden.

I finally pulled myself together to the best of my ability and went downstairs. Once I reached the lobby, Dawn looked at my face, and her eyes got as big as saucers. It was very clear from the swelling of my top lip that there was a physical altercation. She put one hand on my shoulder and the other gently touched my cheek. Shock turned to pure anger in her eyes. We proceeded to the venue, got to our dressing room, and applied ice to my swollen lip. It went down a bit by the time we had to go onstage. That was my first taste of just how jealous Junie was.

He would always apologize once he'd settled down, but the damage was done. I can't say I was ever head over heels in love with Junie, as our relationship was complicated, but I had a *strong* love for him. A part of me connected with him, searching for spirituality and a quest for love. He told me about how he was raised, and I thought my love and undivided attention would revitalize him. I even prayed that my love would change him. I guess I was on some kind of mercy mission. I was also searching for a love that would empower me to become the best woman I could be. I realized later in life that no human could do this for me.

As Lynn Mabry uncovered deeper and more complex layers in her pairing with Junie Morrison, Dawn Silva continued in her tumultuous and volatile relationship with P-Funk guitarist Michael Hampton.

WILLIAM "BOOTSY" COLLINS Dawn and Michael? A mug was in love. The love thing will always have some kind of downfall. Love makes you do crazy things. But then, how do you get around it? Things happen. That's the way the funk is.

The funk don't give a funk, and it gets *funked* up.

You sing, play, and spend your whole time together on the road. Somebody's coming over to see you, and the next thing you know, y'all hooked up. Sometimes, people get lonely out there, and they get sidetracked. We didn't get many days off, so what do you do when you get one? You start messin' around. Then you're with somebody else, and then she's with somebody else, so now you got friction.

My philosophy then was, "I can't fall in love because I'm already in love with what I'm doing." I was so focused on my music that I couldn't focus on anything else. When showtime came, a mug had to hit the stage. Everybody still loved each other, but there were moments of serious friction. And there was nothing you could do about it.

LYNN MABRY Dawn and Michael's situation was extremely complex. When it was good, they were like a love story. But when it was bad, it was like World War III. When Dawn and I came up front as The Brides, Michael started seeing the men in the audience reacting to Dawn and her sexuality onstage. That really bothered him and further complicated their relationship. His jealousy came from how the male fans adored her. Michael's own insecurity manifested itself as obsessiveness toward Dawn. It was like he was stalking his *own* woman.

DAWN SILVA Michael was extremely jealous. The fact that I used my sex appeal onstage was a big issue for us . . . but that was a part of my job. I'm a flirt onstage. I used my sex appeal, and it made me powerful. The men in the crowd loved it. I would use my sensual seduction techniques onstage, and the men in the audience would go crazy. Instead of Michael getting pissed at the fans, he got mad at *me* and threw things at me from the sidelines.

One night, he came out onstage, swung his guitar, and tried to hit me in the head. What was worse was that the organization would allow him to do stuff like that to me. I was stupid for staying and allowing it. I should have left, but I wouldn't let Michael run me away. Also, Michael had a problem being faithful, and I knew how to piss him off if I caught him with a groupie.

Kidd Funkadelic: Guitarist Michael Hampton in 1978.

One night, when The Brides' set was done, I was walking down the stage stairs, and Michael grabbed me and pushed me to the ground. We ended up fighting in the mud, under the stage as the band played above us.

I often went to Lynn's room to escape from Michael when things got out of hand. He would never do anything to me if Lynn was around. She protected me. But she got so wrapped up in Junie that she no longer defended me. I think George brought Junie in to drive a wedge between Lynn and me. I think he thought we were *too* close.

CHERYL JAMES Dawn was a looker. She had those beautiful legs. She had everything going for her, but she picked a young guy like Michael Hampton to mess around with. I never understood that. She was older and more experienced. He was young and in love. Whatever she put on him, he couldn't handle it. If somebody else looked at her, he would go nuts. He did a lot of childish things, but she provoked some of it too . . . she knew how to push his buttons. Dawn liked smiling, shaking her ass, and talking to other men to piss Michael off. She drove him crazy and made him do wild shit. He had no control. It got to the point where he would spit at her, smack her, anything he could get away with. Once, we had to put makeup all over her back so the audience wouldn't see the bruises from a fight they had earlier in the day.

One night, Dawn was on her way to the stage, and as she walked past

The Brides (Lynn Mabry and Dawn Silva) attend their wedding reception at Osko's Disco in Los Angeles in 1978.

Michael, he threw a glass of red wine all over her expensive white foxtails. That was it! I was fed up with his bullshit and lost it. I chased his ass into the men's room. He ran into a stall and locked it so I couldn't get to him. I'd had enough of Michael beating up on Dawn. But it didn't matter; she always went back to him. After a while, it just became a regular occurrence that they fought.

During the United States leg of the One Nation Anti-Tour, a promotional wedding reception to celebrate the success of The Brides of Funkenstein was held in New York. *Rock & Soul* magazine wrote "The Brides of Funkenstein made a special visit to Disc-O-Mat in Times Square to meet their fans and autograph copies of their debut LP, *Funk or Walk*. Highlighting the occasion was a mock wedding reception with entertainment by a troupe of fire-eaters, coneheads, and outrageous dancers."

Another lavish wedding reception was planned at the famed discotheque Osko's in Beverly Hills. Osko's became famous as the fictitious Zoo Club in the legendary disco film *Thank God It's Friday*. The event got significant press coverage in many Black and music publications.

LYNN MABRY We thought we were going to a party thrown by George at Osko's in our honor. I didn't realize Atlantic Records created this massive party to promote their artists. We pulled up at Osko's, and a crowd of photographers was in front. We had no idea that a barrage of cameras would be waiting. When Dawn and I exited the limo, it was a full-on moment of fame. That was my first experience with the paparazzi. I don't think I'd seen so many cameras take pictures of us like that. It would have been different if we had experienced it gradually. It didn't happen like that for us; it was overnight. The visual in my mind of flashes and the sound of the rolls of film spinning in the cameras was like, "Jesus is on the main line, and you better get a picture."

The club was packed. Atlantic Records was out in full force, including the company's president, Jerry Greenberg. There were celebrities, recording artists, and record executives in attendance. I knew we were popular, but I didn't realize we were *that* popular until *that* moment. That party made me realize that Dawn and I now had something honored by the record company and our fans. We were doing record store promotions in different cities, and the places were jam-packed, with lines around the block. It let me see there was more to this pairing of Dawn and me than

I expected. I was now assured that The Brides of Funkenstein was not just a group; we were a moneymaking conglomerate. Dawn and I would now expect better treatment from George and the organization. We had earned it. We weren't just members of Parliament-Funkadelic anymore. We had proven that we were successful on our own . . . as The Brides of Funkenstein.

Bob Lucas of *Black Stars* covered the gala at Osko's in a three-page feature article, "A Close Encounter of the Grooviest Kind." In an excerpt, he wrote:

> The bridegroom was not present, and details about the wedding ceremony were sketchy, but the wedding reception for The Brides of Funkenstein blasted off at Hollywood's disco, Osko's like the Mothership headed for a remote new galaxy. We met the lovely brides—Lynn Mabry and Dawn Silva—toasted them with champagne, and nibbled on the towering multi-tiered wedding cake. In the midst of all the activity, *Black Stars* managed to get the lovely brides in a quiet groove to talk about the social and musical event of the season. For *Black Stars*, the highlight of the evening was meeting two beautiful sisters, who both like Chinese food and have boyfriends but are not yet thinking of marriage, and were shiny-eyed excited leaving on a tour that took them to Germany.

CHAPTER 18

ONE NATION UNDER A GROOVE

By the conclusion of the United States portion of the One Nation Anti-Tour in November 1978, Clinton and Thang Incorporated reenlisted Parlet for the European leg. P-Funk was booked for fourteen shows in Holland, Amsterdam, Germany, England, and Paris. Billed overseas as the World Funk Tour, they filled halls across the continent. Clinton loaded the Mothership to take across the ocean. The P-Funk mob stepped off the plane decked out in military fatigues, letting everyone know that Uncle Jam's Army had arrived to storm the continent. Publicity was at full throttle when the caravan invaded Europe. Funkadelic's *One Nation Under a Groove* and The Brides of Funkenstein's *Funk or Walk* LP's UK releases were scheduled for December 1 to coincide with their arrival. Parlet was hitting the country cold, as their debut album had yet to reach European record stores.

CHERYL JAMES This tour was supposed to be "One Nation Under a Groove," but everybody wasn't groovin'. Parlet wasn't groovin' for months, and I was trying to keep everything together. Things began to change positively when we were informed that Parliament-Funkadelic was going to Europe. The first show was only a few weeks away, and George wanted me to fly over to manage The Brides. The initial plan was to leave Mallia, Jeanette, and Shirley in Detroit. It was like Parlet was on punishment. I didn't understand why they were being treated this way. They were a wonderful live act. They were strong vocally and visually.

After begging George to take Parlet to Europe, he said, "OK, I'll take them. Do you know anyone who could help with The Brides?" I phoned my roommate, Andrea Thomas... everyone called her Andi. She was once an educator in Europe, teaching German students English. I knew that she was perfect for the job.

ANDREA "ANDI" THOMAS (ROAD MANAGER) Cheryl came home one day and said George needed someone to go out with The Brides. What hooked me was that the tour was in Europe, and I had just returned from there and loved it. I took a leave from my nine-to-five job and joined the tour.

No one knew who I was except the girls and a few guys when I showed up. When I arrived at the tour bus, Archie Ivy, one of the managers, thought I was a groupie trying to hook up with the band. When he was told I was working with the organization, he still had a sexist attitude toward me, like I couldn't possibly know what I was doing. He was shocked that I had a credit card and an international driver's license. He couldn't believe I spoke German fluently until he had to ask me to translate for him. Once he needed me for something, I finally started getting a little respect.

We boarded an Air India flight at Detroit Metro Airport to Germany. We were flying over the Atlantic Ocean, and the plane was jammed. It was so crowded that you couldn't even walk around. I had a drink to relax, and Cheryl tried to get some sleep. I heard a commotion; then I saw people running. Cheryl and I jumped up and ran to the back of the plane. Frankie "Kash" Waddy and Lynn were in the bathroom smoking a joint. They decided to light some perfume in a cap to mask the odor. The plane shifted, and the ignited perfume spilled all over the sink. Lynn ran out of the bathroom and grabbed my drink to douse the flame. She thought it was water. It was vodka. She threw it on the flame, and the fire followed the alcohol straight up the wall of the lavatory. Lynn panicked and ran out of the bathroom and down the aisle to her seat, as smoke billowed out of the washroom.

The flight crew put the fire out, and the pilots wanted to know who was in charge. Cheryl reluctantly raised her hand and was taken to the front of the plane. She had to go to the cockpit to assure the pilots that there would be no incidents for the rest of the flight. Cheryl came back down the aisle and talked to the band of grown people like she was scolding a bunch of children, "Everybody better sit down, shut up, and do nothing else for the rest of the flight!"

LYNN MABRY I don't remember the plane incident being as dramatic as everyone else. Maybe it's because I was so high that I didn't know the gravity of the situation. I do remember going into the bathroom and smoking a little weed. I also remember the smoke alarm going off and rushing to my seat in sheer embarrassment. That's what I remember most: being embarrassed about the whole situation.

CHERYL JAMES Our first touchdown was in Germany, and police were waiting for us with big guns. The authorities decided they would send us back to the United States because of the fire. George didn't travel with us; he flew to Europe separately on the Concorde. So it was on me to fix this. I was ushered into a separate room where German officials were waiting. I tried to talk to them, pleading and begging them to let us stay in Europe.

I said, "We have a big tour booked over here. It's a lot of money, which can turn into many lawsuits. It will be havoc for everyone involved if we don't stay here and do these shows."

I assured the German officials that there would be no further issues. I was able to convince them, and we were allowed to stay. Before we left the States, George set up a private screening of the film *Midnight Express*. Hopefully, this was a warning for anyone caught with an illegal substance while crossing foreign borders. I had to gather everybody together and put my foot down.

I told them, "No marijuana, no hashish, nothing can travel from country to country. Whatever drugs you have, you must do it wherever you are and destroy all evidence before moving on to the next country. If it's illegal, get rid of it!"

That was the rule, and if you got caught, it was a fine of five hundred dollars, and you were immediately sent back to the United States.

The first show was in Neunkirchen, Germany. It was like being at home because the audience was filled with Black troops from the US. When the curtain went up on that first night, we looked at the mostly Black crowd in amazement. They knew who P-Funk was, and they loved Parlet and The Brides, which made those German shows great.

GARRY SHIDER The Brides and Parlet were in top form in Europe. All the girls were pretty confident in their own sets by that time. Lynn was strong in her voice and personality. She knew how to command a stage and get the audience involved. Dawn was confident in her beauty and sexuality. She was great onstage. The Brides had all of that working for them.

Parlet had those qualities, too, but it was different. The Brides seduced you into giving up the funk; Parlet was gonna *make* you give it up. They were loud and more "in your face" and aggressive. Mallia was a force of nature vocally and onstage. She was a great frontwoman. Jeanette was probably the most daring of all the P-Funk Girls because she wasn't scared of anything. Shirley was beautiful and had a strong voice. They were all great, and their bands were tight.

LYNN MABRY There was always a sense of competition with the women. You constantly felt like you had to prove yourself in P-Funk. When I saw Parlet live on tour, I thought they had a better show than us. They were funkier and more visual, and, in my opinion, their singing was far superior to what The Brides were working with at the time. I was impressed and a little jealous. I did realize that we had our own dynamics onstage. So, once I got over feeling a little green, I concentrated on The Brides of Funkenstein being the best we could be. The more we focused on ourselves, the better our shows got. And we had a fantastic band.

SHIRLEY HAYDEN After Germany, I remember riding around Amsterdam on a giant double-decker bus. The guys in the band were excited about smoking weed in public and going to the red-light district. Seeing the "ladies of the evening" silhouettes in the windows was fascinating as we made our way down the narrow streets. Everyone was having fun, and we were all jovial. The tour was going well, and the Europeans loved us.

As we made our way to England, I could feel tensions rising. One of the Bridesmaids, Babs, was married, and the organization let her husband come to Europe with her. She would tease the other Bridesmaid, Sheila Horne, and make fun of her. Babs was messing around with drummer Frankie "Kash" Waddy when her husband wasn't around. That was an open secret in the organization. While we were on the tour bus traveling to England, Marvin Gaye's song "Got to Give It Up" blasted over the speakers. When the song got to the chorus, Babs looked at Sheila, smirked, and said, "Sheila Horne's got to give it up."

Parlets Shirley Hayden and Mallia Franklin bring the Pleasure Principle to fans in Amsterdam, Holland, in December 1978.

Bride Dawn Silva high-kicks in Amsterdam with the Horny Horns (Rick Gardner, Maceo Parker, and Richard "Kush" Griffith) onstage in December 1978.

Sheila looked at Babs and her husband and said, "Babs already *gave* it up."

Babs's husband looked at her with daggers coming out of his eyes. The tension between them was so thick for the rest of the bus ride that it was palpable; you could cut it with a knife.

CHERYL JAMES We didn't know that Babs's husband was crazy. He took it upon himself to beat the shit out of Babs when we got to the hotel. Amid this beating, he sank his teeth into her flesh several times. She literally had bloody teeth marks on her body. That moment traumatized all the girls. I had never witnessed anything like that before, so I came unglued. I knew a human bite was one of the worst you could have.

We had to get her to the hospital, but we had to deal with her husband first. Andi and I let him know that he had to go. He thought he could just beat her ass without repercussions, but he didn't realize how determined Andi and I were. We found George and told him what happened. We insisted that her husband leave because of what he did to her. George agreed and immediately got him a ticket back to the States.

We took Babs to the hospital, and the doctor said, "This is horrible. What animal bit her?" I had to tell him that it was a human. The doctor was shocked. He treated her wounds and gave her a tetanus shot. The next day, we ensured her husband was packed in a taxi to the airport and returned back to the US.

Our next stop on the tour was London. Parliament-Funkadelic was invited to the government's Houses of Parliament. Many people don't get to do that, and I think we were one of the first rock bands ever invited. It was Parliament at the Houses of Parliament. I gave everybody pep talks about how respectful we need to be because the Brits are really into protocol. I wasn't worried about the girls, but I had to tell the guys in the band, "Be quiet and act like you got some sense."

We arrived in a procession of about thirteen black Bentleys; George's Bentley was white, leading at the front of the line. We got out of the cars and stood in front of the Houses of Parliament. A group of photographers and reporters waited for us. George carried a stuffed monkey around Europe that he named Logic. The dignitary, Sir Victor Goodhew, who invited us, introduced himself. George wouldn't speak to him directly. He made the man talk to the stuffed monkey. We laughed hysterically because this stuffy dignitary was talking to the little monkey. George didn't care that this was a dignitary; he'd make him do tricks if he could.

They invited us into the Houses of Parliament, and the band members

Parliament meets Parliament: The P-Funk Mob with Sir Victor Goodhew in London, England, at the Houses of Parliament in 1978.

lost their minds when we got inside. They didn't follow my rules. They were loud and acted like fools. They jumped on tables, pulled out cameras, and took pictures. The Brits weren't fazed and enjoyed letting them cut up. After all that chaos, they served us a superb dinner. I was thankful that they didn't throw us out. That day was a day that Parliament-Funkadelic and the British Houses of Parliament will never forget.

MALLIA FRANKLIN Europe was a game-changer for the girls. We did photo sessions and interviews for some of England's most prominent music magazines. Parlet was hot! We were killing all the shows. We had so much energy penned up inside from being unable to perform that we just exploded once we could get onstage. Those were the best shows Parlet did. We got fabulous reviews, and the European crowds were even more receptive to us than [those] in our own United States. For once, I felt Parlet was getting some of the shine we should have gotten all along.

We were excited about the new Parlet album we were working on, *Invasion of the Booty Snatchers*. We had already recorded two or three songs. I think we even performed "Ridin' High" [from the forthcoming Parlet album] a couple of times in Europe. We were kicking ass every night, and

One Nation Under a Groove: The whole P-Funk Mob lands the Mothership in London, England, in December 1978.

George and the organization were finally taking us seriously . . . and that felt so good.

Night after night, we changed our shiny outfits into variations of army fatigues and joined Parliament-Funkadelic onstage to land the Mothership. The Brides and Parlet were the vocal assault force, with Garry Shider, Ray Davis, Ron Ford, Gary "Mudbone" Cooper, Robert "P-Nut" Johnson, and the Bridesmaids.

LYNN MABRY I will always remember Manchester, England. Dawn and I walked out onstage, and everyone in the audience raised candles and lighters. It was a sea of light. I felt the love and admiration for The Brides wash over me like a wave from the audience to the stage. I had never felt that. I remember looking over at Dawn in disbelief.

"Do you see this? Can you feel this?"

That was mass adoration for The Brides of Funkenstein. George Clinton was not on that stage.

Later that night, it was announced that we were all getting royalty checks when we got to the final show in Paris . . . five thousand dollars each. We were so excited! At that moment, it felt like all the work and struggle were paying off. We had the fans' love overseas, and we would finally see some real money for all our hard work.

(Left to right) *Mallia, Lynn, Jeanette, Shirley, and Dawn pose for the cover of England's* Black Echoes *magazine in 1978 for their Christmas issue.*

The Brides of Funkenstein and Parlet were definitely making a splash in Europe. Pictures, pinups, and articles filled various periodicals. The most prominent was in the weekly music newspaper *Black Echoes*. The women of P-Funk graced their Christmas cover, and George Clinton was also interviewed in the same issue.

George stated about his female protégés, "We don't usually feel we have to compete with anybody until we see The Brides lighting up the stage, and we know we got to follow them. Shit, I really thought we were out of that competing thing, but having to go onto a red-hot stage when the girls just burned it . . . And Parlet, they're the youngest, and they really smoked on the last two shows in Germany." George shakes his head and smiles, "Shit, ain't they got no respect for their elders? We'll take that from Bootsy, but not three little girls. I'm going to get my temperamental shit together."

DAWN SILVA The day after the interview for *Black Echoes*, The Brides and Parlet had a photo shoot for the magazine, which was surreal. Because this was for their Christmas issue, the photographer dressed us in Santa Claus robes. I remember the magazine staff being excited, and I don't believe they expected to find such gracious guests. Perhaps they were prepared for five egotistical funk artists, par for the course for young females riding their first wave to stardom. But they instead found women who seemed to love and respect each other. Women who were entertaining, funny, humbled, and happy, and the photographer and his crew went out of their way to accommodate our every need.

However, it couldn't have been further from the truth. Before that photo shoot, we had never collectively respected each other's artistry or celebrated the fruits of our labor. But on that cold, sunny day in London, someone treated us like stars, and those beautiful photos captured every delightful moment.

CHAPTER 19

FUNK OR WALK

By the time the World Funk shows reached London, England, disgruntled musicians coined it the "Dog Food Tour" due to mounting financial hiccups. Some of the group's more tenured members, like drummer Frankie "Kash" Waddy, Horny Horns member Richard "Kush" Griffith, and others, threatened to strike as the tour approached its final show at Pavillon de Paris in France on December 16, 1978.

In an excerpt from his 2021 memoir *Rock and Roll Warrior*, David Libert (P-Funk's former booking agent) recalled his time on the road with the band and a typical conversation between Clinton and one of the road managers, Larry "LB" Benjamin:

"We took in $125,000, George."

"OK, give it here," said George, with an outstretched hand.

"George, George. We have bills to pay. The bus company is after us for falling behind in the payments. The Mothership is about to be repossessed, and our equipment is in need of repair. I can't just hand you $125,000."

"OK, give me $100,000. Pay $25,000 in bills."

LB pleaded, "George, please. We have to pay the band. We have to pay the crew. There are things that we simply have to cover in order to keep the show on the road!"

(Left to right) *Dawn Silva, Mallia Franklin, Shirley Hayden* (top), *Lynn Mabry, and Jeanette Washington* (below) *in a rare picture from the 1978* Black Echoes *photo shoot in England.*

"OK. Give me $75,000. Pay $50,000 in bills. That's it!"

As the stack of cash was handed to George, he deposited it straight into his boot.

Libert cleverly named Clinton's custom-made platform boots "The Bank of Funkenstein," writing, "The Bank of Funkenstein had one unbending, absolutely nonnegotiable rule: once the money went into the boot, it never came out again. It was George's money, unpaid bills be damned."

JEROME ALI The beginning of the tour was fine, but somehow it went south. Mallia started saying that she was going back home to the United States. I remember telling her, "Mallia, don't do this! Finish it out. I know you and Jeanette are at each other's throats, but we'll get this done and go home." It also had a lot to do with the finances, so I understood where she was coming from. I'll speak for the whole group; everybody was dissatisfied with the money.

Bernie Worrell's wife, Judie, couldn't stand George. I remember her being in the dressing room with Cheryl James and me in England, and she was venting like a hurricane. "I'm sick of this! Bernie's being mistreated. He doesn't need to be with P-Funk anymore. He needs to move on!"

I was taking it all in. To think that this could be happening to somebody so *important* as Bernie made me think about some things. Ron Dunbar and George talked to Mallia; whatever they said calmed her down, and somehow it worked out.

BERNIE WORRELL I feel for people; that's my job . . . to help and teach. The girls were all my babies. I loved Mallia, but she could definitely be a diva at times. There were others also. I'm not going to get into who the divas were, but when they would get into trouble, I would try to calm them down, help them get through situations and not quit. Mallia really wasn't in a position to quit Parlet, but she wanted her money, which I could relate to. I had to calm her down in Europe so she could get through the rest of the tour.

DEWAYNE "BLACKBYRD" MCKNIGHT The European tour was one of the most spectacular experiences I've ever had in music. All of us were touring the continent together. It was the first time I experienced Parlet as a live act because they didn't tour the States with us. It was one big show. Here we are, this great big band of Black folks, and everybody was talented. I thought, "Wow, how do you handle all of this?" I often wondered how George kept it all together without going nuts.

The Europe tour was also the first time that I didn't get paid. The first of many times, unfortunately. We were in a hotel in England and were told that one of the road managers ran off with all our money. Mugs were hungry. Many of us said, "If we're not getting paid, then we're going to eat." From then on, we ordered room service around the clock. I can't even imagine how big the room service bill was. Everything started so great... didn't end so great though.

BRUCE PETERSON As the management staff, we always had to be the bearers of bad news. When George spent money and didn't pay people, I'd always say, "We're going to take the blame for this." We were in a bad position. The band looked at us as "George's people." When we wanted to pay the band, George looked at us as if we were choosing the band over *him*.

Archie Ivy was his "yes" man. He went along with whatever George wanted. We always told Archie, "You have to be a manager, not a *FAN*-ager! Why are you saying 'yes' to everything?"

If one of the other managers had the payroll, George would want to take the money and say, "We'll pay the band tomorrow." I remember a gig when one of the road managers, Brem, opened the hotel room window, took the stacks of cash, put his arm out the window, and threatened George and Archie to toss the cash out from the top floor, saying, "If we can't pay the band, *nobody* will get their money!"

Threatening to toss the money was the only way we could get the band paid. We tried to take care of business but had only so many pieces of the pie. Then George hired *more* people, and now more people want their cut. It became harder and harder to divide the pie.

CHERYL JAMES We finished the shows in England and were on our way to the last show in Paris. Everyone was packed and loaded onto the bus—everyone except Mallia. I went to her room, and she was still in her nightgown. Her fiancé, Donnie [Sterling] was up and dressed, but she wasn't.

I said, "Mal, why aren't you ready to go?"

"I'm not going," she said.

"What do you mean you aren't going?! You have to go. Mallia, do you know what this would do to the girls?"

Mallia wouldn't budge. She decided she would make demands on George, and if he didn't fulfill those demands, she was not doing the last gig in Paris. And there was no way I could talk her out of it. She wanted her money. I didn't understand why this day was different from any other day. George *always* owed us money.

We had to go on without her, and I had never seen Jeanette so upset.

(Left to right) *Gary "Mudbone" Cooper, Junie Morrison, Nene Montes, Bernie Worrell, and Rodney "Skeet" Curtis in a dressing room in 1978.*

Her anger that night was overwhelming. Jeanette was pissed off because she felt powerless. She didn't have a contract like Mallia, which was a big source of her angst with George.

Parlet was born out of tragedy, losing Debbie in the beginning, then picking up the pieces with Shirley. Now Mallia? I was thinking, "How do we recover from this?" Pulling off the Paris show without her was going to be like pulling a rabbit out of a hat. It helped that Parlet had a band behind them that was so strong.

SHIRLEY HAYDEN Mallia wouldn't give me an explanation of why she wasn't doing the show. She was my friend and support system, and I followed her lead. I knew "professional" when I saw and heard it, and that was Mallia. Now I was left with Jeanette, and I couldn't follow her at all. She was not a leader. She couldn't lead me. I'll just say it, Jeanette didn't really like or care about Mallia. Jeanette was more concerned with wanting the position or power she thought Mallia held. Mallia would also tease Jeanette about her shortcomings vocally, which didn't help their relationship.

Parlet joining the European tour was a major shift for us. Parlet went over there, and we kicked ass. We went out onstage, wanting to be our best. Europe really wanted Parlet. I could see where we could have continued as a group on our own. But we were young and weren't in control. George had a strange look on his face as we left the stage on those first shows in Germany. I'll never forget it. We'd evolved as a group, and I think he was insecure after seeing how powerful we had become. The higher-ups could also see what was going on. I think George saw where he could possibly lose us, and he had to nip the power of Parlet in the bud.

I was terrified that Mallia wasn't going out onstage with us in Paris. But we had to do what we had to, and Jeanette and I had to go on without her. We were in the dressing room in Paris, getting ready. I was a nervous wreck. How are we gonna pull this off? I grabbed Mallia's silver crown and put it on my head. I needed a piece of her to be with me on that stage because she'd left me. We walked toward the stage, and George stood behind the curtain, waiting for us. He approached Jeanette and me, saying, "Just do it! Don't be afraid." As soon as we got out onstage, I could feel a coldness from the audience. It may have been the language barrier, but the French fans were not as enthusiastic as other countries. Jeanette and I were singing, and Donnie was *trying* to sing Mallia's leads, but the whole thing wasn't working. A lot of that show is still a blur for me.

When the set was over, I walked toward the side of the stage. I saw George. He was smiling, clapping, and whistling. As soon as I saw him, I started to hyperventilate. He said something to me as I approached, but I couldn't hear him because the sound went out of my ears, and my vision went blurry. The next thing I remember is opening my eyes. I was on the ground looking at the ceiling, with people milling around me. Junie Morrison and Cheryl James were leaning over me. Junie was pulling off my costume, and Cheryl put a paper bag over my face.

She was screaming, "Breathe, bitch! Breathe!"

Someone lifted me off the floor and took me to a couch nearby. The situation was so stressful that it physically took a toll on me. It devastated me because it was clear from her actions that Mallia Franklin was no longer interested in being in Parlet . . . and that broke my heart.

JEROME ALI We got through the Paris show, but it was sad. We all had to encourage Shirley and Jeanette. "Mallia made up her mind, that's it! You two girls will have to do your best." It turned out OK, but it wasn't the same. The three girls were a powerhouse together. But when you are talking about funk and rock, that was Mallia's specialty. Mal was a rock star. She had a voice that penetrated. Plus, Donnie wasn't hiding his desire to do his own thing. He wanted to be a solo artist, not in Parlet's band. That wasn't something that was hidden. He made it well known to us that this was now his main goal.

Parlets Shirley Hayden and Jeanette Washington take the stage without Mallia Franklin in Paris in 1978.

RON DUNBAR I went to Mallia's room in Paris and tried to talk her out of leaving the group. I knew how important she was to this Parlet thing. I think she thought she was irreplaceable. But in George's eyes, *anyone* is replaceable.

I said, "Mallia, you need to think about your actions. George will keep moving on, with or without you." She ignored me.

Mallia wanted to do a solo thing. She had the talent. She was good enough to do that, but it didn't work out that way. George shined a lot of light on her in the studio. Still, he was not up for doing a solo situation for anyone outside of Bootsy. He never let anybody influence him otherwise. It was George Clinton and Parliament-Funkadelic.

We had some great male vocalists. That didn't change the fact that no one except Garry Shider or Glenn Goins was in the front. But even in those cases, the focal point of P-Funk was always going to be George Clinton. He purposely did that. He didn't want one individual to stand out from the pack.

Mallia leaving Parlet changed that whole situation, and I knew it would hurt the group even more. From an A&R perspective, the public perception was that Mallia was white. That made Parlet different, and it was a selling point for them to cross over. That element was gone. As I said before, to George and me, she was the focus.

DAWN SILVA I saw Mallia after the show in Paris. She was mad and hurt. I understood her frustrations, but she couldn't have picked a worse time to strike. George needed an excuse to eliminate Parlet anyway because they were becoming a nuisance. This was the perfect opportunity. George wasn't threatened by Lynn and me. He was threatened by Parlet. He said it himself in *Black Echoes*, "I'm not gonna let three little girls kick my ass." He meant that. I was angry at Mallia because she didn't step up. She let influences around her cause her to lose her spot. Mallia got upset, and I think that was the first time I ever saw her cry.

Mal was tough. She wasn't a pushover. Sometimes I felt bad for Donnie because I've seen Mal slap the shit out of him if he didn't do what she wanted. Then she'd turn to me and say, "Silva . . . you got to train these niggas!"

There was so much dissension from everywhere that it was easy to be manipulated into doing the wrong thing. She left the group hanging. She wasn't thinking about what her decision would mean for Jeanette and Shirley. George wanted her to play her position, and when she went on strike in Paris, it messed up his plans. He needed her in Parlet. They were *dead* without her.

GARRY SHIDER Mallia was the first girl I ever met with P-Funk. I didn't even have a driver's license yet. She was cocky. Most of Mal's attitude was due to her relationship with George, Bootsy, and Dunbar. It was different from the other girls. George and Bootsy lived in her home. She fed us when we didn't have no food. She was like the Della Reese character from *Harlem Nights*. She was the woman that could sit in the room with the men. That was "Big Momma." Mallia's weaknesses were her ego and her mouth. That "Mal mouth!" It always got her in trouble.

I also think Donnie Sterling set her up when it came to leaving Parlet. He wanted to do his own thing and knew how to play her on that passive-aggressive tip. I also think that losing Debbie hurt Mallia to no end. She never really got over that. The Paris show was the biggest test for her. Mallia needed to step up to the plate for Parlet . . . and she didn't. She deserted them. When Jeanette and Shirley went onstage in Paris without her, that was it. Mal handed Lynn and Dawn the whole damn game. The competition was over . . . The Brides won.

GEORGE CLINTON I don't know what happened with Mallia's strike in Paris. Ron Dunbar was handling that issue pretty much. Whatever the politics were at that point with Donnie Sterling and Mallia, I didn't know about it. Everybody was falling out of love by then. Lynn and Junie were starting to have problems overseas too. The whole thing was like a big soap opera. It was like *Peyton Place*.

TOM VICKERS I think George treasured Mallia. They were friends for a long time, and she was instrumental in many things and his connections with musicians. He always looked at her as a core member of his inner posse. As a result, she had an important role not just as a singer in the group but in the whole Parliament-Funkadelic thang.

If it weren't for her, he would have never met Bootsy. That meeting changed everything for George. Bootsy was coming in from James Brown, and he knew the power of "the one." He spread the word of "the one" to George, which took Funkadelic from being a loose, unfocused Black rock band into a mindset and point of view that was unique and compelling.

Mallia was a key group member like Eddie Hazel, Bernie Worrell, Garry Shider, and Bootsy. She was in that vaunted place. I considered her an architect in the whole P-Funk thing. She was important. That's how she always came across to me from George's perspective.

MALLIA FRANKLIN By the show in Paris, everything was a fight, and I was fed up. I was fighting the organization to get the money I should have been paid. I was tired of being in the "worker bee" syndrome. You would think that we, Parlet and The Brides, were favored since we were the artists. That wasn't how the organization worked. We always thought things would change if we could get to George with our gripes. He would tell us they would change, but it would only be temporary *if* they did.

Then there was a constant power struggle with Jeanette Washington. Jeanette was competitive. It was a plus because she would go that extra mile to be the best onstage. She could dance. I mean, Jeanette could go, and whatever choreography we did, Jeanette came up with it. She was ballsy, and I loved that about her. That was her strength. She did shit like leap off the stage down into the audience, and I encouraged all of that because it made Parlet's show more dynamic. Let me say our relationship wasn't always bad. I loved Pussycat [Jeanette], and sometimes I felt genuine love from her, but I wasn't going to fight her for position.

And there was a lot of pillow talk between Donnie and me. I found out that I was pregnant by the Europe tour. When I joined Parlet, I was at the top of my game. I always had weight issues, and now I'm getting fat because I'm pregnant and depressed that we weren't getting paid or being allowed to work. I had an abortion because I was unsure about everything. There were things that Donnie wanted to do outside of Parlet. Everything didn't move as fast as he thought it should. He wanted to do another group, Sterling Silver Starship, and he wanted me to do that with him.

CHERYL JAMES I think Donnie had no problem with Mal not going to Paris. It was the moment he had always been waiting for: "Make her go away so I can step up front and show George what I can do." Mallia was a pretty woman, and there was nothing she couldn't do vocally, but Donnie made her feel insecure. He had his own ambitions of being a star. Mallia *was* a star, and Donnie spent a lot of time filling her head with insanity. He played Parlet down and made her feel like she was wasting her time. She fed into it, and that was her downfall. She would make statements to the other girls in so many words like, "I'm the shit." That caused tension. You don't say that! Everybody knows you're the shit; you don't have to remind them.

DONNIE STERLING (PARLET BASSIST) I never talked Mallia into leaving Parlet. We didn't want to break up Parlet, so to speak. Her problem was with Jeanette and Cheryl James. Cheryl was catering to Jeanette instead of catering to the group. It became one-sided. Mallia got upset with the whole thing and didn't like what Parlet was turning into.

Moneywise, a lot of things didn't go well on the Europe tour. We had the gigs, but something happened to the budget. We didn't know if we would step off the plane and have money to do anything. The money was always late, and, at some point, Mallia said to George, "I will not deal with how I'm being treated in Parlet! George, we are going to have to renegotiate!" George didn't want to make decisions. He would try to make everybody happy, but he couldn't. He told Ron Dunbar to handle it.

George and Dunbar had already given me the go-ahead for *my* project, Sterling Silver Starship. George said he wanted someone to take out "Brick

Brains," which was George's nickname for Rick James. When I said I was leaving as Parlet's bandleader, Mallia said she was going with me. She didn't want to be there anymore.

Although she would continue as a Parliament-Funkadelic member, Mallia Franklin never returned to her position in Parlet after the strike in Paris. She and Donnie Sterling planned to marry and create their new band . . . a namesake, Sterling Silver Starship, for the Thang Inc. organization.

LYNN MABRY After the show in Paris, we were told that George or one of the managers would contact us to deliver the five-thousand-dollar royalty checks we were promised in England. Once we settled in at the hotel, we heard that people started receiving theirs. George called our room.

He said, "Oh, by the way, we don't have The Brides' royalty checks. Atlantic Records has your checks. But I have something for you."

That didn't make any sense to me. This isn't for Brides of Funkenstein; this is for Funkadelic, of which we were members. Dawn and I were very upset and confused that every man in Parliament-Funkadelic got a five-thousand-dollar check. Junie had his check; even the dancer Sir Nose, Larry Heckstall, did. We should be getting a royalty check like everybody else in the group. Maybe he got a little nervous because George knocked at our room door shortly afterward.

He said, "Listen, I want to discuss your royalty checks. Don't worry. I'm going to make sure you get your money. I promise you. But in the meantime, let's chill out, and we will deal with this tomorrow."

Of course, he then pulled out the buffer . . . the cocaine. We snorted a little bit, smoked a little weed, and drank throughout the night, and our checks were no longer a subject.

As women in that organization, we were considered "lesser." How is it that every man, including the dancer, got a check, and women who brought real talent, money, and substance to this organization got nothing? Maybe Mallia found out about not receiving the checks beforehand. When the women didn't get their checks, perhaps that fueled her motive to strike in Paris. I'm not sure. But it would make perfect sense.

Dawn and I never saw our five-thousand-dollar checks. I think George cashed them. Thang Incorporated had our power of attorney, which we didn't know then, to cash any of our checks. The Brides had a hit record and an album on the charts, and someone was reaping the harvest. It sure wasn't Dawn and me. We were not being replenished financially or otherwise.

George had the power to make decisions that would be a win for all those involved. You will have casualties if you don't have that quality in a leader. And let me tell you something: The Mothership was a nation of casualties. That was disheartening because I thought George would be looking out for us. He didn't have an emotional connection to us anymore. We were now musical toys he played with. By the end of the European tour, I realized that The Brides of Funkenstein were just pawns.

We were pawns in George Clinton's "Big Game of Funk."

CHAPTER 20

After the European World Funk Tour's success, Parliament-Funkadelic was back on the road with a brand-new stage show within a month. The album, *Motor Booty Affair*, hit the Billboard Soul charts at number one, with a hit single, "Aqua Boogie (A Psychoalphadiscobetabioaquadoloop)," also in the number-one position.

The album's cover drew on Detroit-born artist Overton Loyd's unique talents. A gatefold cover featured a pop-up rendition of the city of Atlantis. Illustrations included cartoon portraits of some of the characters mentioned in the songs, including Mr. Wiggles the Worm and his ladies, Giggles and Squirm, Octavepussy, Queen Freaklene, and Rumpofsteelskin. The live show brought the album's concept to life. A stage equipped with fountains (real and faux), a fifteen-foot marijuana smoking skull, and a giant replica of the screeching bird from the album cover made the Aqua Boogie show possibly the most elaborate of all the P-Funk tours.

The Brides of Funkenstein continued as the opening act, changing from their trademark foxtails into scantily clad, glittery worms—Giggles and Squirm—night after night. Mallia Franklin's decision to leave Parlet thwarted the group's slot on yet another P-Funk tour.

With the Rubber Band returning to Bootsy after the European tour,

Mr. Wiggles the Worm and his ladies, Giggles and Squirm, welcome you to the Motor Booty Affair in 1979. Dawn Silva, George Clinton, and Lynn Mabry.

The Brides hired new recruits, genius-drummer Dennis Chambers and keyboardist Gary Hudgins, to join their band.

In 1979, The Brides of Funkenstein was voted the #1 Top New Female Group R&B by *Record World* magazine for the single "Disco to Go" and their album *Funk or Walk*. With awards and promising accolades, The Brides were positioned for success, but festering internal conflicts began to emerge, with the relationship between Lynn and Walter "Junie" Morrison being the most troubling. Compounded by the Clinton organization's financial struggles, Lynn and Dawn's once-rock-solid sisterhood was being chipped away.

LYNN MABRY By "Aqua Boogie," we weren't perceived as real people anymore. We were all George's cartoons that ultimately built his empire. Think about that . . . that's heavy. Maybe that was George's way of staying disconnected from us . . . to put on all these personas and alter egos. Dr. Funkenstein, Sir Nose, Mr. Wiggles. The wilder George got, there was less connection and sense of integrity with the band.

My relationship with Junie was taking unexpected turns. One day, during a session, I was singing in the booth, and I saw Junie walk into the studio with his big sunglasses on and a bigger smile. A woman walked in behind him, and they sat together in front of the recording booth's picture window. When I was done singing my part, I came out to greet them. I innocently extended my hand to introduce myself to Junie's guest.

"Hi, I'm Lynn."

Junie quickly interjected, "This is Carol . . . my wife."

I was shocked. Junie always told me that they were divorcing and not in contact. I stayed quiet. After the session, I returned to my hotel, still perplexed by the meeting. The next time I spoke to Junie, I asked for an explanation.

He said, "Although we are divorcing, I need her in my life spiritually. Carol is a Christian woman and my spiritual advisor."

Sometime later, during a break from the tour, Junie asked me to come to his home in Ohio. He'd convinced me that he was separated and his relationship with Carol was now platonic, and I was looking forward to spending time with *my* boyfriend for the first time in his environment. We arrived at his ranch-style house with a manicured lawn and garden and entered the entryway. His wife, Carol, walked out of the kitchen. I thought that Junie lived alone, but her casual and welcoming demeanor seemed as if they were still living together as husband and wife. I was totally blindsided.

After her gracious welcome, she made tea and offered me some. I politely accepted. My instinct was to remain as normal as possible. I did not want to let on that Junie and I were in a relationship. Junie seemed unfazed and reacted as if having me in their home was like welcoming a new friend. It was challenging to sit there, realizing that the man I had been with for months was still in a full-fledged marriage. She brought my tea, and we visited for a while, exchanging smiles and pleasantries.

At one point, Junie left the room. Carol turned to me, grabbed my hand, and said, "Please don't take him away from me. I'm trying to win his soul for Christ." How do you respond to that? She was often on the road with us and even at recording sessions from that moment on. Junie and I would now sleep in separate rooms when she came out on tour to "advise" him. Some nights, he would be in the room with me, and some nights with her, depending on how he felt.

DAWN SILVA Lynn and Junie's relationship became more bizarre when Junie's wife, Carol, joined the Aqua Boogie Tour. My most vivid memory of the games Junie played was when we were riding down the highway, literally hundreds of miles away from our next show. I watched Junie and his sister-wives, Lynn and Carol, roll alongside us in his Rolls Royce from the tour bus window. Lynn was behind the wheel while Junie was relaxing in the passenger seat, and Carol lounged in the back. Lynn was smiling and waving at us like she was a fan. The band was looking at her like she had lost her mind. I was embarrassed for her and confused. The irony was that she was driving past her own state-of-the-art custom tour bus, equipped with twelve bunks, a sound system, video games, a bathroom, and a refrigerator. All the P-Funk band members may have respected Junie Morrison's talent. Still, many did not approve of his pimpish lifestyle in general. Lynn was totally sucked in. I was so upset about the whole situation and filled with uncontrollable rage.

LYNN MABRY After the revelation of his wife, Carol, I was *sure* that Junie had relationships with other women. He played awful mind games and manipulated a situation to get a rise from something or someone. While we were together, he told me he had a "connection" with Jeanette Washington. I couldn't believe it. I called her on the phone; this may sound strange, but she and I had a wonderful moment discussing our mutual relationship with him and what he was doing. She said what they did was typical, but the most important thing to her was that he allowed her to open up to him. We even cried together about the situation. Afterward, I asked him, "How could you have a relationship with Jeanette *and* me?" He had no real answer. It was apparent that having multiple women was a cycle for him.

CHERYL JAMES Lynn's heart truly belonged to Glenn Goins. After he died, she was quiet. She was looking for someone to share her heart with. Junie came along, and he was very demanding. Lynn was young, and Junie felt he could *mold* her into someone he wanted her to be. Junie was an Ohio Player . . . and he was a real "player." Whenever I turned around, Lynn was hauling his stuff and driving him around, and many of us were concerned about those things. She was always catering to Junie, always following Junie. If he said jump, it was all a matter of how high. We didn't understand it. I loved Lynn and didn't like what Junie was doing to her. Junie was brilliant; I can't take that away from him, but I found his actions toward Lynn utterly ridiculous.

Junie came to Detroit to record, and he and Lynn moved in with me temporarily. He was into pyramids and all the energy they give off, so he brought multiple pyramids into the house. He also brought his Rolls Royce and parked it in my driveway. Maybe he thought I was impressed, but I wasn't.

At one point, Lynn, Dawn, Jeanette, and Junie lived at my house. We all knew that he and Lynn were an item, but the next thing I knew, he and Jeanette were an item, too. Lynn and Jeanette were catering to his every whim. I would see them all lying together and conversing . . . it was bizarre. The best way to describe their behavior was the "Stepford Wives" . . . like they were in some trance waiting to willingly do his bidding. It was like Junie had everybody in the house programmed.

One time, I remember him wanting something trivial from the grocery store, and he sent Jeanette out in below-zero weather, walking in a blizzard to get it. She willingly went out in the cold for Junie . . . just because he wanted something. He went back and forth to Ohio and primarily used Lynn as his driver. Lynn did everything Junie told her, which was not always best for her or The Brides. But because of her attachment to him, she did it anyway.

He was a man who didn't like me because I was a strong, aggressive woman. That was not his cup of tea. He would do this thing with his hands like he was putting a hex on you. We called it a "whammy." He was always trying to put his whammy on me. It was important for Junie to try to bring

The Brides on the Aqua Boogie Tour in Washington, DC, in 1979.

me over to his side of thinking. Probably because I was aggressive and independent, he felt his plan would run smoothly if he could break me in mentally. It didn't work, and things got very tense in the house.

Junie produced a session with The Brides and Parlet on a Parliament song called "Deep." I was in the studio with them, and he asked me to say something in the song like I was arguing with a man. Junie didn't like the fact that I cursed. I went into the booth and recited the lyrics that he had written. He entered the booth after me and said, "Shut your garbage mouth, woman!" That was his way of taking a dig at me.

After a month of craziness, this Junie setup wasn't working. I asked myself, "What the hell is going on in my house?!" Junie and I had a big argument. I got pissed and told him, "If anybody's going to pimp in my house, it's going to be me! You can get the fuck out!" Junie left and returned home to Ohio.

GARY HUDGINS (BRIDES KEYBOARDS) The first night I joined The Brides of Funkenstein's band was for the Aqua Boogie Tour in Atlanta at the beginning of 1979. I was placed behind Junie Morrison and told to watch and learn everything he was playing and *how* he was playing it. After a night or so, I could play everything he was playing note for note.

I thought The Brides were great as a live act. George used Lynn and Dawn's sex appeal to sell the group. Not that they weren't talented, but watching the fans, who were mostly men, react to them in their sexy costumes got the biggest reaction. I looked at Dawn more as the boss. She was the one I would go to if I had any ideas or concerns. I think that she was the one that held us all together during that time.

I knew Lynn and Junie had a situation going on, and tensions were brewing between Lynn and Dawn shortly after I arrived. I also knew a possible love triangle existed between Dawn, Michael Hampton, and The Brides bass player, my friend Jeff "Cherokee" Bunn. However, I always tried to stay out of the drama and just do my job.

DAWN SILVA As the Aqua Boogie Tour went on, Lynn distanced herself more, and The Brides shows became sloppy. Garry Shider came to me and said, "Dawn, you're going to lose your band unless you take control of this situation." That was the wake-up call for me to step up if The Brides of Funkenstein were going to survive.

We were in Philadelphia, and I went to Junie's hotel room to get Lynn for sound check. Junie told her that she didn't have to be at sound checks anymore, and she started missing them more frequently. I knocked on the door. It opened, and I walked into a dark room with only the glow of candlelight. Lynn sat on the floor having some kind of séance with Junie's wife, Carol, and Jeanette Washington. Junie was sitting in a chair observing his triangle of women. He always believed in doing things in threes . . . even when it came to women.

I said, "Lynn, we've got to go. We've got sound check."

Lynn said, "Be quiet! Dawn, can you feel it? The energy, Dawn. Can't you feel it?"

Whatever it was, I didn't want to feel it.

Junie said, "Nah, she don't feel it."

I said, "Come on. We're supposed to be at sound check."

She said, "I'm not going. Junie said that I didn't have to go."

I looked at Junie and said, "Shouldn't you be coming too? Aren't you supposed to be The Brides' musical director?"

Junie ignored me, and Lynn just sat on the floor. I left for the arena without her. He had been filling her head for some time with ideas that The Brides would be nothing without her. He tried to lure me into the same egotistical thinking. He told us to fly to shows, not ride on the bus with our band. He called them "the employees." They were our band, and I continued riding the bus with them. Lynn started flying with Junie. I didn't want to be around him, which meant I wasn't around Lynn either. He was successful in separating her from everybody, including me.

She never showed up to sound check that day but arrived in time for the show, and the show sucked. One thing that I hate is being embarrassed. I was ashamed of what our hard work had now become. After the show, we returned to the dressing room, and I went *off* on Lynn in front of the Bridesmaids. I could have handled it differently and talked to her privately, but I was so mad at her attitude toward what we built together that I lost it. Lynn was my best friend. That was the first argument we had ever had in *all* our years of friendship.

Babs was no longer a Bridesmaid by now, leaving Sheila and Mackie, and they were waiting for Lynn and me to fall apart. They weren't thrilled about singing background for us anyway. They wanted to be in Parliament-Funkadelic, and singing background for The Brides was just a vehicle to do it. I'm sure they felt their talents were being wasted, and maybe they were. They didn't have much to sing, basically doubling Lynn and me. It was all becoming chaotic, and it was because Lynn didn't care anymore, so no one else cared.

We were somewhere in Ohio, and The Brides had to be onstage at eight. I started applying my makeup around 7:15. Lynn was nowhere to be found. 7:30, still no Lynn. By 7:45, I started getting nervous because no one had heard from Lynn *or* Junie. One of the road managers knocked on the dressing room door, telling us we had fifteen minutes to showtime. I nervously looked over at Sheila and Mackie.

I asked Mackie, "You know all Lynn's parts, right?"

She excitedly replied, "Yes!"

I told them to grab some of The Brides' LeGaspi costumes. They screamed and tore their cheap Bridesmaids' spandex outfits off. Sheila didn't care about what she would sing; she was just glad she would finally be up front.

As we walked toward the stage, I got strange looks. The staff and onlookers realized that we were going onstage without Lynn. I'm sure many wondered, "How is Dawn going to do this without her?" We walked out to a packed house and started the show. From song to song, I kept turning around, looking for Lynn. As the show went on, I really started to worry. "Was she in an accident? Did Junie hurt her?" I didn't know.

We got halfway through the set to the ballad "Vanish in Our Sleep." That was one of Lynn's favorite songs to sing. It was always the most emotional song of the set. I had to sing it that night alone, and I felt myself getting teary as I sang it. Maybe I knew in my soul that Lynn was gone and she was not returning. In my eyes, Lynn was the leader. My job was to look cute, dance, put my notes in, strut across the stage, and be sexy. But that night, I surprised George, many others . . . even myself. Without warning, I had to become a leader.

Mackie sang most of Lynn's parts, and Sheila filled in the rest. Whatever we were doing, it was working. Mackie and Sheila were aggressive onstage because they wanted to prove to George that they deserved to be lead singers, not in Lynn's and my shadow. We got to the finale, "Disco to Go." When I heard the crowd cheering for the three of us, I knew The Brides of Funkenstein that was Lynn and Dawn was over. Everything we built together faded away, and it was because of Walter "Junie" Morrison . . . I will always believe that.

DEWAYNE "BLACKBYRD" MCKNIGHT I remember the night before Lynn went AWOL. She was in the dressing room, upset and crying. That was unusual for her. Junie came in and kicked everybody out. The next night, Lynn and Junie were gone. My first thought was, "Oh shit! What are we going to do?" I'm not sure how we pulled it off without Lynn, but we did.

I didn't know Junie well then, but I remember him calling an impromptu meeting with The Brides band. Junie told us he wanted us to leave P-Funk and go with him. I didn't want that. I wanted things to stay like they were. As a band, we were all working well together. Collectively, Parliament-Funkadelic, Bootsy, Brides, Parlet . . . that was the band. I didn't intend to leave, and the band collectively declined his offer.

LYNN MABRY No one understood how unhappy I was. I was going through challenges, personally and with our performances. My spark was gone. Whatever dancing I was doing stopped. I wasn't doing anything special with how I looked. By then, I had serious doubts and problems with George, and I was bucking heads with some of the management staff. I felt like I had lost Dawn. She was my best friend, but her focus was entirely on performing, being a Bride, and nothing but the funk. I was emotionally drained, hopeless, and found myself neither connected nor invested. I talked to Junie and told him, "I am so incredibly unhappy. I don't think I have ever been this unhappy before."

He looked at me and said, "Do something about it."

I started to cry, "I don't know what to do. I am physically and emotionally exhausted. I've been on the road with these people for over two years, and it's been a struggle. I feel like I want to run away."

He said, "Is that what you really want?"

I replied, "At this moment . . . yes. But I don't know if this is the right time."

He said, "It's never the right time. The right time is when you've come to the end of your rope."

I had a few drinks to numb myself while struggling with my decision. I realized that my contemplation to leave culminated in my experiences with P-Funk from day one. From the first day I met George, while we were with Sly, there were systematic points I dealt with. Everything from my decisions to sleep with the men I slept with in the group. The decisions to do the drugs, the decisions made for me musically, the issues I had with the other girls, even Dawn. She was now upset with me most of the time.

Junie watched as I downed glasses of Hennessy, and he said, "If you want to leave, I'll leave with you."

That shocked me because he was a member of P-Funk too. I know that he didn't make that decision because he loved me so much. He was probably tired as well. I'm sure situations were going on with George and others in the organization, making it easy for him to bow out. I wasn't thinking about Dawn or the Bridesmaids. I wasn't concerned about how they were going to handle the show. What was sad was that we only had three more weeks of the Aqua Boogie Tour. In retrospect, I can see how irresponsible even contemplating leaving was. We had been on tour for four months, and I couldn't hold out for three more weeks? Of course, I could have.

When someone leaves a situation, they see an open door to do so. My life was full of stress, problems, pain, sorrow, and death. I was finally able to say, "I'm tired." I was never able to say that before. I couldn't share those feelings with Dawn because she was going full steam ahead with The Brides. Our perspectives were now totally different. Her position was, "We've got to keep going." As a friend, Dawn couldn't hear or console me because, in her mind, we had made it. If I had been more mature, I would have finished the tour and had a conversation with Dawn and George to say, "I'm done." But I was twenty years old. We were in Canton, Ohio, close to Junie's hometown of Dayton, so we just jumped in his Rolls Royce and left.

Dawn told me that she thought Junie convinced me to leave The Brides, but that's not what happened. I didn't go to be with Junie. But Junie, being older and more experienced than I was, didn't discourage me from leaving so abruptly either. He encouraged my immature decision, which was sad in the end.

LAST YEAR WE ANNOUNCED "HERE COME THE BRIDES."

THIS YEAR WE SAY, CONGRATULATIONS FOR "DISCO TO GO."

Record World R&B Awards:

R&B Albums
#1 Top New Female Group/Brides Of Funkenstein
#4 Top Female Group/Brides Of Funkenstein

R&B Singles
#1 Top New Female Group/Brides Of Funkenstein
#4 Top Female Group/Brides Of Funkenstein

World Funk Headquarters
6253 Hollywood Boulevard (At Vine Street), #807
Hollywood, California 90028 (213) 464-Funk

Brides Best: Record World *magazine voted The Brides of Funkenstein "Top New Female Group R&B" of 1979.*

MALLIA FRANKLIN I'm not one to get into someone else's love affair, especially when I had my own shit going on with Donnie. But Lynn was someone I cared for. Lynn was younger than the rest of us, and I saw how Junie played on her need to be loved by him. I was in a hard place because Junie was my friend. I brought him into the situation and loved him like a brother. We all had dys-*funk*-tional love things going on. Hey . . . it was the seventies. I always felt that Lynn and I were being used as bargaining chips for Junie and Donnie against George. We were used as pawns in some ego trip. Because we had intimate relationships with these men, they had a different control than George had over us. It was all the pillow talk, all the "If you loved me . . . " conversations.

When you are in love, sometimes you don't see past yourself. If we had been more mature and business-minded, we would have realized how much power we had in this situation. If we had known, Lynn and I could have parlayed the situation into something more beneficial for both of us. But we were young, in love, unhappy, and pissed off.

GEORGE CLINTON Lynn leaving was a big letdown. She was some of the glue that kept P-Funk vocally tight . . . the harmonies and things. Everybody would rally around her. She would keep them together even with people that were hard to get along with.

The whole Junie "coup" was going on, and I didn't know about it. He was undermining and trying to take over. When I found out, I told him, "Give me a contract, and I'll go with you too!" I was serious. It didn't matter who was running it; that ain't the point. Let's just keep it going. I wasn't all caught up in being in charge. I didn't care. That shit didn't bother me. If anybody was good enough to run it, he was.

The Brides was one of my favorites. When you have something that important involving that much money, you should be coming to rehearsal and getting along with people. It's so important that you're not fighting over no women or men, not even a little bit of money. You can get the money if you can get past the bullshit. The money you're fighting over can't take the place of the *real* potential of the shit. Lynn and Dawn didn't truly understand the potential of what they had. If they did, they would have hung in there together. I figured that Junie and Lynn couldn't go that far. Where were they gonna go? I didn't think Lynn would give up the whole Brides of Funkenstein thing like that. I felt that she would easily come right back . . . But she didn't.

CHAPTER 21

INVASION OF THE BOOTY SNATCHERS

In April 1979, as the Parliament Motor Booty Affair Tour concluded, Parlet's sophomore album, *Invasion of the Booty Snatchers*, hit record store shelves. Long before songs about twerking, Parlet was singing in praise of the rump. According to George Clinton, Casablanca had prepared heavy promotion for *Invasion* . . . after Parlet's success as a live act on the European tour. "They were just about to get their break when that second album came out," George said. "But Casablanca was pissed at us by then. Parlet didn't get a real shot at the brass ring like the rest of us did."

With Mallia Franklin's vocals on half of the album despite no longer being a group member, Clinton and Thang Incorporated released the songs "as-is," with her credit as an "additional" vocalist.

Her replacement was Detroit native Janice Evans, who was quickly piloted into the studio to complete the album's last two songs. In a 1979 article in *Record World* magazine, "Parlet Finds 'Permanent Funk High,'" new recruit Evans said that "although singing the funk is a definite shift from what I was used to singing [she sang with the Beverly Glenn Concert Chorale for five years], the music is free and uninhibited, you can overemphasize it, dramatize it, and be as creative as you want, but whatever you do, it's got to be funk. I'm still trying to get used to all the new words."

Though the reviews were good, they did not boost sales for a group that had lost two-thirds of its founding members by the second album. Like many Black girl groups, Parlet had become a revolving door of members. The first single, "Ridin' High," would become the groups highest-charting release, peaking at number forty-nine on the soul charts. The album would stop climbing at number seventy-three.

MALLIA FRANKLIN We started recording the *Booty Snatchers* album in the fall of 1978 before going to Europe. "Ridin' High," which was originally called "Disco Lover," and "Huff-N-Puff" were the first songs we finished. They were both written by Donnie [Sterling]. We also started vocals on "Booty Snatchers" and "No Rump to Bump," two more of Donnie's songs. Donnie and I were also writing other songs for the Parlet album; one was a ballad called "To Give," but we kept it for Sterling Silver Starship after we left Parlet.

SHIRLEY HAYDEN After Mallia left, the organization staged another all-out search for a girl. It was an emergency. I'm unsure how they found Janice Evans because Jeanette and I weren't involved. Janice was in a local Detroit trio called September with her sister, Gwen Dozier, and their cousin Diane.

Janice came into the group, and we befriended her. She had a lovely voice, but she was a church girl, and she didn't have that "sex machine" look and attitude that P-Funk Girls made famous. We did a lot of socializing outside of Funkadelic, but I wasn't sure if I really trusted her. I knew it was vital for her to prove to George that he hadn't made a mistake. But she could be bitchy. For whatever reason, Janice always compared our voices and thought she was a better vocalist than me. Then she would say, "You stay in the mirror too much." We were at rehearsal one day, and Eartha Kitt was on TV. Janice turned to me and said, "You remind me of Eartha Kitt. You know how she's from down south but has that *fake* French accent? That reminds me of you." In other words, she was calling me a phony.

Ron Dunbar came to me with a concept for a song called "I'm Mo Be Hittin' It." It perturbed Janice that Ron would come to me first with this idea and that I would be the first to lay a lead vocal . . . it was more of a rap. I know it was one of the first *female* raps done. I laid the rap down, and we took a break to get some ice cream. I could tell that Janice was pissed. She looked at me and said, "If I were George Clinton or Ron Dunbar, I wouldn't have you doing lead vocals on nothing!"

Booty Snatchin': Shirley Hayden, Jeanette Washington, and Janice Evans become Parlet in 1979. Casablanca promotional photo.

I couldn't believe she would be so bold to say something like that to my face. I was so shocked that I couldn't even respond.

By now, Parlet had gone through several phases. People were becoming a little disenchanted. The group is looking unstable. Replacing girls repeatedly had a lot to do with George's contract to fulfill with Casablanca. So we had an album to finish, and Janice Evans was it.

RON DUNBAR I was producing Parlet full-time for the most part by the second album. George was in the studio here and there. He spent more time with The Brides by this point. My dilemma now was that Parlet didn't have a lead singer in my eyes. When George initially instructed me about Parlet's sound, Mallia was my lead reference. As the only original member, Jeanette Washington stepped out front, and everything changed from that point.

Janice Evans came into the fold. She had a good voice, but it didn't inspire me as a songwriter and producer. There was nothing I could sink my teeth into. It just took Parlet's material in a different direction. Their music was still funky but became more sing-along and had fewer solos than Parlet was known for on the first album.

CHERYL JAMES Shirley entered Parlet so early that she could *pass* on the first album cover. Replacing Mallia was more problematic because of that voice, and she looked different from the other girls. Don't take this as a negative, but Janice Evans came from an entirely different environment as far as singing. Funk was something new to her. Janice had no real knowledge of the P-Funk family except for what she heard on the radio. That makes you an outsider when it's time to participate. Some of that hardcore funk was missing. That's not to take away from her singing ability. She was a great singer.

When it was time for the girls to take new pictures for the *Booty Snatchers* album, I got word that Parlet wasn't getting any money for wardrobe. The clothes they wore in the promotional pictures were things they already had. Some pieces were mine. There was no support for Parlet from George or Thang Incorporated after Europe.

Some time passed, and George finally came through. He flew us to New York. A limo picked us up and took us to the designer Larry LeGaspi's studio in Manhattan, and George paid the bill. We picked out a few thousand dollars' worth of costumes. LeGaspi had racks of wild spandex outfits. Bodysuits with one leg and one arm, gloves with oversized gold cuffs and three fingers, skull caps, and hats that looked like flying saucers.

SHIRLEY HAYDEN After *Booty Snatchers* was released, Jeanette, Janice, and I flew to Los Angeles to promote the album. I was excited because I had never been to the Funk organization's LA office, World Funk Headquarters. I thought it would be a beautiful office space. It was nothing like I expected, mainly desks and boxes everywhere.

As representatives from record companies commonly did back then, the people from Casablanca would accompany us to record store signings and interviews. They arrived at the office, and I instantly felt the label reps' uncomfortable vibe. I remember their faces when we were introduced and they were handed our new promotional pictures. The pictures we took for *Booty Snatchers* caused controversy back then. At that time, pointing at each other's booties was very risqué. But Funkadelic was wild and controversial, so I'm sure that's the reason George chose that picture in the first place.

The Casablanca staff looked puzzled . . . *startled* is a better word. It was apparent that this wasn't the same group from *Pleasure Principle*. Neil Bogart was a fan of Mallia's, and it was obvious that she was gone. George still had to deliver them two more Parlet albums that she was contracted to do. She bailed. I'm sure there was some concealment to Casablanca on Thang Incorporated's part.

Knowing George, he probably said, "Let's just keep Mallia's vocals on it, put a generic album cover on it, and get it out."

Casablanca's reps presented Jeanette with a gold record for something she sang on for Parliament, and they accompanied us down to a record store on Sunset Boulevard. It felt like there were stares and whispers between the Casablanca staff. I saw one of them pick up the phone to make a call. For all I knew, they could have been calling Neil Bogart. I didn't feel good about the vibe of it at all. It made me nervous. It felt like this *new* Parlet was already a letdown to the people at Casablanca.

TOM VICKERS No offense to Parlet, but there *was* a lack of support. I don't think it was a conscious effort on George's part to put all his eggs in The Brides' basket and kick Parlet to the curb. The changes with the group and at Casablanca created this house of cards to be blown over and fall apart. That's what happened. I won't say that Parlet became an afterthought or that George's focus shifted from them, but, frankly, with Neil Bogart having issues at the label, the money focus that had gone into Parlet and Parliament during Casablanca's heyday just wasn't there anymore.

At the same time, Atlantic Records, where The Brides were signed, was a viable label through Warner Brothers, with tons of money and distribution. They were in the game a lot heavier. The mindset was, "Let's go with the power." The power was with Atlantic Records and The Brides of Funkenstein.

By May of 1979, a string of music festivals featuring Parliament-Funkadelic, Bootsy's Rubber Band, the "revamped" versions of The Brides of Funkenstein and Parlet, and a collection of other popular groups like Rick James, Con Funk Shun, The GAP Band, GQ, Instant Funk, Mother's Finest, and Sister Sledge dominated the concert landscape well into the summer months. The all-day events would start around two in the afternoon and wrap up close to midnight.

The Brides of Funkenstein was still a fan favorite, coasting on the success of their first album, *Funk or Walk*. Parlet debuted new material from *Invasion of the Booty Snatchers*. With Donnie Sterling defecting with Mallia Franklin, Parlet brought in bassist Jimmie Ali, the twin brother of guitarist Jerome Ali, to replace him.

DAWN SILVA After Lynn left The Brides, we had about a month before the big summer Funk Festivals of 1979, starting with a massive show at the Los Angeles Coliseum. That gave us a little time to retool The Brides' show. That's when I first started to see Sheila Horne's *other* side. She was now having a sexual relationship with George, and members of The Brides band were beginning to really dislike her. Sheila debated what parts she would sing and informed me of what parts she *wasn't* going to sing. I could foresee that this was going to turn into a big problem. She was overenthusiastically taking ownership of a spot she hadn't been given "officially" yet. Now that she was messing around with George, she wasn't that sticky, sweet, accommodating girl anymore like when she was a Bridesmaid. Now she felt that she had some kind of power.

GORDON CARLTON (PARLET GUITARIST) I thought the Parlet band members started having more freedom by the Funk Fests of '79. Before, when Mallia and Donnie were in the group, our mindset was always, "The girls are up front! As the band, we must do all we can to make *them* look good." But after Mallia left and Janice Evans came in, the musicians thought, "We need to start showing what *we* can do. It's not just about the girls being in front anymore. Now, we will interject ourselves and become more part of the show." The girls weren't the priority. In a way, the Parlet musicians took the show over.

GARY HUDGINS The '79 Funk Fests were my first shows on the bill with Parlet. The one thing I remember about playing shows with them was that there was always a lot of tension between Parlet and The Brides. The musicians were just as competitive with each other as the girls were. It was always stressful when we were on a show with them. It was The Brides-Baltimore musicians versus the Parlet-Detroit musicians. I wasn't into that kind of atmosphere, so I wanted those shows to be over.

When Lynn Mabry left, everything switched. The group changed with Sheila Horne and Jeanette McGruder coming up front. Sheila got really cocky. It caused issues, especially with Dawn. Sheila was combative, and we had to change things up in the show to suit the new Brides. It was different playing behind them because what made The Brides special to me was the charisma and chemistry between Lynn and Dawn . . . and now it wasn't the same.

The "new" Brides of Funkenstein (Sheila Horne, Jeanette McGruder, and Dawn Silva) take the stage at Oakland Stadium in 1979, with bassist Jeff "Cherokee" Bunn in the background.

Parlet (Shirley Hayden, Jeanette Washington, and new member Janice Evans) performs at the Pontiac Silverdome in 1979.

CHERYL JAMES Festivals were always great . . . like a big competition, and you got a chance to hang out with the other bands. The Los Angeles Coliseum was the first, and it was crazy as hell. It had to be one of the biggest festivals for us. There were one hundred and three thousand people in the Coliseum that day. We returned to the hotel, and it seemed like all of America was there. We couldn't walk down the halls, down the stairs, or get in the elevators. Wherever we went, people were screaming our names. Fans would follow you into your room. It was a crazy time and a nonstop party.

The Funk Festival at the Silverdome in Pontiac, Michigan, was another memorable and crazy show. It was a hot summer, with hot groups and lots of drugs. The fans were in full-party mode. They wanted to be closer to their idols and rushed to the stage. They crashed the barriers and rendered security helpless. There was nothing to quell the chaos. Group members scattered; many headed backstage to avoid injury. The crowd continued pushing forward, and people were being trampled right in front of us. Some groups watched the turmoil and began to help the wounded by pulling them on the stage. A fleet of ambulances had to be called in. They stopped the show, and people were all around us on gurneys being carried out. It took a while to regain order so the show could go on. I had never seen that kind of mayhem in my life. That was a first for me, and it was terrifying. Everything was chaos. It was an unfortunate foreshadowing of what was on the horizon for P-Funk.

CHAPTER 22

NEVER BUY TEXAS FROM A COWBOY

In the fall of 1979, Funkadelic had their second number-one hit with the Junie Morrison–produced "(Not Just) Knee Deep," the first single from their new album, *Uncle Jam Wants You*.

With Sheila Horne and Jeanette McGruder now positioned up front with Dawn Silva, The Brides of Funkenstein's sophomore disc, *Never Buy Texas from a Cowboy*, was also released in the fall of '79. The album's title cut was the first single, peaking at number sixty-seven on the Billboard Soul charts. The album stayed for six weeks on the charts, peaked at number forty-nine, and cracked the Pop 100 Album Charts at number ninety-three.

In 2001, *Never Buy Texas from a Cowboy* was listed at number twenty-six on *Rolling Stone*'s "The Fifty Coolest Albums of All Time." Robert Christgau, the self-proclaimed Dean of American Rock Critics, wrote of the album: "I prefer it to *GloryHallaStoopid* [Parliament] or *Uncle Jam Wants You* [Funkadelic]. It's gratifying to hear women asserting themselves in what has always been a sexist setup."

The album cover features three pairs of legs in platform heels under one giant cowboy hat in the desert. Both Brides' album covers were examples of anonymous sexual symbolism. Keeping group members unknown

The Brides of Funkenstein (Dawn Silva, Sheila Horne, and Jeanette McGruder) in their Larry LeGaspi costumes for Never Buy Texas from a Cowboy.

became a trick of the trade for the Clinton organization; unidentifiable members were easier to maneuver. Ironically, in some ways, this could be interpreted as Clinton's "fear of commitment."

After the album's release, *Blues & Soul* magazine wrote, "The Brides of Funkenstein have expanded to three girls, and they have a new Atlantic album on the streets this week. Only Dawn Silva remains from the original duo, with Lynn Mabry 'retiring' and settling down in Dayton, Ohio, with another former P-Funker, Junie Morrison. Though Junie still contributes towards the movement, rumor has it that he is now working on his own solo album with Lynn generally aiding and abetting."

DAWN SILVA When it was time to start recording The Brides' second album, Lynn and I were still The Brides of Funkenstein, as far as Atlantic Records was concerned. We were the only Brides with contracts. When Lynn left so abruptly, George was walking on eggshells with the record company. He was in a dilemma about who would now be The Brides. Some of the first sessions for the second Brides album were initially done, with Mallia and me laying some vocals. He asked me if I had any suggestions for the new Bride. Then [he] finally asked me if I wanted to promote Sheila and Mackie permanently. He'd already made his decision but did give me the respect to ask, even though my opinion wouldn't have mattered. It would be who *he* wanted anyway, and that was Sheila and Mackie.

MALLIA FRANKLIN Sheila and Mackie reaped the rewards of what Lynn and Dawn had already worked toward. It was a great scenario to step into. It wasn't a comfortable situation, though. Dawn was trying to maintain control of the group, which they weren't making easy for her. Girl groups are a trip in general, and many in the organization wondered whether this new Brides thing would work. Ron Dunbar had Dawn, and I lay foundation vocals on some of those first songs like "Texas and Holding You Responsible." Sheila had a great voice and did most of the leads, and Dawn was sangin' her ass off on those songs. I had never heard Dawn sing like that. I remember shouting in the studio, "Sang, Silva!" She wasn't going to let the *new* Brides upstage her.

DAWN SILVA With these new Brides, I had to decide who I was going to blend with. Will I blend with Mackie's tone and let her be the boss? Or do I blend with Sheila's tone and let her be the boss? They weren't going to follow my lead, and I sure wasn't going to follow theirs in *my* group. They wouldn't blend with me, so we were all fighting vocally in the studio, and George capitalized on it. It was like we competed for his attention. I had to do something amazing in the vocal booth to get him to notice and get some kind of praise. When you listen to the second Brides album, you hear all our voices fighting for control. But, in the end, it was just as rewarding as the first Brides album because *Texas* had more of a rock edge.

By now, George was totally fascinated with Sheila Horne. She was amusing to him . . . a new toy. She excited all his senses—musically, emotionally, and sexually. He loved her voice and produced a lot of the second Brides album with her in mind. She was his muse for the moment. When their relationship got deeper, I think he was giving her the illusion she could take over the group, and that's what she started trying to do. Sheila was a bit naiver than the rest of us, and she probably thought George would make good on his promise to make her a star.

We recorded the song "Smoke Signals," and George wanted Sheila to moan in the song. She walked into the sound booth while we watched her through the huge glass wall. She started moaning and looking at George. Then she started feeling on her breasts and squealing, "Oh, mother's hot . . . mother is hot," like she was having the best orgasm of her life. George was totally fixated while she rubbed her tits. He started screaming, "Yeah! Momma's hot!" like a dog in heat. Mackie and I looked at each other in disbelief. She may have been entertainment for George, but we were not amused. By then, Sheila's ego was out of control. Whenever you disagreed with her, she whined, "I'm gonna tell George!"

I would respond, "I don't give a fuck . . . tell him!"

GEORGE CLINTON I was proud of both versions of The Brides. But these *new* Brides weren't supposed to be as good as they turned out. Sheila Horne was excellent, Jeanette McGruder had her own sound, and Dawn really stepped out. Lynn overshadowed her so much on the first album that Dawn became really strong on this one.

It was a different sound from Lynn and Dawn. Of course, it was easier to record Lynn and Dawn because anything they do, they *can* do . . . just like that. *Funk or Walk* was ridiculously bad. It was smooth, almost like doing Bootsy. But *Never Buy Texas from a Cowboy* was one of the *baddest* albums I have ever done. It was a workout to produce this Brides album because there were so many egos in that motherfucker by then.

Mackie was always cool. She was like my buddy . . . so funny and always had me laughing. She also kept little, loud-ass Sheila in check. Sheila was a brat when she and I were together. She had to understand that she couldn't just think she could get away with shit because she was with me. I loved working with Sheila because of the Diana Ross sound in her voice, and I could easily get her to do what I wanted vocally. But when you do that with someone like Sheila, it comes off like you favor her.

I told Sheila, "You can't make it look like I favor you. I favor your singing, but you make it look like something else."

It was harder recording with her than with the others because of our personal thing. I never had any kind of personal thing with Dawn. I didn't even want to *look* her in the eye. Nope! I never even looked *near* that one... hell, no! After I saw how crazy Michael Hampton was, I said I wasn't fucking with *that* one, so it was easy to work with Dawn, and I was thankful for her being there. She never said to them, "This is *my* group, and y'all need to sit down and shut up!" And she could have. But I had to keep Sheila from fucking with her. I told her, "I will not be on your side if you get in trouble with Dawn." But you can't help nobody who thinks she's cute.

RON DUNBAR I won a Grammy Award for Best Rhythm & Blues Song in 1971 for a song called "Patches," written for Clarence Carter. "Patches" was really a country song in the vein of soul music. George wanted me to write a song for The Brides like "Patches." He wanted a country-funk feel in it. George said he wanted a song that would win us a Grammy. I translated the whole country theme of "Patches" into "Never Buy Texas from a Cowboy" for The Brides.

By now, we were recording primarily at a studio in East Detroit called Superdisc. We still recorded sometimes at United, but The Disc, as we called it, was our main studio now. I was looking for a lead vocalist I could showcase in the new Brides. By the second album, the lead vocalist in my mind was Sheila Horne. That girl sure could sing. When Sheila became involved, I altered The Brides' sound compared to Dawn and Lynn. I preferred writing for Sheila as a songwriter. She had the voice that I leaned toward.

DAWN SILVA I started coming out stronger as a performer and singer when Lynn left. I had no choice. Lynn and I had worked too hard to build The Brides up. Even though she had abandoned it, I wouldn't let anybody else come in and destroy what we created. This was a new chapter in my life because I could now shine for myself. I didn't have to worry about wearing something too sexy or downplaying my talent and creativity. I had to step up my game. I wouldn't keep quiet and stay in the back seat anymore. No!

I'm in the driver's seat now. But the three of us were fighting about the group's direction.

It wasn't about friendship with Sheila and Mackie like with Lynn. The three of us were never really a group; every female was for herself. It was like, "I respect you, but if I find a position for myself, I'm taking it!" With that aggressiveness between us, Sheila's rock and roll edge, my stage presence, and Mackie's theatrical voice, we unknowingly stepped into another genre—the rock and roll arena.

When it was time for pictures for *Texas*, we went to designer Larry LeGaspi's studio in New York. He measured the three of us for cowboy and Indian costumes that would coincide with the album's concept. I was an Indian, Sheila was a cowgirl, and Mackie was a buffalo princess. He made a giant buffalo headdress with claws and fur, but Mackie didn't like it, so Larry made a second one with silver chaps and foxtails . . . but she did wear the buffalo onstage a few times. Sheila got upset that Larry designed the Indian outfit for me. It was the most presentational and sexy. It was gold with bright yellow feathers and a beautiful Indian headdress. Sheila claimed that I stole it. How could I do that when they were custom-made for us? I'm 5'6", and she's 5'1". You can look at the outfit and tell it was made for me. But the costume got the most attention, so she figured it was hers.

We took beautiful promotional pictures for the album. There were so many great shots to choose from. We finally got the picture back that would be released to all the magazines, and George picked the most unflattering image in the bunch. Sheila was so upset with him. When it was time to do press for the album, that caused problems with me and the other Brides. Lynn was gone, and they didn't recognize the other two. I was the one the reporters wanted to interview. I was the one the fans identified and wanted to talk to. That was something Sheila and Mackie couldn't handle. When *Never Buy Texas* was released, I understood that The Brides was no longer a group . . . I was out there alone. We were three individuals onstage giving up the funk.

As we started rehearsals for our set on the Uncle Jam Tour, Sheila became increasingly demanding. She didn't want to do all her vocals on the album. George had her do a lot of screaming on the record, which affected her voice. As rehearsals went on, Sheila sang over Mackie and tried to take her parts.

I said, "Sheila, let Mackie do her parts; let her sing what she does on the album. Sing what you sing, and I'll do what I do. The parts are already set."

Sheila replied, "I want to sing what I want!"

I looked at Mackie and said, "You want her to have your parts?"

She said, "No!"

Sheila decided that she would sing what she wanted to sing anyway. Things weren't shaping up how she expected. She wasn't getting her way, and her whining to George wasn't working.

CHAPTER 23

SMOKE SIGNALS

Parliament-Funkadelic launched their Uncle Jam Wants You Tour in October 1979 with a string of shows at the legendary Apollo Theatre in Harlem, New York. The P-Funk review, billed as "George Clinton's Production of Popsicle Stick Starring Parliament-Funkadelic," featured P-Funk (without George Clinton), The Brides of Funkenstein, and Ex-Spinners member–turned–solo artist and newest addition, Philippé Wynn. After the Apollo, the band filled venues across the country. In November 1979, Parliament released a new album, GloryHallaStoopid (or Pin the Tale on the Funky), which reached number three on the Billboard Soul Album charts. Their run at the Apollo was so well received that the band returned a few months later, in February of 1980, for another two-week stint.

Author Ted Fox chronicled a performance in excerpts from his 1983 book, *Showtime at the Apollo*:

> Clinton and "P-Funk" were heroes in the ghettoes of America, the leading proponents of the wild style and free philosophy known as funk. Their shows, over the weekend of March 1, 1980, the last live shows at the Apollo, were spectacles

> abandon perfectly in keeping with the theatre's grand tradition. The M.C. introduced the opening act, The Brides of Funkenstein, and the Apollo's new gold curtain parted, to the cheers of the crowd. Three gorgeous women, provocatively dressed in tight, revealing costumes, lured the teenagers to the edge of the stage, and the kids met the Brides with a forest of outstretched hands that the performers grabbed whenever possible. There was a new addition to the Apollo: a tongue projecting from stage center about eight or ten feet into the orchestra section. As in the old days, each performer worked to outdo the others. Each of the Brides took her turn wriggling and wailing down the appendage, doing the damnedest to outdo her sister.

RON BREMBRY (MANAGER) After Lynn left, Dawn would be up front naturally as the leader of The Brides. Sheila Horne had a big attitude about that. Every night when the band struck the first note, Sheila would cut in Dawn's way and run out to the front of the stage. It never failed . . . and it pissed Dawn off. Dawn went to George and complained about Sheila's behavior.

He told Sheila and Mackie, "Y'all two, stay back and let Dawn go up and do her thing."

They would always say, "OK."

But night after night, Sheila would push her way ahead of Dawn to the front of the stage.

DAWN SILVA When we got onstage, Sheila would talk and sing over everybody. I was fed up, and Sheila knew it. We were onstage one night, and she was singing something she wasn't supposed to, and it just hit a nerve. Finally, I snapped.

I said in the mic, "You little bitch! Do it again! I'll push your ass off this stage! Sing your parts or get off the stage!" The crowd cheered.

I was tired of Sheila's shit, so I went to George and said, "George, if you don't want me to hurt her and go to jail, seriously, you better tell her something."

George told Sheila, "You need to stop messing with Dawn. Sing your parts and leave Dawn alone."

I think he didn't really mind what she was doing. He created that monster. He was screwing her and fueling her with drugs, so he loved it. It was at those times that I was most upset with Lynn. She deserted me, and now

Dawn Silva onstage in Hampton, Virginia, in 1980.

I had to deal with this behavior. Sheila and Mackie didn't care about me. They cared about themselves.

The Brides' album *Never Buy Texas from a Cowboy* and constant touring garnered them loads of attention. They achieved something no other P-Funk group had accomplished. The Brides of Funkenstein won the 1980 Black Music Award for Top New Female Group and performed on its televised awards special. This was the first time any P-Funk act would perform at an awards show.

BRENDA ADAMS-PIERCE P-Funk was in Oakland, California, when multiple gold records for Parliament's album *GloryHallaStoopid* came to the LA office. I rented a station wagon and drove the gold plaques to Oakland to deliver them to the band.

When I returned to Los Angeles, George called and confronted me, saying someone in the LA office told him they found drugs in my desk drawer. I asked George, "Who told you that?" He said it was Nene Montes. That hurt me. I worked hard and would not do anything to jeopardize my position in the organization. Who was Nene anyway? And why was he allowed to run the office at will? I was glad that George trusted me enough to tell me some of the stuff that was going on behind my back.

That exchange started a solid relationship between George and me, but it brought some animosity from the other guys I worked with in the office. Before, if I had questions I needed answers to, it was like pulling teeth to get a response. Now, I could get George on the phone directly when I needed productive answers. I could feel tensions rising from the guys in management who thought they had the final word on everything. I was uncertain about who had my back . . . if *anyone* did.

Harold Jackson of the Black Music Awards came to the Thang Incorporated office. He wanted to give The Brides of Funkenstein an award and wanted them to perform on TV. George didn't like his acts on shows like *Soul Train*, *Midnight Special*, or *American Bandstand*. I think Bootsy was the only P-Funk act that ever did one of those shows. That was why the girl groups weren't particularly recognizable to the public. This would be an opportunity for the ladies to be exposed to that kind of visibility. They earned the right. I didn't ask for anyone's permission. I just took a gamble and said, "Yes." It took me about two days to approach George and tell him what I had done.

I said, "Harold Jackson wants The Brides to perform on the Black Music Awards show, and I accepted for them."

He looked at me without expression and flatly said, "OK."

I didn't get any resistance. I think George knew I was doing my job. I followed that up with, "I want to work with The Brides on a management level."

He said, "Hmm. Do you know what you're asking me? Give me a couple of days to think about it."

About a week and a half later, he called me and said, "OK. Meet us at the Apollo in New York on Friday. Get ready for boot camp."

I worked with a young lady at Black Radio named Debra Lett. I hired Debra, and she came over to handle the Funk office while I went to New York.

I told The Brides about the award show when I got to the Apollo. They were quite excited. The greatest difficulty was getting a clear understanding from the ladies of where this opportunity could take them. I wanted them to branch out and be an entity of their own, but they weren't sure about that. They had been entrenched in an all-male society for so many years that I think they were nervous. But there was a bit of apprehension on *my* part as well. Was I doing this alone, or was George behind it 100 percent? Were there going to be any repercussions? There was no communication with George anymore about the awards show. He really wanted nothing to do with it . . . no "Good luck," no "Break a leg" . . . nothing.

DAWN SILVA My recollection of the award show is very different from Brenda's. I was in Detroit at Mallia's house when I got a call from her. She said, "The Brides are nominated for an award, and, if you win, all these unbelievable doors will open for you." I never thought George would support that. We were getting more than everybody else was, and he was jealous. If you are a member of P-Funk, you get punished if you become successful.

A staff member who worked in the Funk Headquarters office in Detroit was playing as a double agent for us. We needed our costumes for the show. She snuck the costumes out of the office in a pillowcase and brought them to Mallia's house before we caught the flight to Los Angeles. She didn't tell anyone; she just said, "Good luck," and handed the costumes to me.

I knew there were going to be roadblocks around this show. Brenda needed the instrumental TV mix of "Party Up In Here" for us to perform because it was about to be released as a single. She found out the day of the show that the Funk organization never sent it. We decided to lip-synch from the album. The show's producer wanted us to do Ron Dunbar's ballad "Didn't Mean to Fall in Love." I was upset about that. We were supposed to be these outrageous P-Funk females going up onstage in wild costumes. Now we're going onstage to sing a little R&B ballad? We could have lip-synched "Never Buy Texas from a Cowboy." He said, "The ballad or nothing." So we did it.

We were up against popular acts like Sister Sledge in our category. We worked out a script if we won. Brenda wanted me to go up and say, "I want to thank George Clinton." We argued about that because he didn't want us to do the show in the first place. I wanted to say, "Thank you," and walk off.

Brenda said, "Just thank George as the producer."

Sheila said, "I want to talk!"

"No! Dawn's going to speak for the group."

Musician Ray Parker Jr. and actress Jayne Kennedy introduced our category. Jayne said, "The winners are The Brides of Funkenstein!" It's one of the greatest feelings when your name is called. We walked out, and Jayne extended the award to me. Sheila went to grab it, but Jayne quickly pulled it back and handed it to me. Backstage, Sheila had been flirting with Jayne's husband, Leon Isaac Kennedy. Sheila walked *around* me to the microphone and said, "We'd like to thank our producer, the funk master, George Clinton." Mackie and I stood there glaring at her. Brenda was pissed. What do I say after that? Nothing. Sheila already said it. I lifted the award, the audience clapped, and we walked off.

BRENDA ADAMS-PIERCE I knew there would be retaliation from the other managers at Thang Incorporated for The Brides winning an award and being on TV. The fact that I could make something happen so important and positive, and George allowed me to do it, made me a threat. I knew I didn't want to be in a situation where guys could take shots at me just because they could.

I didn't go to the office after the awards show the next day. Once again, I knew I would be cut off from George. The only people I would be in contact with were Archie Ivy, Raymond Spruell, and Nene Montes. I didn't feel I could give all I wanted to the organization anymore. My last task was to ensure The Brides walked across that stage and collected their award. I was done. I never looked back. My days with Thang Incorporated were finished, and I could honestly say, "Job well done."

DAWN SILVA After the awards show, The Brides returned to the GloryHallaStoopid Tour with P-Funk. Michael Hampton and I hadn't been together for some time. I was now seeing The Brides' bass player, Jeff "Cherokee" Bunn. Cherokee was a young, muscular guy, and I felt he could protect me. Cherokee and I started rooming together, and Michael was outraged. It didn't matter that he was screwing groupies in every state and had been for years; he was upset with me because I'd moved on.

In May of 1980, the tour got to Fort Worth, Texas, and Michael couldn't control himself any longer. One afternoon, Sheila and I were rehearsing in my room. The next thing I knew, the glass from the picture window was shattering. A hand was reaching through to unlock the door. Sheila started screaming. The door flew open, and Michael rushed in. He was enraged.

I jumped up from the bed. I tried to stay calm and reason with him, "Michael . . . what do you want?"

He walked over and said, "You want to be with him?!"

I turned around to run into the bathroom when I felt a forceful blow, followed by a sharp pain. I grabbed my shoulder . . . then I saw the blood. I realized that Michael had stabbed me in my shoulder blade.

Sheila ran down the hall screaming, "Michael's killing Dawn! He's killing her!"

The Brides of Funkenstein win "Top Female Group" at the Cashbox Black Music Awards in 1980. Singer Cheryl Lynn, second from right, is pictured with the Brides (left to right, *Dawn Silva, Jeanette McGruder, and Sheila Horne) backstage.*

I hit my knees while blood poured down my back. At that point, Michael got scared and ran. A few seconds later, Cherokee ran in. He was startled when he saw the blood. He got a towel and applied pressure to the wound and called an ambulance. I went to the hospital and got about six stitches to close the wound. After all the years of fighting, that day, I *fully* understood that Michael could have taken my life.

Later that evening, I was released from the hospital and returned to the hotel. My phone rang, and it was Archie Ivy. I don't think he even asked me how I was feeling. He just informed me that showtime was in an hour.

He said, "Shake it off. It's not that serious."

His comment reiterated that the P-Funk staff didn't give a damn about me. When Andi [(Thomas] was still The Brides' road manager, Michael would be arrested every time he hit me. The organization would bail him out and tell her, "Stop calling the cops! Why are you wasting our damn money?" After Archie's "shake it off" comment, I knew it was time to go.

The next day, Michael found me again. He pulled off his shirt. He had taken the same small knife he'd stabbed me with and carved my initials on his body. His chest was bleeding from the letters D. S. He wanted to show me his wounds like some form of apology. I *had* to leave . . . it just wasn't safe. Cherokee left with me and came back to my home in Sacramento. George wasn't happy because we had only one or two more shows. Mackie and Sheila did those as The Brides without me. I'm sure they were OK with that. That's what they wanted anyway.

When the tour's final leg went out two months later, George called and asked me to return because he wanted The Brides to be the opening act. I declined. George was desperate and offered me more money. This time, I would make more than *double* what the other girls were making . . . that was some sense of redemption. I was reluctant but eventually agreed. I flew back to Detroit to rehearse with Mackie and Sheila. This time, everything was different. It wasn't fun anymore. It wasn't creative or inspiring. Now it was just a job.

LYNN MABRY After leaving The Brides, I didn't follow what Dawn and the other girls were doing. I was still dealing with my relationship with Junie. Not long after we left P-Funk, Junie and his wife, Carol, finally split. He moved out of their house, and we ended up briefly back at Cheryl James's home in Detroit.

I started feeling weird physically. I took a pregnancy test and found out that I was indeed pregnant. My first thought was, "This is fabulous!" I envisioned us being a family, living together, and having children. The idea of being a mom was everything that I ever wanted. I went to Junie and told him, expecting him to be as excited as I was. His reaction was the total opposite.

He said, "We're not in a position to have a baby right now. We don't have a place to stay. We're not touring with P-Funk anymore, and I'm trying to get a solo record deal. What are we going to do with a baby?"

After about a week of me attempting to come to grips with the possibility of terminating this pregnancy, he reconsidered and said, "Let's do it." I was relieved because there was no way that I was giving up my baby.

Junie finally got a record deal on Columbia Records and started recording his album *Bread Alone*. We eventually moved into an apartment together. Junie would stay out recording most nights until the wee hours of the morning. Sometimes he didn't come home until the next day. A woman named Theresa Allman was one of the Wilamina background singers. They sang on his album, and she would call him often.

"Is Walter there?" She never called him Junie, and that was strange.

Jeanette McGruder, Dawn Silva, and Sheila Horne on the Uncle Jam Tour in 1980, with former Friends of Distinction vocalist Jessica Cleaves (far right) *who joined P-Funk in 1979.*

I would give him the phone, and he would leave the room.

"Why is he so secretive about these phone calls with her?"

I finally asked him, "Is there anything I need to know? Is something going on with you and Theresa?"

"We're close," Junie replied.

That comment let me know they had a relationship. I was pregnant, and I wasn't going to put up with that.

After frequent sleepless nights, hormonal and depressed, I told my mom I was unhappy and wanted to come home. She sent me a plane ticket, and I flew back to Berkeley.

About a week and a half passed, and Junie called, asking me when I was coming home. I insisted I could not return under the same conditions I had left. After many attempts to get me back, he started explaining how *I* was breaking up the family. Weirdly enough, Junie convinced me that it was *my* fault, and I found myself apologizing to *him*.

I was crying and saying, "I'm sorry. Please forgive me."

My mother overheard our conversation, came into my room, and said, "Did I hear you ask him to forgive you? What did *you* do?"

"Mom, I didn't give him time to explain, and he wants me back."

She sternly said, "You are not going back to him!"

"He wants me back, and I'm going. He's going to make it right."

Three weeks later, I returned to Junie and gave birth to our daughter, Akasha. Unfortunately, Junie *didn't* make it right as he promised . . . he was still seeing Theresa. I'd had enough. Akasha and I returned home to Berkeley. My relationship with Junie was finally over.

CHAPTER 24

PLAY ME OR TRADE ME

Parlet released their third and final album for Casablanca Records in July 1980, *Play Me or Trade Me*. Comic renderings by Ronald "Stozo" Edwards, who also drew the art for *Invasion of the Booty Snatchers*, of a giant green hand lifting the trio to the heavens graced the cover. Open at the wrist, the hand litters the sky with balloons, money, and advertisements for "mouf" (a P-Funk term for sex). There is also a Booty Snatcher (Parlet's cosmic rival) flying away with a cash register full of money.

Much can be read into *Play Me or Trade Me*'s title and cover art. Was this a statement of Parlet's demise? The double entendre in the lyrics of sports and love—"I'm not a benchwarmer, I'm a heart warmer" or "Play me or trade me, turn me loose, let me go"—suggested the reality for the trio. It was, indeed, the group's final inning.

Two singles from the album charted: "Wolf Tickets," a duet between Jeanette Washington and George Clinton, reached seventy-three on the Soul Singles Charts, and "Help from My Friends" reached sixty-seven. But the album itself failed to crack the Soul 100.

By the time of the album's release, Janice Evans was expecting a baby and was replaced temporarily by her sister, Gwen Dozier.

GEORGE CLINTON When Parlet did "Wolf Tickets," I tried to feature Jeanette more as the leader. I was so caught up in what I was doing that I was looking for leaders. She amazed me so much when we recorded that song . . . the way she followed me on that track. I didn't know Jeanette could do that. I was like, "Oh shit! Maybe I *do* have somebody here who can lead this."

SHIRLEY HAYDEN The third Parlet album, *Play Me or Trade Me*, was strong, but the title said it all. Three strikes, you're out! The lyrics solidified it: "Play me or trade me; I got to have a game." George was telling us that the game was over.

Parlet wasn't really getting along when we started recording the last album. Jeanette told me she was out for herself. That hurt me deeply because I thought we were finally building a bond. She was bulldozing over everybody, trying to get the spotlight. Our first single, "Wolf Tickets," even reads, "Parlet, featuring Jeanette Washington." What the hell was that?!

We stayed in the studio recording for all of P-Funk's acts, but we weren't getting paid. I didn't want to beg George for anything, but I couldn't let everybody know how fucked up everything was. My mom told me, "They're using you!" But I couldn't tell her that they *were* using me. I allowed myself to be used because I didn't want to leave. I hoped that, eventually, the company would work out its issues.

The GloryHallaStoopid Tour went out, and Parlet was again left behind. We were major recording artists, now relegated to playing small local clubs that smelled of old liquor and Pine-Sol. At best, we played the state fair. It was embarrassing and unfair. Why couldn't we go on tour like The Brides? They had a different kind of relationship with George than ours. It was more *personal*. George does for whom he's in admiration at that moment, and some members of The Brides were in personal relationships with him. I didn't want to sleep with him. Parlet didn't have intimate relations with George like that.

When the GloryHallaStoopid Tour made its way to Detroit, I could feel the anxiety welling up on my way to Joe Louis Arena. Seeing P-Funk but not being allowed to perform was not a happy experience. I walked up to the stage door and entered the backstage area. I worked my way to the side of the stage to watch the opening Brides set. The houselights went down, and the crowd started roaring.

When the lights came up, Dawn, Sheila, and Jeanette McGruder strutted onstage wearing Parlet's LeGaspi spandex outfits we picked out in

"I'M NOT A BENCH WARMER" Jeanette Washington

PARLET:
PLAY ME OR TRADE ME

Benchwarmers? Gwen Dozier, Jeanette Washington, and Shirley Hayden play their final inning on Parlet's last album in 1980.

New York. Jeanette Washington was standing next to me, and to see Dawn Silva, whom she couldn't stand the sight of, traipse around in her costume was torture. At that moment, it felt like George had just thrown us away. The Brides had everything. They got beautiful costumes. They got the shows, the press, and all the attention. They were the queens. And now they got what little scraps Parlet had left.

CHERYL JAMES Parlet wasn't touring, but I did stints on the road with The Brides to make a living. I was catching hell out there . . . it was not fun. Being a woman in this big group of men was very challenging, mostly from my *own* team. Road management is not easy, and I always do it the right way.

Some of the male managers in the P-Funk organization had a problem with me because I wouldn't sleep with them. With all the women and groupies all over the country, they were upset because they couldn't have *me*. They didn't like me; it was just something they hadn't *tapped* yet. I remember telling one of the producers I needed something for one of the groups. He said I could have whatever I *needed* if I did what he *wanted*. In other words, this is a trade-off; to get what I needed to do my job, I had to *fuck* for it.

One of the other managers even *raped* me. I'll never forget it. After the incident, I had to pull myself together to do my job. I was in a room with a bunch of the guys. One of the band members noticed that something was very wrong.

He called from across the room, "Cheryl, what's wrong with you?!"

The perpetrator yelled, "Oh, she's just mad because I *fucked* her!"

Just like that, he said it, and some of the guys laughed. Even rape was no big deal to this cast of characters. Nobody cared how hard I worked or how well I did my job.

I returned to Detroit, and Parlet was angry because they were not given any work. One of the guys in Parlet's band, Gordon Carlton, had access to a Winnebago, so we hit the road on our own.

It was August 1980, and we piled equipment, clothes, and bodies into the camper and hit the highway to go to a big festival I booked in St. Louis. We did the gig, and after the concert, I went to the trailer where the promoter paid everybody. When I stepped in, Ron Banks, the lead singer for the Dramatics, who was also on the show, was in the trailer getting his money. I was glad to see somebody I knew from Detroit. I hugged Ron, turned to the promoter, and said, "I'm here to collect Parlet's pay."

He said, "We ain't got no money."

I said, "Excuse me? We are a long way from home and don't have any money. We need our money."

He said, "I told you . . . ain't no money!"

I looked at Ron and said, "Can you talk to him?"

Ron walked out and left me standing in the trailer.

I turned to the promoter and said, "I can't leave here without money. We're stranded."

He pulled out a gun and put it to my forehead. "Bitch! I told you . . . ain't no money!"

I eased out of the trailer and told everybody that we didn't get paid and we were stranded in St. Louis. I finally broke down and called George.

P-Funk was in Atlanta, preparing to perform at the annual Jack the Rapper Convention. Jack the Rapper was a radio DJ and was considered by many to be the "father of Black radio." He started a music convention for Black radio executives. It became the place for artists to hobnob and showcase their new material to radio stations and programmers. A couple of hours passed, and George wired money to St. Louis so we could get to Atlanta. Our reimbursement for getting us out of St. Louis was for Parlet to perform at the convention for free.

SHIRLEY HAYDEN Parlet wasn't scheduled to perform, but George and Jack the Rapper were friends. That particular year was a big deal because it was held at the grand opening of the Peachtree Hotel. The event was star-studded. Minister Louis Farrakhan addressed the convention that year. George sent enough money for Parlet to fly. The band members drove the Winnebago and met us. I was becoming very vocal about my issues with Parlet, and it was pissing Cheryl and Jeanette off.

Janice Evans was pregnant when *Play Me or Trade Me* was released, and her sister, Gwen Dozier, stepped into her spot. Gwen was so happy to have the Parlet gig that she had no opinion about *anything*. She didn't want to rock the boat, but the boat needed to be rocked.

When we touched down in Atlanta, I saw Martin Luther King's widow, Coretta Scott-King, and Daddy King at the airport. For me, that was a thrill. The next thing I knew, the girls left me stranded at the airport because we'd argued on the flight. I caught a ride with some of the roadies to the hotel and checked in. I didn't see anyone, then I found out that Cheryl was somewhere smoking weed with Bob Marley.

The next morning, Parlet took the elevator to the main floor and was whisked into the hotel's ballroom. The band started playing, and Gwen and I took our places at the microphones. Jeanette was supposed to be right behind us. Seconds passed, and Jeanette was still not onstage. Jeanette strutted out in a rhinestone-studded bra, panties, and stockings with garters. The men in the crowd went wild. That wasn't part of the plan. Everybody, including Cheryl James, who bought this little ensemble for her, was hell-bent on making Jeanette the star. They saw Grace Jones perform the night before, which inspired Jeanette's outrageous outfit.

We were doing our routines, but Jeanette wasn't following the routine. She was going to do what she wanted. I was stuck in the back with Gwen, trying to keep it together. A couple of songs later, Jeanette saw her moment and took a flying leap from the stage. She landed on top of Ray Parker Jr.'s table, bent over, and put her ass right in his face. She slid off the table, sat in his lap, and shimmied.

Cheryl and others on the side of the stage were screaming, "Wooooooooooo! Yeah, bitch! Work that motherfucker!"

I was totally beside myself. By the end of the show, it was sheer pandemonium. We left the stage and tried to get through the crowd as people congratulated us. I was too stunned by what just happened. It was a feeling of sadness. The organization made it clear that it wasn't about Parlet anymore; it was about Jeanette. She finally got what she wanted from day one . . . the spotlight.

The next day, everyone was packing up to leave Atlanta and return to Detroit, and no one was speaking to me. I wasn't planning to return to Detroit because Linda and Garry Shider invited me to their home for a dinner party that evening, but I needed to change my plane ticket. Cheryl James walked into the room, and I asked about my return ticket.

She said, "You get home the best way you can . . . Bitch!" slamming the door behind her.

I went to Archie Ivy. He said the tickets had already been booked, but I had to get to the airport. In a panic, I just decided to go home. Once again, the girls jumped in a taxi and left for the airport without me. I jumped in a car with one of the road managers, Ron Brembry.

I was upset and crying at the airport when I saw Garry Shider walk through the doors. He approached me and said, "C'mon, let's go."

I was mentally exhausted when I got to Garry's home. I went into their guest room and fell asleep. A few hours passed, and I was awakened by a man's voice . . . it was George. I was terrified. I just knew that he was there to fire me. I got out of bed and cautiously went to the kitchen, where everyone had gathered. George and I discussed what happened at Jack the Rapper and how I felt about Jeanette's antics.

GEORGE CLINTON I didn't realize how fragile Shirley was. She was a nervous wreck and crying about the situation with Jeanette. I told her they don't pay you any attention when you play for the record industry.

I said, "They ain't paying for shit to be here, so you got to get their attention. If they won't listen to you, do the 'Betty Davis' on them and pull your shit out. If you're gonna take it that far, you might as well be damn near naked. That's what Jeanette did."

I did the same thing when I hit the stage at Jack the Rapper. I took a tablecloth off one of the tables, cut a hole, and took all my clothes off. I walked past a girl that used to date Bootsy. I stopped, looked at her, and she looked at me. She noticed that I was looking at her wig.

She said, "No! No, George!" I grabbed it.

She was trying to hold on to it, but I pulled it off. There were four nappy braids underneath. I put her wig on my head and walked down the hallway. People were leaving the show.

I screamed, "Get yo' asses back in there!"

They followed me back in. All the executives started coming back down in the elevators. This white dude was looking at me strangely as I walked by. I stopped, lifted the sheet, put it over his head, and farted.

He screamed, "You nasty motherfucker!"

I kept walking and hit the stage.

I said to Shirley, "Dry them tears. That's how you do this! You got to be outrageous. That's how you get bigwigs to pay attention to you."

CHERYL JAMES After Jack the Rapper, Parlet tried to keep going. There were no shows . . . nothing. Nobody wanted to invest in Parlet. But George was negotiating for his own labels with Casablanca [Choza Negra] and Uncle Jam Records with CBS. The ladies had their hopes and dreams of a successful career wrapped up in the vision of Uncle Jam going global. It was a symbol of some kind of hope. I thought it could be my second chance at a career in an industry that is not kind to women. I wanted to work hard, learn the craft, and make something happen for me in the record industry. I wanted to do what it would take to succeed, even if my gender was an issue.

Jeanette found out she was pregnant. She sunk everything she had into Parlet and could never get anything out of it, and after four years with P-Funk, Jeanette Washington finally threw in the towel. There was no need to fight or convince her to stay because there was nothing worth staying for. She asked George for a one-way ticket to California. She got on the plane and never returned.

SHIRLEY HAYDEN After Jeanette left the organization, George and I met in his office, which was the studio's bathroom. He wanted to have a "confidential" conversation with me about Parlet. He said he now wanted to build the group around *me* and asked how I felt about that.

He said, "Shirley, I know you can work with anybody, but can they work with you?"

That question made me think. George put it out there but never followed up.

A short time passed, and my phone rang early in the morning. It was

Jeanette Washington calling from California. In the angriest tone I had ever heard, she said, "Bitch, you will *never* be the leader of Parlet . . . EVER!" and slammed the phone in my face. I was frozen. I don't know how she learned about George's and my conversation, but she did. And she let me know that she was not going to let that happen.

CHAPTER 25

THE BIG BANG THEORY

By 1980, George Clinton solidified his deal with CBS to distribute his label, Uncle Jam Records. In a 1980 article with *Blues & Soul*, he mentioned new albums from Parlet and The Brides of Funkenstein on the horizon. He talked about new bands: Roger's Human Body (a spin-off from Bootsy's protégés, Roger Troutman and Zapp), Sweat Band, Trey Lewd (a band that featured George's sons, Tracy and Darrell), Jessica Cleaves, and Sterling Silver Starship, featuring Donnie Sterling and Mallia Franklin. Despite Clinton's ambition, the P-Funk organization's internal enemies, conflicts, and increased drug use threatened to bring this mighty musical force to its knees.

MALLIA FRANKLIN Everything for all of us was riding on Uncle Jam Records. All of George's acts were going to be under one umbrella. George would finally get the dream of his own label. That was his goal all along. We hoped this could be the organization's move to positively change everything.

After leaving Parlet, I put all I had into Sterling Silver Starship. It sounded like a great idea when Donnie was explaining it to me. It would be a concept group featuring Donnie and me as a couple . . . much like

Mother's Finest. Their album *Mother Factor* was a template of what I thought we wanted to do. We could write and produce with George, have a more direct working relationship with him, and get a more significant piece of the pie as songwriters.

We brought in guitarists Tony Thomas, Rodney Crutcher, and Lonnie Greene on drums. We negotiated an advance with Ron Dunbar for fifteen thousand dollars. Donnie and I also became staff writers for Don Davis, the owner of United Sound Systems. Don was becoming heavily involved in the Sterling Silver project, and we recorded an album full of material.

While negotiations were underway, I got a call from Cecil Holmes at Casablanca. The label was aware that I had left Parlet. He asked me about possibly doing a solo project away from Parliament-Funkadelic. I didn't want to leave my family. I told Cecil that Donnie and I had contracts in the works with George for Sterling Silver Starship. Honestly, I felt positive about it. So I declined to even discuss another offer. That was probably the biggest mistake I have ever made in my professional career.

LESLIE VOCINO (OFFICE MANAGER, FUNK EAST, DETROIT) I always knew that Mallia wanted to be solo, but George would never sign her as a solo artist, although that's what he promised. He would blow her off as he always did, which frustrated her. Then Donnie and Mallia did their own group together and presented that to George and Dunbar. It seemed like a good compromise. Mallia and I had gotten very tight. I was dating Sterling Silver's guitar player and was really into what they were doing. I asked Dunbar if I could manage them.

His response was, "No. We aren't going to do anything with them."

I knew that Sterling Silver Starship was doomed at that point. I think Ron Dunbar played rotten games with Mallia and Donnie's relationship. I think there was also some jealousy on Dunbar's part. He really wanted to be a star himself. Ron was controlling Donnie pretty much and was such an abuser of power at that time. He did some awful stuff, but George gave him the authority to do it.

MALLIA FRANKLIN Donnie and I started having a lot of problems, and, as the project progressed, it became more about this being *Donnie's* band. That wasn't the plan we discussed. That's when I started feeling like I had been played. It wasn't about *us* anymore—it was about *him*.

The closer we got to the record deal, the further Donnie and I grew apart. We broke up, and Sterling Silver Starship was put on the shelf. I realized that I allowed Donnie to influence my decisions professionally. He didn't support that it was *my* time and that his time would come. I missed out on furthering my career for four to six years.

After we split, Donnie left Detroit, returned to Los Angeles, and got a record deal on A&M with a band called Kiddo. I stayed in Detroit with the P-Funk organization and continued as a member of Parliament-Funkadelic. George kept some of Sterling Silver's best songs, like "Agony of Defeet," and put them on Parliament records.

HENRY MAYERS (RECORD PROMOTIONS) I worked at Mercury Records but was still good friends with George. I talked to him all the time. He was telling me about his plans for starting his own label. I would be the promotion manager and A&R director for Uncle Jam. That's what George wanted me to do. I told him that the next big thing in music was this new thing called new wave. So I found groups like Gary Fabulous, the Mutants, and the Cadillac Kids to sign them to Uncle Jam. When I worked with George, one of the groups we discovered was Roger Troutman and The Human Body . . . well, Bootsy was the one who actually found them. I videotaped them a few times for George, and they were going to sign with us.

GEORGE CLINTON Roger was supposed to be on my label. I produced his band, Zapp, as a favor to Bootsy. I took a piece from the song "Funky Bounce" and looped it. I made that into "More Bounce to the Ounce." Roger didn't like the song, but it was a smash! I gave Roger Troutman all the credit . . . all of it! Is my name on that record? No! Then Zapp's album was released on Warner Brothers and became a smash. I didn't ask for any production credits or money on that deal. I said to Roger, "This is yours." In exchange, Roger's solo album was going to be on Uncle Jam. Roger accepted my offer, and I gave him twenty-five thousand dollars. We paid for the whole Roger Troutman solo album, *The Many Facets of Roger*. We spent about two hundred and fifty thousand dollars in total. Roger finished the album pretty quick and pocketed the rest of the money from the budget.

BRUCE PETERSON Roger would be the big blowup for Uncle Jam, and we expected a lot of money from that. There was some money due to Roger for the Zapp album from Warner Brothers. Someone new at Warner called George and said, "We have a check here for Roger. Where should I send it?" George had them send him the check. He got the money and disappeared. Now Roger is asking us, "Where's my money?" All the education in the world doesn't prepare you to answer those kinds of questions. That's a perfect example of us as managers being undermined. It's not that hard to pay people when you have the money. But if the money isn't there, meaning somebody took it, you got problems. Roger went direct to Warner Brothers and cut George and Uncle Jam out of his solo record deal. Our biggest artist was gone.

Then there was the Choza Negra record deal with Casablanca. Choza Negra was really Nene Montes's deal. It was the label name *and* a band. The band Choza Negra was comprised of some P-Funk members, like Frankie "Kash" Waddy, but the music was geared toward the Latin market. There was a Cuban master drummer, Francisco Aguabella. He was Nene's buddy and the point person for Choza Negra. We didn't want Nene in the middle of our business with Uncle Jam Records, which was our priority. That was the last place that Nene Montes needed to be. So Choza Negra was his own "toy."

By this time, the cocaine was out of control, and George was spending more and more money on it. Nene was in the mix, sprinkling "dust" everywhere and creating problems for us as managers. One of our guys was even carrying coke on his body on commercial flights for Nene, got busted, and went to jail.

GEORGE CLINTON While we were recording the Uncle Jam projects in the studio, our managers and labels set it up for us to mess up. I didn't realize it back then. The record companies made sure that Uncle Jam wasn't going to happen.

Sly Stone came back around, and I think it scared the record industry when Sly returned. They thought that Sly would be on the Uncle Jam label with us. They wanted it to be phased out because they were scared it would be too big . . . it would be another Motown. Ron Dunbar tried to help but couldn't play the record industry politics. He also believed that *I* knew what was happening with the record companies.

People were trying to shut the shit down before we could get it started. I look at legal papers now and say, "Damn! They were planning on fucking that shit up right then." I see now that it was designed to fail. We had big money coming to our organization, and our own managers were planning our demise. Nene Montes negotiated all the contracts for our labels. I didn't know that Nene was making his *own* side deals with the record companies. He made a deal with Warner Brothers and gave them Roger

Troutman's solo album. They stole the master tapes from the studio in New York; he and Roger did that together. Nene Montes ruined everything for everybody.

LESLIE VOCINO That Uncle Jam Records shit was crazy. There was no rhyme or reason to anything, and George tried to do a hundred things at once. There was crap going on with the new management company he hired, Lewis Levin Management, about them not getting paid by George and him being in trouble with the IRS. Anytime it came to what kind of money George owed management companies and stuff like that, he kept that behind closed doors. Even Ron Dunbar didn't know a lot about that stuff. Warner Brothers was about to drop Funkadelic. They didn't want *anything* to do with George at all. The secretaries at Warner would only talk to Bootsy or me . . . that was it. Bootsy was smart. He always distanced himself enough away from George that it didn't affect his money too much. That's why he's still successful today.

By the end of 1980, as Thang Incorporated's debts increased and record sales declined, many claimed that George Clinton allegedly invested more in cocaine than capital. With different theories of how his addiction started, Clinton has refuted this: "As far as drugs were concerned, people thought we were doing more drugs. It looked like we were doing more drugs because we were struggling. But we were doing fewer drugs because we had less money. We should have had a lot of money then but didn't." However, in his 2014 memoir, George wrote:

> Another source of pain seemed like pleasure at first. Near the end of the year, I was doing coke with a limo driver, a girl, and she turned to me and said, you've got to try this. Right there in her hand was a freebase pipe. I took it. I tried it. The first motherfucking hit off the pipe, I thought I had found acid again. It was so good and powerful that it was like busting a nut. When the first high passed, I knew I had to have it again as soon as I could. What I didn't realize at the time—what I couldn't have known—is how long I would spend trying to find my way back to the initial surge of good feeling and what the cost would be.

TOM VICKERS The end was near when cocaine started to be smoked and was transformed into what they called "freebase," the early term of what would be known as the cheaper version "crack" down the road. Freebasing was much more expensive because it was pure cocaine; it hadn't been cut down with additives. A single freebase rock was two hundred bucks. George found a new way of ingesting a drug that he was fond of and was going through massive amounts of money to support this habit he had developed. At that time, no one knew how addictive it was and how it could consume your money. I don't think he went into it thinking it was as addictive and would take over his financial picture so quickly, but it did. All those changes put George through changes, and everything started to flatline.

SHIRLEY HAYDEN I knew things were starting to fall apart when I went to Superdisc studio to do a session in 1980. As I came up the stairs to the control room, I was startled, "Oh my God! That's Sly Stone!" I was so excited. Unfortunately, after the first few minutes, that disappeared. The truth was that he was in really bad shape when he came to P-Funk. He was unkempt, walking around the studio with no shirt or shoes. He wore blue jeans that Mallia's sister, Jenifer, gave him from her closet because he had no clothes. He'd worn those for easily a week.

Bootsy was trying to get Sly in the vocal booth to record a song he was producing. Bootsy was the sweetest. He was *annoyed* but patient with Sly. Sly sat on the floor with his legs crossed and picked up a pipe and butane lighter that emitted a huge flame. This was the beginning of the freebasing era. Sly was the first person that I ever saw freebase cocaine. Bootsy just wanted to get the part down. Sly wouldn't budge. The pipe was his focus.

LINDA SHIDER When Sly came back in the eighties to work with George and taught him how to freebase cocaine, that was the beginning of the end right there.

LESLIE VOCINO There was a girl that Archie Ivy hired in Los Angeles. This girl and Nene Montes were best friends, and I believe *she* got George into freebasing. She came to Detroit, and Ron Dunbar brought her to our office to do payroll. I was getting overwhelmed, but I didn't want her there. She never did any work. I would have rather had someone like Debra Lett from LA.

When the record companies would send checks to the office, she would grab them from the Federal Express guy before I could get them. If I got it, I would take it to the bank, deposit it, and pay off some of the debt, the musicians, and the staff. She would get the checks, forge George's signature to pay off the dope man, and then buy more dope just to keep George freebasing. He would sit in the studio for hours, even days, and suck cocaine up in the pipe. That's all he cared about now. It took a good year to fuck George up, but she did it.

CHERYL JAMES Sex, drugs, and rock and roll—P-Funk took that to a whole new level. That was a part of the entire experience. Many people didn't survive it. Eddie Hazel, Tiki [Fulwood], and many in the original Funkadelic band didn't; they caught hell. Drugs took them out. When we were snorting cocaine, the hangers-on loved P-Funk because of who we were; they wouldn't do anything to hurt us, but now things had changed. When everybody started freebasing, that brought a whole different group of people around who were really shady. They didn't give a damn about us; they wanted money or drugs. People got skinny as hell because they all stopped eating. Drugs became the priority, and I saw people in the band do things I never thought they would do.

As freebasing took over the organization, many band members ended up at a local motel in Detroit, ironically called the Crystal House. It was the spot where anything goes, with no shortage of drug users and hoes. P-Funk made it an infamous piece of Detroit history. Group members were stashed there for months in any given year. Many were abandoned at the Crystal House because they were off the road and not in the recording studio.

George never had any money available, so the band members depended on whoever they could to meet their needs. There were always lots of women coming and going, referred to as "Crystal House Mouf" because they kept the fellas in the band satisfied sexually and financially.

Now, I must say, there may not have been much money, but there were always plenty of drugs to be found. People were doing really mean things to each other, and drugs played a part. People were popping pills, doing cocaine, and some were even fucking with heroin. But hey... such was life with the funk.

WILLIAM "BOOTSY" COLLINS I think that freebasing was the ultimate change right there. When that happened, it was not about music anymore. It was about getting high. We started joking about it. We started calling getting high "the music." We should have known something was wrong when we started doing that.

It was a saying, "OK, who got the music?"

We were making music, but not even making no *real* music. We all got sidetracked. The deep thing is that I can't say I would go back and change anything. I think everything went down the way it was supposed to. Did I like the way it went down? No, not at all! Did I want to see my comrades go down? No. But at the same time, I know we all had to go through some things. Experience is really the teacher.

When I was with James Brown in 1970, he told me not to do drugs. That very thing right there was what made me want to try it. So when I got with Parliament-Funkadelic, it was like, "Anything goes!" That was freedom . . . music, chicks, getting high, anything you wanted to do. That was the ultimate. But when anything is out of balance, things start to get deep.

We just let it get *totally* out of balance.

RON DUNBAR I never did drugs, so I always tried to control the drug use with George and others. I was so nervous about freebasing. This wasn't doing a line or two of cocaine. George and the band were smoking rocks the size of baseballs. It was now so prevalent that it was difficult to rein it in. The drug situation got so intense that it was impossible to keep the structure in any positive perspective because the money was being drained. We had a huge situation where freebasing was being done, and we had to support the habit financially. We couldn't support it.

I told George several times during that period, "Man . . . this thing here is about to fall apart."

Bootsy always had a different mindset. He wanted to do things *his* way . . . different from George's. I talked to Bootsy about freebasing when I learned he was indulging with George.

I said, "Man . . . I hate that you're getting involved in smoking that stuff."

Word got back to George, and he confronted me.

He said, "Don't you *ever* tell Bootsy nothing like that again! This is *my* money, and I can spend it however I want to spend it! If Bootsy wants to get high, that's what he wants to do!"

George got so mad that he threatened to fire me. In all our years together, George and I had never fallen out over anything. But now we were falling out about *cocaine*. The bottom line was if Bootsy continued to get high, George could keep Bootsy under his thumb, and he wouldn't go anywhere. When George threatened to fire me like that over freebasing, I was 100 percent sure that all of us—George Clinton, Parliament-Funkadelic, and Uncle Jam Records—were in serious trouble.

In Bobby J. Brown's 2016 documentary *Tear the Roof Off: The Untold Story of Parliament-Funkadelic*, Bride of Funkenstein Jeanette McGruder talked particularly about the former manager and alleged drug supplier Nene Montes and the effect drugs had on her during her time with the organization:

> [Nene] was tall with a beard. He was a character and an advisor to [Fidel] Castro. He was a radical. The color of [cocaine] was pink. But we all wanted to smoke it. You had to cook it three or four times before it turned white, and it was so much of it. We were passing around the pipe, and I took a hit. It was so strong that it knocked me out, and I fell to the floor. When I came to, they were still passing the pipe around. I stood up, and the first thing that hit me was, "Did I miss my turn?"

CHAPTER 26

THEME FROM THE BLACK HOLE

With Uncle Jam Records in turmoil shortly after the ink dried on the contracts, Dawn Silva started making moves to distance The Brides of Funkenstein from the organization. In an article in *Blues & Soul* magazine in 1980, she said that The Brides needed to be more independent: "The key is to find our own identity . . . Only then can we escape the stigma of being an offshoot to them, and that is something that I am looking forward to professionally."

DAWN SILVA When you are with George, you don't have proper management, and he has control over whether you will be successful or not. I didn't realize how many people knew who The Brides were until we won our Black Music Award. We started getting offers to tour with the Commodores, Blondie, and other groups independent of P-Funk. The Commodores came to me directly to ask if The Brides would go on tour with them, and I remember asking George about it. He turned it over to Archie Ivy and Nina Hoover at Thang Incorporated. Nothing happened; it just got shut down, and there was no explanation. The same thing happened with Blondie. That's when red flags went up for me.

I would listen to the songs they gave us for the third Brides album,

Shadows on the Wall Shaped Like the Hat You Wore, and I didn't like them at all. Atlantic Records wanted to keep The Brides, but they no longer wanted to deal with George and his production company. They tried to pay George off and release the third Brides album without him. George said, "No!" He didn't want to sell us off to them. I was constantly asking myself, "Why is he doing this? Why is he trying to stop us and not allowing us to grow?"

I lived at Mallia's house mostly when I was in Detroit, and we often went to the studio together. Drugs were deep in the organization. Everybody was partying and getting high whenever I went to the studio. There was one recording session where Mallia and I were the only ones in the studio, except for the engineer, Greg Riley. We were waiting for everybody to come upstairs. They were too busy in the basement partying. George would bring in boulders of cocaine as big as his fist. He would break them up and throw the pieces all over the floor. People would crawl on the ground, looking for pieces of cocaine . . . George called it "Easter egg hunting."

We sat there waiting for hours. Greg, the engineer, said, "There are a lot of tracks here. Let's pull up a track and see what we can come up with."

Greg pulled up one of Garry Shider's rock-inspired tracks. In about two hours, Mallia and I finished a song called "Wild Thang." That was my first attempt at producing and writing anything. Sly Stone was at the studio that day. I remember Sly and George finally coming up from the basement when the song was finished.

George said, "What's that? Play that again!"

He listened and said, "That's the shit!"

He looked over at Sly and gave him a high five for *his* production.

I said, "Wait a minute! That high five goes over here to Mallia and me."

Greg said, "The girls did that song."

George was shocked that we could produce something so good *without* him. Being females back in those days, we stayed in a specific place. The song got buried and was never released.

I finally asked myself, "What am I doing here? I've spent all this time away from my child. There's no money and I'm starving." I was sick of it all, and I finally decided that I was going to leave.

By early 1981, Sheila, Mackie, and I were actually getting along. I knew we had a chance to leave the organization and continue as The Brides. I campaigned for that, and, eventually, Sheila and Mackie agreed.

Just The Brides: Dropping the "of Funkenstein," Jeanette McGruder, Sheila Horne, and Dawn Silva try to reinvent themselves as a new wave act in 1981.

On March 20, 1981, the *Detroit Free Press* ran a story, "The Brides Divorced Funk for New Wave." The article's primary function was to promote their first show as a new wave act at the Detroit rock bar Bookies. The piece states: "The three women who comprise The Brides (they have dropped the 'of Funkenstein') are determined to rid themselves of the Funkadelic bias fans may have placed on them." Dawn Silva proclaimed, "In order for us to grow in the public's eye, we have to get rid of the stigma and go musically into other areas. Our destiny lies with the public. We really like the raw aspect and lyrics of new wave and rock, and we hope it works for the public, too."

These statements in print signaled that The Brides were determined to succeed on their own terms. Unfortunately, P-Funk's family demons continued to plague the trio's efforts.

HENRY MAYERS One night, Mallia Franklin called me and said that Dawn was in the freezing cold outside of a motel in Detroit and instructed me to go get her. I picked Dawn up and told her she could stay at my place. She told me everything that was wrong with George and that she wanted a change. That's how I got involved in helping her. I don't think that Dawn has ever seen how big of a star she really is. She's always had men in her life who pushed her down on her talent. The only man that I knew who nurtured her was Sly Stone. When Dawn said that she wanted to take control of her career, I told her that the first thing that she should do was register the group's name. When my lawyer looked it up, I was surprised that The Brides had no trademark. We registered The Brides of Funkenstein *and* The Brides.

Dawn, Sheila, and Jeanette McGruder were recording their last album. I started turning Dawn on to some of the new wave music then. I suggested she do The Brides as a new wave group. She didn't fully grasp it until they started playing the music at rehearsals.

The Brides could have been *bigger* than George. That's why he stuck his nose in all of it. I don't think he cared whether he was a positive influence or not. It's ironic because, at the time, he was encouraging me to manage and promote them. He said that he wanted me to help, but at the same time, he was distracting Sheila with drugs and sex. Jeanette McGruder didn't think Sheila was taking the group seriously, so eventually, she was contemplating leaving.

DAWN SILVA I called Michael Hampton and asked him to put our first new wave rock band together. During the conversation, Michael apologized for hurting me, and I forgave him. We used his cousin Lige Curry on bass, and two former Parlet band members, Kenny Colton on drums and Ernestro Wilson on keyboards.

George showed up at our first gig at Bookies nightclub, and at the end of our set, he jumped onstage and said, "Let's hear it for these bitches!" That's what I remember most about that gig; George closed our show by calling us *bitches*. But the show was successful, and, soon after, we got an offer for a gig at Harpo's, another more prominent rock club in Detroit, opening for Grace Jones. She was interested in taking us on tour, and this show would be a showcase.

I was *so* done with George and P-Funk by then. The organization had been trying to shut The Brides down for years. Sheila and George's relationship was always distracting. George started sending Sheila with drugs to rehearsals. She would walk in the door with a three-and-a-half-gram boulder of cocaine, gleefully saying, "Look what George gave me for rehearsal today!" As we prepared for the Harpo's show, Sheila and Mackie were getting high, and it got messy. Eventually, they started missing rehearsals altogether. Two weeks before the show, I gave them an ultimatum . . . come to rehearsals or don't come at all! They ignored me, so I fired them. George told me I *couldn't* fire them.

He said, "They'll be coming back."

"No, they won't! If The Brides are going to be shut down, you won't do it . . . I will!"

Sheila and Mackie never returned, and George was pissed off.

Parliament's last album for Casablanca, 1980's *Trombipulation*, was consistent, driving, and laced with features from Parlet and The Brides, most notably Jeanette Washington, Sheila Horne, Jeanette McGruder, and a vocal tirade by Mallia Franklin on "Peek a Groove," at the album's conclusion.

George Clinton recalled, "When we did 'Peek a Groove,' Sly [Stone] said, 'Let Mallia go in the booth by herself, and let her do her "Soul Chicken" and keep the rest of the chickens out. Let's see how much funk she got in her." Yeah, she was the "Queen of Funk" from that day, and I'd still crown her that today.

The Donnie Sterling–penned "Agony of Defeet" cracked the Billboard Soul charts for Parliament at number seven. However, the empire Clinton built on the shoulders of his P-Funk troops was crumbling like the ancient sphinx depicted on the *Trombipulation* album cover.

With Neil Bogart no longer at the helm of Casablanca, whatever support remaining for Clinton evaporated. Bogart succumbed to lymphoma in May of 1982 at the age of thirty-nine, after being ejected in 1980 from his own label by the executives at PolyGram, the company that merged with Casablanca in 1977.

Funkadelic's last album for Warner Brothers, *Electric Spanking of War Babies*, released in April 1981, featured standout parts by Shirley Hayden as she engaged in an extraterrestrial conversation with producer Junie Morrison at the album's opening, and Mallia Franklin, who joined Clinton, Bootsy, and Sly Stone on the song "Funk Gets Stronger (Part 1)." The album stopped at number forty-one on the Billboard Soul charts, the lowest of any Funkadelic album since the group's 1970 inception, with the first single, the title cut, peaking at number sixty on the Soul Singles charts.

Parliament-Funkadelic's influence on dance floors, turntables, and cash registers was thinning. With the infiltration of drugs at a record high, the Uncle Jam Records label in freefall, and funds at an all-time low in the organization, many members of the "World's Biggest Black Band" were trying to find ways to get by or get out.

In the spring of 1981, Parliament-Funkadelic was scheduled to embark on its last large-scale tour as major recording artists. Venues like Chicago Stadium, Charlotte Coliseum, and the Omni in Atlanta were preparing for the Greatest Funk on Earth Tour. Bootsy Collins, Sly Stone, Zapp, and various acts rounded the tour's lineup.

Clinton also brought former Friends of Distinction, now P-Funk vocalist, Jessica Cleaves, hoping her forthcoming debut solo album, *Eyes of a Dreamer*, would still get a release date among the Uncle Jam Records upheaval. Mallia Franklin was the only female to participate in the Greatest Funk on Earth Tour for its duration. Being the lone woman onstage with the band allowed Franklin to rebrand herself after the crumble of Sterling Silver Starship and put the "Queen of Funk" solo concept bestowed to her by Clinton and Sly in motion.

MALLIA FRANKLIN We were losing all the record deals, and many of us in P-Funk were getting high because drugs were the only thing in the organization that was plentiful. Everything George had achieved seemed to be taken or given away, which meant whatever little bit we were getting was being taken away too.

George told me that he wanted to feature me during the show. I was

The Greatest Funk on Earth Tour: Mallia Franklin (right) *and Parliament-Funkadelic's* (left to right) *Michael Hampton, Maceo Parker, Larry Fratangelo, Cordell "Boogie" Mosson, Ray Davis, Jerome Rogers, Rodney "Skeet" Curtis, Greg Boyer, Lige Curry, Larry "Sir Nose" Heckstall, Benny Cowan, Greg Thomas, Garry Shider, Robert "P-Nut" Johnson, Larry Hatcher, David Lee Spradley, and Dennis Chambers on their last tour as major recording artists in 1981.*

excited since Sterling Silver Starship didn't work out, and I wanted a solo career. It seemed like George was finally hearing me. He featured me in the studio on songs like "Freak of the Week," "Peek a Groove," and "Funk Gets Stronger." Although the organization was in trouble, I still believed in George . . . always have. I thought this was only a low period but [that] he would turn it around.

CHERYL JAMES I saw the 1981 Greatest Funk on Earth Tour start with everybody being passed *sacks* of cocaine. Everybody had their own sack! When I saw that happen, I said, "This tour is doomed!" George hadn't said formally, "It's over." But even Stevie Wonder could see that it was over.

Jessica Cleaves was on that '81 tour. She was one of my best friends. She was in the group The Friends of Distinction. Jessica was one of the first females to sing with Earth, Wind & Fire. She started to indulge seriously in drugs, and it didn't take long before EWF fired her. Jessica moved to New

York in the seventies, and I looked her up when P-Funk got to NYC. I took a limo, picked her up, and took her to George, and he was happy to have her come aboard the Mothership full-time. I was always conflicted when it came to Jessica being in P-Funk. At times, I wondered if I had made a terrible mistake.

Like other women, she fell in love with George. She got pregnant and wanted me to help her decide what to do. By now, drugs were a part of her daily routine. The only thing I could say was, "That baby can't survive the drugs you're using, and no one but you can decide to have a child." She decided to abort.

By 1981, everybody got high on something, including me. For the most part, I got high for pleasure, sometimes to give me the energy to keep doing what I had to do as a road manager. There were times I was up for forty-eight hours straight. People would get mad at me because they disliked *how* I got high. I wasn't an addict. I could put it down. I wouldn't let drugs interfere with anything I had to do . . . ever.

Drug dealers met us at every stop. We went places, and random people gave us drugs. I tried to discourage that. "Don't take drugs from people you don't know." We had our own dope dealers that traveled on the road with us. That way, you didn't have to worry about some strange person giving you something that would kill you. I became the "chef." I learned to cook cocaine so we didn't have to deal with strangers. I got so good at cooking that the guys bought me a chef's hat and apron.

Sly [Stone] was also on that tour. That was a trip! We were gigging in Northern California, and I left Sly at the hotel in the previous city because he wasn't ready to get on the bus for his own personal reasons. We went to the next city, and I got a phone call. It was Sly. He was in town, and he didn't have any money, so I had to go get him. Sly got in the cab and wanted to get high. That turned into a fight on the way from the airport. He got to the hotel and insisted that he needed his own personal package of dope or he's not doing the show. So I had to find him a stash somewhere to get him to the stage. He was a pain in my ass because it wasn't easy to take care of his drug demands.

MALLIA FRANKLIN Jessica [Cleaves] missed almost every show because of her habit. Cheryl and Jessica got into a horrible fight on that tour. Cheryl punched her and almost knocked her out. They had been friends forever, but it was just an intense, drug-fueled vibe on that whole tour. Sly was billed as a special guest. He would make it to the stage some nights, and some nights, he wouldn't. And when he did, he wasn't up there more than fifteen minutes. George also brought the Mothership out for the first time since Europe in 1978.

George had Sly come out of the Mothership a couple of times. One night, Sly came out of the smoke, and you could hear the crowd's applause when they saw him at the top of the stairs. He started walking down, and another puff of smoke exploded. When the smoke cleared, it was George. He was butt-naked, balls hanging, walking down the stairs behind Sly. The crowd screamed louder, and Sly turned around, saw him, and was livid. He told George, "Don't you *ever* do that kind of shit to me again! Come up butt-ass naked behind me with your dick out!" We all cracked up. That was one of the funniest memories of that tour.

CHERYL JAMES While we were on the road, I discovered I was ill and had to be hospitalized. I took a leave of absence, and didn't hear anything more from George. It took me about a month to recuperate. When I was finally back on my feet, there was no longer a place for me in the P-Funk organization. To them, I had become useless.

Ironically, I landed a job as a director at a substance abuse agency. I was a natural. My own abuse and witnessing others' extreme drug use enabled me to understand what the program residents were going through and support them through their journey back to sobriety. P-Funk taught me a lot, and, in the end, I positively utilized those lessons.

On June 7, 1981, the Greatest Funk on Earth Tour's final performance took place at the Joe Louis Arena in Detroit. With the remaining five shows being canceled, this night would be the last that dry ice flowed from the ominous Mothership's exhaust pipes. With this being a hometown show, most of The Brides of Funkenstein and Parlet, past and present, like Debbie Wright, were in attendance for the swan song. They joined Sly Stone onstage for his standard, "Sing a Simple Song." Like most of the preceding nights, after five minutes, Sly excused himself from his organ and retreated to the dressing room.

The Mothership was hoisted to the rafters of the arena, the curtain closed, and just like that, the historic Parliament-Funkadelic Mothership era ended on a hot and muggy summer night in Detroit.

MALLIA FRANKLIN After the last show, my mom came to the motel we were staying at and paid my bill. The motel locked up our luggage, and those not in their rooms were locked out because no one from Thang Incorporated paid for the lodging. Guys in the band were throwing hotel TVs out of the windows in protest. She paid several other members' bills on her credit card because no one in the company had money . . . that was the claim.

If you lived in Detroit, as I did, you didn't get any money. You were supposed to be happy that you made it home. The band members who didn't live locally were given fifty bucks and a bus ticket. Some of the guys were literally crying in the lobby of the motel. Some stayed at my house until they could get home. It was a sad end to that big P-Funk era.

RON DUNBAR Everything had fallen apart around us. While we were touring, I got a call from the president of Warner Brothers, Mo Ostin. He was concerned about what was happening with George, the drugs, and the organization. Shortly after, Funkadelic was dropped from Warner.

The IRS put a tax lien on the Funk office in Detroit while we were on the road. They sent a cease and desist and locked the doors. The offices in LA had already been closed. We didn't have the business structured to gain enough activity productively and sustain whatever obstacles we had to overcome. If we did, we would have survived. But the overwhelming drug activity kept the decision-makers from making the *right* decisions.

LESLIE VOCINO I personally packed up and closed the doors of Thang Incorporated on June 10, 1981, three days after their last show. No money had been flowing into the office for at least six months. Creditors were up our asses, and there was no money to pay the rent. Nobody was getting paid by the end. I was working for free, trying to keep it afloat. Dope dealers started coming down to the office and threatening me, telling me they would kill me and blow the office up if they weren't paid. George didn't care. Eventually, the dope men got paid. But that was the *only* debt being resolved.

The Thang employees who didn't do drugs were the ones helping themselves to whatever was left, while musicians and singers who helped build this organization were starving. Ultimately, everything falls on George Clinton's shoulders. All George wanted to do by that time was get high. After all our hard work, all he cared about now was dope, and it was awful. It broke my heart. There are sad memories for a lot of us in those last days. It destroyed a lot of people's lives and careers.

Parliament-Funkadelic didn't have to end that way . . . it didn't have to end at all!

CHAPTER 27

JUST FOREPLAY

The "new wave" Brides conjured some interest after their debut show at Bookies nightclub in March 1981. Outrageous diva Grace Jones looked at The Brides as a possible opening act for a tour to support her biggest hit, "Pull Up to the Bumper." With the exits of Sheila Horne and Jeanette McGruder, Dawn Silva called former groupmate Lynn Mabry, not wanting to squander the opportunity. Their force as a duo had already proven that they had the ingredients to possibly be successful away from Parliament-Funkadelic.

LYNN MABRY Dawn and I talked off and on after I left The Brides. She knew my relationship with Junie was over. I got a job as a waitress to be home with my baby, Akasha. I wanted to spend the first few years with her, not singing out on the road. When Dawn called me in the spring of 1981, my daughter was a little over a year old.

She said, "I want us to do a reunion of The Brides. I've got some gigs, and this whole thing with Sheila and Mackie didn't work out. You and I should just do it."

I fought it. I really wanted to just take time with my baby. But I pondered

Reunited: Dawn Silva and Lynn Mabry reunite as the new wave Brides in 1981.

it and said, "Look, I'm going to do this for *you* because I owe you. I left you high and dry. But after this one, we're straight, right?"

She replied, "Yes."

Dawn sent me a tape of music. It was more of a rock, punk, and alternative sound than we had done in the past. All the new music that Dawn wanted to do was stuff she was into at that time. It wasn't music that she and I would have picked together. I come from an eclectic background, so it wasn't like I couldn't absorb it.

Dawn was staying at Mallia's house while she was out on tour with P-Funk. I flew back to Detroit with my daughter, and we moved in temporarily to rehearse the new show. Dawn had formed a racially mixed band of local Detroit musicians before I came. There was one member we picked together at the last minute. What was cool was that they didn't know me. Even though we were going out as The Brides, it felt like a totally new rock band.

I remember rehearsing with them and thinking they were a completely different caliber of musicians than we were used to. We were used to professional guys who played in front of tens of thousands every night. These were nightclub musicians, but there wasn't as much weight on it because we were doing club dates. Plus, I don't think I perceived these Brides' shows in a way that I had to prove something to the audience. Those who were funk fans interested in seeing the original Brides back together would be satisfied.

DAWN SILVA Lynn and I did the first show with the BusBoys in Detroit, and then we got the gig opening for Grace Jones . . . and hopefully joining her tour. Lynn came into rehearsals and learned the new show in a day or so. I was confident about the performance because I had Lynn back. We were so familiar with each other onstage for so many years, and we knew how to do this together.

We walked out onstage the night of the Grace Jones show at Harpo's. I saw Mackie and Sheila sitting in the front row, and they were pissed. They glared at us the whole time. It was the best performance that Lynn and I had ever done together, in my opinion. Lynn stepped up to my level as a performer this time around, and she was proud of me for stepping up my game vocally since she'd been gone. This wasn't The Brides of Funkenstein coming out of P-Funk; we were doing Labelle songs and tunes by new wave artists like Lene Lovitch and Talking Heads. The audience accepted it, and Grace loved the show.

That night, George sent a P-Funk staff member to Harpo's box office to try and collect The Brides money without our knowledge. But they were too late; we had already gotten paid. Going out and booking dates without the organization's hand in it was not going to fly. So they tried everything in their power to shut us down *again*. Somehow it got to Grace's camp that she would get sued if she took Lynn and me out on the road. She was told we were imposters . . . that Lynn and I were "fake" Brides. That shut the whole Grace Jones tour down for us.

Two weeks after the Grace Jones gig, The Brides were booked at the legendary Mudd Club in New York for two nights in May 1981. The Tribeca nightclub was a hotbed for new wave bands and celebrities like Debbie Harry and Blondie and artists like Andy Warhol, Jean-Michel Basquiat, and his former girlfriend, Madonna. The Mudd Club shows were a major break for The Brides at a venue that catered to the new music genre they aimed to conquer.

DAWN SILVA We were right on the threshold of something great when our manager, Henry Mayers, booked us at the Mudd Club in New York. The Mudd Club had an aluminum garage door for a curtain. The garage door would come down when the show was over, and the crowd would bang on it if they liked you. After our set was over, they beat on that door so hard that we had to do an encore. That signified our success that night. I was so happy because I knew we were only a step away from breaking into the rock world and could cross over to do something else.

HENRY MAYERS I attended high school with Don "Was" Fagenson's sister, Nancy, and met Don years before, when he had a group in Detroit called the Traders. They were an obscene punk rock group. I bumped into Don, and he said that he was working on a project that was going to be different. He told me he got people like Marcus Belgrave, a great jazz musician in the city, and some R&B guys. He was creating this funky, jazzy group called Was (Not Was).

When Don started producing the Was (Not Was) album and needed background singers, Sheila Horne did that. After the Grace Jones show at Harpo's, Don asked Lynn and Dawn if they would go on the road with his group.

LYNN MABRY I wasn't familiar with Was (Not Was). I'd heard their "Out Come the Freaks" record on the radio, but that was about it. It was unfamiliar territory when they approached us to go on tour with them, but they were new and fresh enough to appeal to me. That tour was a lot of fun because of the band members, especially my friend Sweet Pea Atkinson. We had some memorable times.

I didn't realize how brilliant Don Fagenson was . . . I just thought he was a bass player. Then I started digging into him, and he began sharing stories with us. Everywhere we went, everyone knew him, and I thought this guy *must* be some kind of underground superstar. We toured with them for several months in the fall and winter of 1981. We were featured on the show, as well as Wayne Kramer, the guitarist from the group MC5. We did Philadelphia, Chicago, and New York.

After touring with Was (Not Was), The Brides reconnected with keyboardist extraordinaire from Parliament-Funkadelic, Bernie Worrell. Bernie left P-Funk in 1980 to record and tour Japan with the rock-punk band Talking Heads. While in New York, Bernie and Talking Heads members caught the show at the Mudd Club.

With new connections in Japan and the assistance of Judie, Bernie's wife, the new wave Brides, featuring Bernie Worrell, were booked in Tokyo for a string of shows. Worrell recruited P-Funk bandmates Michael Hampton, Rodney "Skeet" Curtis, Tyrone Lampkin, and Larry Fratangelo to replace the band of local musicians who backed The Brides the past six months. They revamped the show, adding P-Funk standards like "Standing on the Verge of Getting It On" to delight Japanese audiences.

BERNIE WORRELL Japan was great! Everything went smoothly. My wife, Judie, handled all the business, and people were getting paid. The band was making a thousand per person per show. I, as the bandleader, as well as The Brides, got more. We had never made that kind of money with P-Funk . . . ever.

LYNN MABRY Japan was a pivotal gig. We had never been there with P-Funk, and the show was well received. We had huge audiences come out because "Disco to Go" went number one over there. The promoters gave us a big banquet; there were media and a lot of hoopla. I realized there was a void that was created when I left The Brides. It showed me the effect that Dawn

Land of the Rising Sun: Lynn Mabry (front), *Dawn Silva, and Bernie Worrell in Tokyo, Japan, in 1981.*

and I, as a group, had on the public. Still, it didn't affect me to the point where I wanted to return permanently because I had matured and become a mother. I felt like I was doing something good, but it wasn't a life-altering situation. After almost a year of returning to be a "new wave" Bride alongside Dawn, I was satisfied that I had fulfilled my promise to my friend.

DAWN SILVA We did shows at Club New York and the Suntory Festival [Tokyo], and Judie had us booked for four or five more shows. After Suntory, the P-Funk organization called the promoter. They told him not to put us on any more concerts. I remember them threatening to sue for advertising it as The Brides "of Funkenstein." Even though I had the trademark, the other dates got canceled.

With a second show booked at the Mudd Club when they returned from Japan, The Brides had all the ingredients to be successful away from George Clinton, but reinvention is not easy for artists who have been essential in cultivating a musical phenomenon. And like many marriages, one Bride was in it for the long haul, and the other was going through the motions, feeling a sense of duty. As with many reconciliations, Lynn and Dawn's reunion as the new wave Brides would ultimately fizzle.

DAWN SILVA Bernie Worrell invited the Talking Heads to our second show at the Mudd Club. After the set, we returned to the dressing room and changed. Lynn informed me about dinner with Bernie and members of Talking Heads. I thought, "Great. We can celebrate!" Since we always did everything together, I said, "Where are we going?"

She said, "*We* aren't going anywhere . . . *I'm* going."

She turned around and walked out of the dressing room. Lynn showed up at the hotel the next morning.

She said, "I'm leaving with Bernie. I'm tired of competing with you."

She handed me a copy of the *Village Voice* newspaper with a review of the Mudd Club show. The critic Robert Christgau praised the show. He wrote: "The Brides are amazing . . . Dawn Silva *is* The Brides." I guess that pissed Lynn off. She packed her bags and left me again. I wasn't the same girl that Lynn left in '79. She wasn't the leader this time, and I wasn't in her shadow. Fighting for position with Sheila and Mackie for two years made me different. That was it. The Brides was over. I packed my bags and went back home to Sacramento.

LYNN MABRY Dawn and I have *incredibly* different memories of how The Brides ended. That's not what happened. Anyone who knows me knows that that's not my character at all. I had no jealousy toward anyone in that P-Funk situation, definitely not toward someone I considered my best friend at the time. We initially did this whole Brides of Funkenstein thing together, and *she* asked me to come back. I returned to The Brides because I needed to pay my debt to my friend. In those two years after I left, I grew up a lot, and, most importantly, I now had a child that I had to support. Taking care of her was the most essential thing in my life. After the Was (Not Was) tour, The Brides was pretty much over, and Dawn and I went our separate ways . . . it's that simple. There was no *dramatic* exit. I went back to Berkeley and took a hostess job in a restaurant to make ends meet for my daughter and me.

BERNIE WORRELL I was approached by Jerry Harrison of Talking Heads to do some work with them in 1980. I didn't know who the Talking Heads were. He asked me if I was interested in playing with them, and my question was, "What kind of music is this?" They invited me to a New York studio to hang out and listen to them. I liked what I heard, and they were P-Funk fans. I started working with them almost immediately.

They brought in Nona Hendrix from Labelle as a vocalist, and the band behind them was primarily Black. After Nona bowed out, they asked me if I knew any background vocalists, and Lynn was the first that came to mind.

I told them, "I'll bring Lynn Mabry from The Brides of Funkenstein."

That really got them excited.

LYNN MABRY Bernie called me. He said that the Talking Heads were looking for a singer. I welcomed the change because this wasn't Brides or P-Funk, and Bernie promoted them in such a positive way.

Bernie said, "I'm trying to get you into this situation. I think you would be perfect. It would be good for you. This would be like no tour you've ever done. These people are really cool. We're going to great places. They'll take good care of you . . . and they pay well."

Bernie asked me to come to a rehearsal. I met the Talking Heads, and we just clicked. Dolette McDonald was the other background vocalist with them at the time. They called Dolette and got us together for an audition. I auditioned, and they offered me the tour on the spot.

I had mixed emotions about Talking Heads because this would be the first major tour that I would be on since I had my daughter. Akasha came with me on The Brides mini-tour, but this tour with the Talking Heads would be the first one where I'd be away from her. I needed to make a living for us. I was on my own. Junie was a long-distance father and not active in her life at that time financially. After wrestling with my decision for a while, I asked my mom if she would help me by watching my daughter while I was gone. She jumped at the chance.

While rehearsing for the tour, something happened with the other background singer, Dolette McDonald. We realized we had to find somebody to replace her. The band was freaked out because the tour was around the corner. The group let me audition the new singer because that person would have to sing with me. A few girls came in, but the one who stood out was Edna Holt. Edna had an amazingly happy personality. She wasn't nervous; she was ready to work. I told her that she had to be a quick study, and she was amazing. We clicked, and we're still friends to this day.

When I got out on the road with the Talking Heads, I was exposed to

Stop Making Sense *tour: Edna Holt, David Byrne, and Lynn Mabry onstage in 1983.*

another music genre and another type of people. I was now in the rock and roll world in a big way. And it was a completely different situation than P-Funk.

I thought to myself, "Wow! Here are people in a band who are sane. They're not abusing themselves like Funkadelic."

It was a whole new world, but I knew there was still a lot of growing for me to do because I noticed I was still defensive from what I had come out of a few years prior with P-Funk.

After months on a successful tour, I was informed that we were filming our show for a movie called Stop Making Sense. The film was a success. I made more money with David Byrne and the Talking Heads than I ever did as a Parliament-Funkadelic member or a Bride. I was single-handedly providing for my daughter and me. I was now sure that I didn't *need* Junie to survive. I never did. I could do it on my own. That was a blessing from God.

DAWN SILVA I was back home in Sacramento when I got a phone call from Val Young in the spring of 1982. Val and I maintained a friendship over the years after she was fired from the Bridesmaids in '78. She said she was at the Black Radio Convention in LA and invited me to come. I drove to Los Angeles to meet her and ran into The GAP Band. They used to open for The Brides and P-Funk back in the day.

Charlie Wilson was the leader of GAP. They had a big hit at the time, "Burn Rubber on Me." They also had "Oops, Upside Your Head," a song that stole the intro from The Brides' "Disco To Go" note for note. He told me they were going on tour and would love to take some P-Funk Girls out. Val lied and said she was a Bride of Funkenstein, but Charlie knew better. I wasn't working; The Brides were over, and I desperately needed a gig. After Charlie Wilson's invitation, Val Young and I went on the road with The GAP Band in the summer of 1982.

The GAP Band situation wasn't the first time Val misrepresented herself as a Bride. In 1980, Val booked a recording session with R&B/jazz great Roy Ayers. I was in LA, and Val asked me to come to the session with her. Roy was recording at Total Experience Studios. Val and I entered the studio, and Roy extended his hand to me.

He said, "The Brides of Funkadelic! Ladies, I'm honored to work with you."

His statement confirmed that Val told him she was a Bride. I just smiled and said nothing. It didn't really matter, nor was it important at the time to reveal the truth. Roy seemed excited that the Brides were there singing his song. In return for my silence, I was paid generously for the session, and that was the end of Val's "Brides lie."

At least, that's what I thought.

CHAPTER 28

ATOMIC DOG

After the 1981 Greatest Funk on Earth Tour crashed into a fiery heap of debt, drugs, and disillusionment, P-Funk's holy chariot, the Mothership, was seized by concert promoters, ending up, oddly enough, in Clinton, Maryland. The vessel, which had become almost as iconic as the group itself, was now sitting stagnant, rusted, and wasting away in a neighborhood garage. The tarnished remains would eventually be stripped and sold for parts like a car abandoned in an old junkyard, where the last bones of the Mothership would ultimately end up.

The Mothership's destruction was a sad metaphor for the state of the now-disassembled band that was Parliament-Funkadelic. Now separate pieces, some members would become important components of other musical machines. In contrast, others would remain attached to the P-Funk vehicle they were all too familiar with, riding on the ship's fumes with Clinton to new and unknown destinations.

MALLIA FRANKLIN In 1982, I was invited to Dayton to record with Roger Troutman and Zapp. P-Funk vocalist Ray Davis, horn player Larry Hatcher and I went to Dayton together. We recorded the *Zapp 2* album. We did songs like "Doo Wah Diddy (Blow That Thing), and I was featured on a song called "Do You Really Want an Answer?" Roger and Larry Troutman talked to me about joining a project they were developing with Billy Beck from the Ohio Players called The Human Body.

One thing about the Troutmans was that they were all about business. That's one of the main reasons the George Clinton–Roger Troutman partnership didn't work. They owned tons of property and were basically *running* Dayton, Ohio. Ray Davis and Larry Hatcher stayed with the Troutmans. The Troutmans were still going through things with George, and I still felt a sense of loyalty to him. Plus, I was focused on my solo career, so I left.

After Zapp, I returned to Detroit and started dealing with the movers and shakers in the cocaine game. Like today, most dope men wanted to be in the music business, and I became the bridge between those worlds. I knew the drug dealers who owned studios and let George and others come in and record on spec time. I did what I always do—I brought people together.

I knew so many people in the music industry, and many of us were freebasing by then. I oversaw the entertainer-dope connections in the city, and I could now get premium cocaine . . . pure from Colombia. Because I was the middle woman, I got lots of free drugs, which afforded us many nights of freebasing. My house was the rendezvous point and safe haven for drug dealers and celebrities to exchange funds and drugs. Famous recording artists and executives could get high discreetly.

After all the years with P-Funk, I started recording my solo album. I used the lessons I learned from George and employed most of Parliament-Funkadelic to play on it. A big drug dealer in the city invested about fifty thousand in my project, and that's how I paid everyone. Eddie Hazel, Gary "Mudbone" Cooper, Garry Shider, Junie, and I did production. The Horny Horns and most of P-Funk's musicians played. Some Brides and Parlets; Bootsy's girl group, Godmoma; Steve Boyd from Five Special; Joe Pep from Undisputed Truth; Arnell Carmichael from Raydio; and Belita Woods from Brainstorm sang. I even funded a show for P-Funk at the 20 Grand in Detroit when George couldn't get a gig.

In a 1996 radio interview in Atlanta, the DJ surprised the Godfather of Soul, James Brown, when he said, "Mr. Brown, I got a special message for you. Queen of Funk Mallia Franklin told me to tell you, 'Hello.'" James enthusiastically replied, "Mallia?! She's a *great* lady and a stone-cold fox!"

The 1984 book *Nowhere to Run: The Story of Soul Music*, by Gerri Hirshey, chronicles the triumphs and struggles of Brown, Aretha Franklin, Otis Redding, and other soul icons. In the chapter "We Sang Like Angels," she writes, "Wide-eyed, the maître d' in the starched dining room of this midtown hotel had to dispatch a crew of waiters to create seating for Mr. Brown's entourage. It is a jolly group of more than a dozen and a half, including one Brooklyn reverend (a.k.a. the Rev), a radio announcer, a bodyguard, a hairdresser, a fashion model impresario, dancer Lola Love (a.k.a. the Sex Machine), and Ms. Mallia Franklin, a lively woman draped in grimacing mink heads and lace."

Few knew that by the book's release, Franklin had been dating her idol, James Brown, for over a year.

MALLIA FRANKLIN I met James Brown at a Detroit nightclub called Henry's Palace in 1981. I was with Bootsy, George, and Maude Boyd, the mother of a man I was dating, Steve Boyd, of the group Five Special. They had a hit on the R&B charts called "Why Leave Us Alone." James had just divorced his second wife, Deidre "Deedee" Jenkins.

We connected, and after talking for countless hours, he sent me a plane ticket to visit his farm in Augusta, Georgia. I learned quickly that James was the leader of his world. He was a dominant man and possessive. If you were his, you belonged to him. We got along well, but he didn't like me wanting to continue recording, even *associating* with George too much. That was an issue for him. He thought that it was a waste of time. My strong personality was also an issue. If James had his way, I would have quit singing altogether and accompanied him around the world as his lady. I was thirty and still longed for a recording career. I wasn't going to quit. James was twenty years my senior and fulfilled *his* dreams.

He spent many hours talking about politics and race issues on the phone with my mother. He loved Mom's knowledge of the world and no-nonsense personality. She had been a successful white woman and politician who spent most of her life in a Black world, fighting for equality for women and Blacks. This fascinated James because he was so politically astute. She'd had a very worldly life, so she wasn't affected by the fact that it was James Brown, the Godfather of Soul, and he loved that he was just JB to her.

I was back and forth to Augusta, and we did a lot of horseback riding on his farm. After six months or so, he proposed. Being the old-fashioned guy he was, he asked my mother for permission. I was torn. I loved and respected him. He was my idol. But I wasn't sure if I wanted to marry him. If I did, I knew I would have to kiss my dreams of singing goodbye. I'm sure I could have had a financially bountiful life. But I have never been "that kind of girl." I loved him, but I wasn't sure I was *in* love with him. So I declined.

Eventually, we grew apart, and he married his third wife, Adrienne Rodriguez. When I saw a picture of them in *Jet* magazine, I thought, "She looks like *me*!" Their marriage was always in the headlines, with accusations of domestic abuse. I respected James. I loved him, but not enough to become Mrs. James Brown.

After the end of the P-Funk Mothership era in 1981, George Clinton made a musical comeback in 1983 as a solo artist with his biggest hit "Atomic Dog." With help from a flashy, big-budget music video that could be played on MTV alongside Duran Duran and Michael Jackson, "Atomic Dog" reached number one on the soul charts, his first number-one record since Funkadelic's "(Not Just) Knee Deep" in October 1979.

GARRY SHIDER When it was time to get George's first solo album together, we pulled a lot of stuff we already had in the can for Funkadelic. Most of George's album *Computer Games* was the leftovers from *Electric Spanking of War Babies*. David Lee Spradley was the main keyboard player for P-Funk after Bernie Worrell left. He was also the guy that did the track for "Atomic Dog." I think David was a friend of Mallia and Donnie Sterling's. Donnie produced "Big Bang Theory" for *GloryHallaStoopid*. He hired David as a session player on the song, and he was so awesome that he ended up taking Bernie's place in the band. David did many of George's hit tracks in the eighties . . . "Man's Best Friend," "Double Oh Oh," "Bulletproof," and "Pumpin' It Up."

David was at the studio, laying a drum track and had the engineer flip the tape and the beat played in reverse. We knew we had *something*, and he built the track on top. When we recorded "Atomic Dog," George showed up at the studio, and he was so high that we had to damn near hold him up. He got in front of the microphone and started hollering a bunch of bullshit. Then he left.

I wondered, "What am I supposed to do with *this* shit?"

I had to arrange something to sing around George's bullshit. The first session was Ray [Davis], David [Spradley], Shirley [Hayden], Mallia [Franklin], and me. We laid the first vocals on it. Mal was like the P-Funk dog-and-cat lady. She created a couple of those hooks for the dogs' and cats' songs. "Puuuurrrrfect, simply Puuuuurrrrfect." She was great for one-liners.

We rolled the tape, and George's rap started, "This is the story of a famous dog . . ."

Mallia started *panting* like a dog.

She looked at me and said, "Come on, Garry . . . come on!"

I started panting, we *all* started panting.

I said, "Damn . . . we can record this shit?!"

Sometimes Mal got on my nerves. She'd walk into the middle of a session and say, "So you didn't call me?!"

Then we would put her in the booth to sing, just to shut her up. But everybody moved out of the way when she got out there. Mal was crazy as a bedbug. But we couldn't get a hit record without her. It was her energy. The last hit record *was* "Atomic Dog."

A couple of days later, George came back and wanted to fix his parts.

I said, "It's too late for that. I built everybody's voices around what you did. I thought you meant that shit you were doin'."

We mixed it, released it, and it was a smash. George was famous for not giving people credit . . . He did it to me and others. One person who's owed a lot is Mallia . . . if anybody wants to show some respect. She brought a lot of people to this group. People that made George a lot of money. She ain't gonna bite her tongue either, but sometimes she needed to. Because when she didn't, she was helping to put *other* people before herself. I would try to shut her up, but she never listened . . . that "Mal mouth."

MALLIA FRANKLIN George's name was like mud in the industry, and most of us from Parliament-Funkadelic were branded as "burnouts. Some left funk behind completely just to work. Lynn did it. She went straight to pop and rock and flourished. The industry wasn't into funk anymore, but it was so deep in my veins that I couldn't do anything else. George lucked up. He signed a new record deal as a solo artist with a company in which he had no prior business dealings, Capitol Records.

Through George I became friends with producer Ted Currier. Ted was a radio disc jockey who became a bigwig at Capitol and EMI. He was very instrumental in George getting his solo deal when no other label would touch him. He produced a song called "Work That Sucker to Death" for an Ohio group called Xavier in 1981. It was basically a P-Funk record with George, Bootsy, and Ted at the helm. There's even a little shout-out to my son by George's alter ego, Sir Nose, who says in the song, "Turk that sucka to Seth."

Ted also introduced me to rap music as a genre.
He said, "Mallia, rap is the future. A lot of it sucks, but this is where the music industry is headed."

Ted was one of the first producers who merged rappers with vocalists like me, singing hooks on their songs. He put me on songs with the rappers the Boogie Boys. They had a big hit called "Fly Girl." He also brought in Gary "Mudbone" Cooper from Bootsy's Rubber Band and did a group called Sly Fox with David Bowie protégé Michael Camacho. They had a big hit called "Let's Go All the Way."

TED CURRIER (PRODUCER, CAPITOL RECORDS) I'll never forget Mallia's voice. She was *the* voice and presence of "Atomic Dog" to me. It was distinct and identifiable. Mallia's voice could deliver shivers when she sang double-tracked high notes. For me, her voice created the signature female sound of P-Funk. She's instantly recognizable on *any* P-Funk song. I intended to record a body of work with Mallia and Garry Shider singing together as a duo for Capitol. That's what I wanted to do, but it never happened.

SHIRLEY HAYDEN By 1983, nothing much was happening for us. Garry Shider was running things in the studio for the most part. He was using Mallia and me on a lot of songs. We were recording George's solo albums for Capitol Records. We recorded "Quickie" at United Sound. That was Mallia, me, and a friend of Mallia and Mudbone's, a singer named Kim Seay. We were doing most of the background on songs like "Last Dance," "Nubian Nut," and "Bio-Friction" with Mudbone, Robert "P-Nut" Johnson, Ron Ford, Michael "Clip" Payne, Eddie Hazel, and Garry.

At that time, Mallia was heavy in with the Kingpins of the Detroit cocaine scene. She was dealing with big-time drug dealers who lived in many of the city's wealthiest neighborhoods. Mallia took me to a guy's house in Palmer Woods. Palmer Woods was an exclusive neighborhood where doctors, athletes, and corporate bigwigs lived in spacious, elegant homes.

We pulled up to a mansion and entered the massive foyer. We went down a flight of dark stairs. Entering the dimly lit basement, we saw it was set up like a nightclub, with a fully stocked bar and stage emerging from the wall. I wasn't doing heavy drugs. I had a daughter at home that depended on me. I was *curious* about partying but wasn't acquiescing because I didn't want to get caught up. But that night, we partied, laughed, listened to music, and snorted cocaine. The owner of the house, who looked like a little bear, kept trying to touch me. Mallia had a business relationship with this guy and felt comfortable with him. I felt uneasy . . . like fresh meat.

All of a sudden, Mallia stripped down to her one-piece leopard unitard. She was brazen and very voluptuous. She grabbed her big purse and pulled out a purple satin cosmetics bag. For a split second, it reminded me of visions of us in the dressing room, preparing for a show. But this was a different kind of performance. This was a "dope dance," and this was her getting-high costume. She unzipped the bag and emptied it on the bar. Cosmetics and perfumes had been replaced with her "works" . . . a free-base pipe, wire stems, cotton balls to make torches, and a small bottle of Bacardi rum to ignite them.

As the night went on, Mallia invited Garry Shider and a few other P-Funk guys to indulge in this abundance of cocaine. There was so much that the host wasted cocaine on the basement floor. The guys started kneeling, crawling, picking it up with their fingers, snorting it, and rubbing it on their gums. After hours of getting high, I was ready to go home. Mallia tried to convince me to smoke *one last* joint. I couldn't get any higher; I had to go. By the time I emerged from the basement, the sun had risen. I got in my car and glanced in the rearview mirror. My nostrils were caked with pure cocaine. At that moment, I knew that I didn't want that life.

There was another time that I remember. Mallia asked me to come to her house for dinner on a Sunday afternoon. I went happily. That was my girl. We talked about music, guys, etc. When I arrived, she was on the phone with Liz Bishop, George's ex. That was the first time I was introduced to Liz. Mallia was waiting for some guys to come in from Ohio. They arrived, and something made me feel uncomfortable. I was wondering how she knew them . . . but she knew *everybody*.

Mallia cooked a big pot of spaghetti, but the guys brought rock cocaine for dinner instead. From their conversation, these guys assumed *I* would be dessert. The next thing I knew, I was surrounded by freebase pipes. They blew smoke in my face and encouraged me to indulge. I wouldn't. One of the guys said, "Let me talk to you," and pulled me upstairs. He tried to convince me to get high.

Mallia came up the stairs and said, "You don't want to get high? Awww . . . you a party pooper!"

She became condescending. My feelings were so hurt. I told Mallia that I was leaving. I realized that she was trying to pawn me off to the dope men. Because I wasn't going to play the game, she had no use for me. It was degrading, and I was so disappointed in her.

She was making a lot of transactions at that time. Sometimes our children were with us, and she put us all in danger. That upset me deeply. I loved Mallia, but I didn't trust her anymore. Her decisions were now all drug related. She was willing to sacrifice our years of friendship and compromise me, compromise herself *and* her own integrity. She was relentless and would complete this solo album by any means necessary. Mallia's actions were now no better than the men's . . . *She* had now become the pimp.

CHAPTER 29

BULLETPROOF

The eighties ushered in flocks of young, new artists that would change the musical landscape once more. A minority of Black acts, like Prince and Rick James, successfully shifted with the times, and the music spectrum was dominated only by a few. The demolition of disco and the punk, new wave, and new romantic movements imported from overseas changed the game for eighties music in America. Many Black artists tried to infuse new styles into their own images and sound, most unsuccessfully, and some women of Parliament-Funkadelic continued to carve roads for themselves in the new music landscape by any means necessary.

In Parliament-Funkadelic's heyday, the female members were deliberately shrouded in mystery. Unless you were a true Funkateer, most people never knew who these women were as individuals or if they were Brides or Parlet members. When it was time to strike out independently, they were unrecognizable singers. They didn't have identities like George and Bootsy. They were caricatures on album covers and voices burned into vinyl. A perfect example of this practice was the 1985 release of Val Young's debut solo album, *Seduction*, produced by Rick James, with Val's claims to the press that she was a former member of the duo The Brides of Funkenstein. This falsehood has adhered to Young's career for decades.

George Clinton told writer Charlotte Morgan in a 1986 *Rock & Soul* article that he was developing a new Brides of Funkenstein for the eighties, featuring former Bride Sheila Horne and new members Patty Curry and Jenny Peters for MCA Records. The Brides' resurrection ultimately fell apart during recording and was never completed, and some of their best songs, like "Do Fries Go with That Shake?," were placed on George's solo albums for Capitol Records.

DAWN SILVA I heard about Clinton trying to put a new Brides group together. They're lucky it didn't happen. The truth is, Lynn Mabry and Dawn Silva were incorporated under that group name and still legally signed to Atlantic Records as The Brides of Funkenstein until 1985.

I was on tour with The GAP Band when I got a call from my mom in Sacramento.

She said, "Honey, are you and Lynn in trouble?"

"Not that I know of. Why?"

She said, "I just had two men from the feds at my door looking for you and Lynn."

I was genuinely shocked. We discovered that George had one of his attorneys set up a fictitious corporation called The Brides of Funkenstein Inc. They used our names and Social Security numbers and forged our signatures without our knowledge. This company also had fake employees with false Social Security numbers.

According to the IRS, millions were being funneled through this company. Clinton or someone at the Funk organization was paying the taxes on this dummy corporation. One year, they didn't pay the tax bill, red-flagging the feds in a major way. I knew nothing about this corporation until the feds came after me. They didn't go after George initially because he *technically* didn't set up the corporation; his lawyer in New York did.

I had to go to the federal building in San Francisco. They put me in an office with a pen and paper, and I had to sign my signature over a thousand times. They compared the signatures and saw that it wasn't mine on the corporate documents. They couldn't prove that Lynn and I earned this money... and I couldn't prove that we didn't. They put a seven-year lien on both of us. We got a lawyer, and the lawyers contacted George. George got scared and paid off the largest federal penalties but didn't pay the smaller ones. He left that for Lynn and me to pay.

It wasn't our responsibility; it was Clinton's. Lynn was making pretty good money. She called me, said the IRS was garnishing her checks, and wanted me to pay half the tax lien.

LYNN MABRY The FBI? Door knocking and threats? I don't think so! I wouldn't forget something that huge. Millions of dollars going through our names would have meant thousands of dollars owed in taxes. I was never hit with a tax lien or garnishment and didn't pay any additional taxes on The Brides' behalf. I wasn't making that kind of money to do something like that.

I recall that situation very differently. We discovered that George had been cashing checks for us for some time. We wouldn't have known, but a new assistant was hired by George, and when IRS checks for Dawn and me landed on her desk, she found us and informed us that they had been delivered. She mailed us the checks. She didn't realize she should have contacted Archie Ivy or George beforehand. We were confused about why we received a tax refund from our taxable contributions to the IRS. I hadn't been active with The Brides since 1979. This was now the eighties. After receiving the check, we tried to contact George, his attorneys . . . anybody who would talk to us. We started asking questions, but no one seemed to have answers.

We called the IRS. They told us that The Brides of Funkenstein had been given a tax break. If we were getting a tax break, that meant money was still coming into the organization through our names. We were confused, as George told us we hadn't made any money for years.

We called Atlantic Records and spoke to a guy who was trying to be as helpful as possible. The instruction was that no information could be released to anyone except Thang Incorporated, their attorneys, or George himself. But by this time, Thang Incorporated had folded.

He said, "I've got records of royalty checks sent to you and Dawn. I see one right here in the amount of twenty thousand dollars for each of you. We sent everything to Thang Incorporated. All the checks we have records of were signed and endorsed by the two of you."

We both responded, "No! We never got those checks."

That meant that someone at Thang Incorporated forged our signatures. I flashed back to Paris in 1978 when every guy in the band got royalty checks, and George said to Dawn and me, "Atlantic is taking care of The Brides. They've got your money."

We were upset about realizing monies had been changing hands, and once again, we didn't see any of it. It wasn't like this massive amount of money was being put *solely* into The Brides. It couldn't have been money for recording because we were riding on the same financial coattails as Funkadelic and Parlet. So where did the rest of it go? Our band wasn't making much, maybe two hundred dollars a week. George may have spent twenty thousand dollars total on wardrobe, but one royalty check from Atlantic would have paid *all* of that.

DAWN SILVA Clinton and the IRS had me so screwed up financially that The GAP Band was the only group I could work for because they were paying me cash under the table. I toured and recorded with The GAP Band for almost a decade. I began a romantic relationship with the leader, Charlie Wilson, about a year after I joined. We were together for nine years. We were engaged, but never got married.

Charlie wanted to produce a solo album for me and got me a record deal on PolyGram. A few years into our relationship, Charlie got deep into cocaine . . . especially freebasing. I even dabbled in it to fit in, but I didn't like feeling out of control. My constitution was stronger, and I managed not to get addicted. There was a point in our relationship when Charlie was sober for a few years, and those years were much happier than when he was getting high. When he was high, he was abusive physically and mentally.

Charlie's drug addiction went from costly freebasing to crack. While we were recording my solo album, he got busted by undercover cops in one of those infamous LAPD stings set up by Mayor Tom Bradley. He got a diversion and had to attend NA [Narcotics Anonymous]. Charlie stopped smoking crack for a while and tried to get clean. When he stopped, the abuse stopped as well. But at some point, he started smoking it again. It turned him into a monster. He became paranoid and believed I was changing now that I had a record deal. Charlie started physically abusing me again. I was living in hell and knew I had to leave or something terrible would happen.

CHERYL JAMES Charlie Wilson was on the *wild* in the eighties, and his relationship with Dawn was bananas. He could pass out an ass-whipping. They came to my house in Detroit, and Charlie beat Dawn real bad in my living room. Dawn was talking shit, and Charlie was telling her to "shut up!" She kept talking, and he jumped on her.

I yelled, "Don't tear my house up, Charlie!"

He picked her off the floor and said, "See what you made me do in Cheryl's house?!"

It was really a bad relationship. But as long as I'd known Dawn, she was in domestically abusive relationships. I almost expected it with her history with men.

Dawn Silva and The GAP Band's leader, Charlie Wilson, on tour in 1983.

MALLIA FRANKLIN I loved Charlie . . . all the Wilson brothers, but I wasn't happy about how volatile his and Dawn's relationship had become. I would see Charlie and Dawn when they came to Detroit. Because of my drug connections in the city, I could always hook Charlie up.

DAWN SILVA We were in our suite, and Mal and I were reminiscing about P-Funk, and Charlie was high and irritable.

He said, "Fuck that P-Funk shit! Fuck P-Funk!"

He said That we were blowing his high. Charlie and I started arguing. He was getting angry, and it was about to get physical. He jumped up and was on his way across the suite toward me.

Mallia said, "Come on, Charlie. Don't do that. You need to calm down."

I said something like, "Yeah! You heard her. You need to calm down."

He raised his fist, and Mallia jumped in front and was hit in the jaw. Charlie was startled. I knew that he didn't mean to hit her. He apologized profusely. Mal took that hit for me.

Eventually, I'd had enough of Charlie's abuse and left. I still had a record that I was obligated to get done for PolyGram . . . whether I was with Charlie or not. I disappeared and went to Fort Worth, Texas. I hooked up with a group called Yarbrough & Peoples to finish the production of my first single. They had a big hit called "Don't Stop the Music." I turned in the song, and PolyGram gave me a release date and scheduled a video shoot for the single.

Charlie found the hotel I was staying at and showed up at my door. He was furious. Reluctantly and stupidly, I let him in. I knew he was high as soon as he walked in.

He said, "Bitch, you think you're going to get away from me?!"

An argument turned into a fight. His forearm was around my neck, choking me, and I bit him. The next thing I knew, Charlie punched me in the eye. The blow was so hard that he crashed in the left side of my face and broke my nose and cheekbone. I suffered a full orbital blowout. Everything was crushed.

As I lay on the floor, Charlie spat on me and said, "Bitch, there's only *one* superstar per family!"

I swallowed a mouth full of blood and bone and could feel it cutting my throat. I thought, "I'm going to die." I was in and out of consciousness, and my life started flashing before me. I was asking myself all kinds of questions:

"Why did I bite him?"

"Why do I get into these abusive relationships?"

The truth was that I wasn't fighting Charlie Wilson or even Michael Hampton. I was fighting the ghost of my father, Lawrence Weber. . . my *first* abusive relationship. Splinters of bone continued going down in my stomach, cutting my intestines. I regained consciousness and saw Charlie in handcuffs, arrested by the police. He begged me not to sign the complaint as they led him to the squad car. It took almost eight years of reconstructive surgery to straighten out the damage that Charlie caused that day. He got what he wanted. The album never came out. PolyGram Records dropped me, and I left the music business altogether for many years.

MALLIA FRANKLIN I spent a lot of time in New York in '85, recording with Bootsy, Black Britain, Boogie Boys, and Ted Currier at Capitol Records. After being in the dope game for a couple of years, one of P-Funk's members who frequently came to my house to get high brought a *friend* who turned out to be an undercover DEA agent. He worked his way into the loop I established with the Colombian cartel.

After several months of drug buys, the shit all came down while I was in Ohio writing and recording "Instant Replay" with Bootsy protégé Mico Wave. The DEA raided my house and held my teenage son, Seth, at gunpoint. Luckily, there were no drugs to find, and they left my son shaken but unharmed. Within a few days, I returned home. My mother and my attorney accompanied me to turn myself in, and I was soon released on my own recognizance.

Within a few months, my three Colombian contacts and I were in front of a judge at the federal building in downtown Detroit. This wasn't a local drug bust; this was *federal* charges. Every day was a circus of reporters, as the fraud trial of millionaire carmaker John DeLorean was conducted in the courtroom next door. After a weeklong trial, the judge found me guilty of conspiracy to distribute cocaine. The judge knew my dad. That worked in my favor when it was time for sentencing. Because I had no prior record and my parents were so well respected in Detroit, I got a year's sentence at a federal corrections work farm in Fort Worth, Texas.

LYNN MABRY After touring with the Talking Heads for a few years, I went to work with Rita Coolidge in 1985 and then with Japanese artist Ryuichi Sakamoto in 1986. While touring Japan, I had a spiritual awakening. I was listening to gospel music by the group Commissioned, and there were some words in their song that spoke directly to me. I played the song repeatedly and started crying.

I said, "Lord, if you could just get me through this period of my life, I'll change. I will become more responsible and take my life more seriously. I will be a better mother, daughter, and woman."

I was hired to sing in a recording session, where I met one of the singers, Kathy, who had the voice of an angel. After becoming friends, Kathy saw a void of sorts in me and asked if she could take me somewhere. She

The Big Apple: Singers Taka Boom and Val Young, with Mallia Franklin in New York City in 1985.

invited me to church. I shared my apprehension about organized religion and the extreme rules that came with it. But she promised me this would be different. Trusting her, I agreed to go.

Once I entered Maranatha, a nondenominational church in Los Angeles, I could feel a difference. The music ministry was stellar. The late pastor,

Billy Ingram, spoke to the congregation, but I swear he spoke *directly* to me. It was God speaking . . . showing me how to love through *his* love for me.

In 1988, there were rounds of auditions in LA to sing with George Michael for his Faith Tour. This was his debut solo project after his successful run as the leader of Wham! I made it through the first and second rounds of auditions. I was called for the final round with Niki Harris, who sang with Madonna. As I patiently waited for my turn, I could hear Niki and George singing his duet with Aretha Franklin, "I Knew You Were Waiting." She sounded so good that I just *knew* she had this gig.

I went in after Niki and sang with George. I concentrated on flow with him and harmony. To my surprise, I got the gig. As we rehearsed, George encouraged me to step out during the show. He put me on a ten-foot platform in the middle of the stage, and the audience's feedback was electrifying. I sang, danced, and did duets with George. I was the only woman in the band and the *only* singer. I wasn't being paid much for a major tour that was making a gazillion dollars, and I eventually went to his manager with my concerns. After a solid stance on my worth and some convincing, I was given a raise.

After the Faith Tour, Sheryl Crow, who just got off tour with Michael Jackson; Dolette McDonald, who was singing with Sting; and I went out with Don Henley. After Don Henley, George Michael called me again to do his next tour, Cover to Cover.

Some women of P-Funk, such as Shirley Hayden, Sheila Horne, Jeanette McGruder, and Mallia Franklin, continued to record with George Clinton throughout the eighties on his solo albums with Capitol Records. Singers like Linda Shider, Pat Lewis, Sandra Feva, and former Miss America Vanessa Williams also contributed vocals.

After four albums for Capitol and not being able to recapture the success of "Atomic Dog," Clinton was released from the label. Music icon and funk aficionado Prince picked him up in 1989 and signed George to his label through Warner Brothers, Paisley Park.

MALLIA FRANKLIN Before I went in, I got word that Janet Jackson heard my demo of the song "Hipnotize." She wanted to do it, but I declined. Janet wasn't a big recording star yet, and I was trying to get my own thing going. I wrote a letter from prison to Janet's producer, Jimmy Jam, explaining my circumstances and my interest in working with him and his partner, Terry Lewis, when I was released.

After being released from the feds in 1988, I didn't return to Detroit. I went from Texas to Minneapolis. I chose the Twin Cities because it was the music hotbed, thanks to Prince and producers like André Cymone, Jesse Johnson, Jimmy Jam, and Terry Lewis. I still had a little fame from Parliament, and the Minneapolis scene greatly respected us.

I first met Prince in Toledo, Ohio, in 1980, when he was on The Fire It Up Tour, opening for Rick James. I met Prince and his bassist and best friend, André Cymone. Prince was quiet; André did most of the talking. Prince asked my sister, Jenifer, on a date that night . . . and she went.

Over the years, Prince always ensured that I was cared for whenever I went to his shows. He hired many P-Funk people to work for him over the years. Guys like Billy Sparks and Greg Brooks worked for P-Funk back in the day. Prince signed George to Paisley Park strictly out of his love and admiration.

One night, I went to Paisley to do a session with George. He was late. I sat in the studio for about an hour when the door opened. It was Prince, and he looked startled.

He coyly said, "Hey."

I replied, "Hello, Mr. Nelson."

He snickered and said, "You don't have to call me Mr. Nelson; you can call me Prince."

I said, "I call you Mr. Nelson as a sign of respect."

"Then I'm going to call you Ms. Franklin."

I had known Prince socially for years, but this was my first time with him one-on-one. I sat on the couch while he was talking to his engineer. He turned to me and said, "I have something to confess. *Pleasure Principle* was important to me."

Shocked, I replied, "Really?"

"Yes," he said.

He was a true fan, and I was honored. That conversation cultivated a friendship with Prince that lasted for years. It felt good that he appreciated my contribution to P-Funk and George's whole thing.

George finally arrived. At the time, he was getting high, big-time. Prince couldn't stand it. George would hit the pipe, get on the floor, and blow the smoke under the door so he wouldn't set off the smoke alarms in Paisley Park.

Prince was setting up to film *Graffiti Bridge* at the time. During the session, he turned to George and said, "I want Mallia in the movie."

In the film, George performs a Prince song called "We Can Funk." Belita Woods, someone I also brought into P-Funk, sang the song, but Prince wanted *me* in the film.

George Clinton kept afloat monetarily by staying on the road with an all-male augmented version of Parliament-Funkadelic, called the P-Funk All-Stars. Female members were exiled from this aggregation of the eighties, but by the nineties, that would change, with former Brainstorm lead vocalist Belita Woods coming aboard.

BELITA WOODS (VOCALIST) I was at United Sound Systems in Detroit in 1982. I was in the hall, and I heard a voice call my name. I turned around, and it was Mallia Franklin.

I hadn't seen Mallia since she was sixteen, hanging out in clubs with Barrett Strong, who was a friend of mine. I couldn't believe she remembered me all those years later. She was recording vocals in the studio with singers Pat Lewis and Sandra Feva. I thought they were working on a P-Funk record because George Clinton was at the session. I did shows in Detroit with The Parliaments in the sixties, but I didn't really know George well.

Mallia pulled me into the studio and said, "Let Belita sing on the song!" Pat and Sandra weren't happy, as George was watching from the mixing board. I didn't want Mallia to get in trouble for putting me on *his* song without permission. It turned out that it was Mallia's session, not George's.

What Mallia did for me that day was let me know that she trusted me, when everybody else in the room doubted my talent. She welcomed me in and had no problem taking me around George. Mallia and I are musical soulmate sisters for life. That opened the door for touring with the P-Funk All-Stars. That wasn't a great thing in the beginning because some of the guys treated me really bad when I first got there. They now had a "no women in the band" rule.

LYNN MABRY I met Sharon Celani, a vocalist who performed with Stevie Nicks, while on tour with George Michael. We became friends. After my second tour with George, I was offered an opportunity to sing with Sharon on Stevie Nicks's TimeSpace: Whole Lotta Trouble Tour in 1991. Everything about that tour was great. The only thing that caused concern was that Stevie was going through some personal obstacles. She discovered that

Sheila E. and Lynn Mabry form Heaven Productions in 1997 and start a nonprofit organization (Lil Angel Bunny Foundation, later named Elevate Hope).

she was diagnosed as bipolar. On top of it, she dealt with some physical ailments and substance abuse issues.

A few of my bandmates and I became very close. One of the members of her band was percussionist Peter Michael Escovedo. Peter is the brother of Prince's protégé Sheila E. I met Sheila once, many years ago, in 1975. We were both sixteen years old, and their uncle, Coke Escovedo, whom I was working for at the time, was excited for me to meet his niece. I greeted her with a smile. In return, I was given a quick handshake, a brief "Hello" . . . and that was it. She seemed either very shy or not interested in meeting me at all.

I told Peter the story of our first encounter, but he encouraged a reintroduction. Near the end of the TimeSpace Tour, Peter invited Sheila to one of the shows. After the show, we were escorted backstage to meet our guests. As I walked toward Sheila, she stood up with a huge smile, said "Hi," and hugged me. This was a far contrast from our first meeting. We visited briefly and agreed to reconnect once the tour was over. I think she needed to meet a person who was grounded. Being someone like Sheila E., you'll meet many people who are all over you just because you're Sheila E. . . . I couldn't care less.

One day, Sheila asked me if I would be interested in singing with her.

She was embarking on a two-week tour in Japan. I was looking forward to that. As friends, we shared our experiences regarding the similarities in how we were brought up. I often invited her to the church I attended. Usually, Sheila declined. After many invitations, she finally came. Just like my first service, Sheila spent most of it in tears. She rededicated her life to the Lord, and it was clear that her life, just as mine, was changing.

While rehearsing for Sheila's Japan tour, I got a call from George Michael's road manager.

He said, "I'm doing a tour with Bette Midler. She needs a strong singer to sing with her and the Harlettes."

I went to one of Bette's rehearsals to meet her. Bette asked, "Do you know any songs of mine?"

I said, "I know 'The Rose.'"

When they got to "The Rose," Bette asked me to come onstage. She pulled out a stool, gave me a mic, and we sang together.

When it was over, she looked at me strangely and said, "It's weird and amazing. It feels like you have sung with me before. You knew exactly where I was going. How did you know where I was going?"

I shrugged my shoulders and said, "I didn't. I just followed my heart and listened."

She turned to me and said, "I'd love to have you come out on tour with me." I accepted.

I returned to Sheila's rehearsal, and, as soon as I walked in, she said, "You got the tour. I know it." I apologized for being unable to go to Japan with her, but she understood.

I worked with Bette Midler from 1993 to 1995. It was fun, crazy, wild, and sometimes a spiritual challenge. But Bette, like George Michael, always complimented and honored me publicly. To be acknowledged was a blessing, and I was very appreciative of that.

After the tour with Bette Midler, Sheila E. and I continued to perform and attend church together. One day, Sheila called me wanting to know if I was interested in partnering in a production company with her. I thought about it for less than a minute and said, "Why not?" I officially became the VP of Heaven Productions Music. Partnering with a woman who was now my best friend was special. It allowed us to work toward a common goal while figuring out how to best navigate through this male-dominated music business.

CHAPTER 30

SAMPLE SOME OF DISC, SAMPLE SOME OF DAT

The resurrected legacy of Parliament-Funkadelic in the nineties came unexpectedly. The introduction of "sampling" to the music industry would push P-Funk's hooks, beats, bass lines, and breaks to a new generation of fans. Many rap and hip-hop front-runners, such as West Coast producers Dr. Dre and Ice Cube, used P-Funk's grooves, incorporating them into their tracks.

"The Humpty Dance" by Digital Underground and "Me, Myself and I" by De La Soul, produced entirely on samples of P-Funk's music, became hip-hop anthems. Artists like Del the Funky Homosapien, Ice Cube, and Jurassic 5 sampled sections of Parlet songs, while Ruff Ryders, Too Short, and Low Profile sampled Brides of Funkenstein cuts.

"Mallia ended up with Snoop Dogg and Dr. Dre and them," George Clinton said in 2008. "She became one of their background singers and did a lot of hook writing for them. Mal gave them a lot of that P-Funk *legacy* that they ended up with."

DAWN SILVA In the early nineties, word got out that rap artist Ice Cube wanted to meet The Brides of Funkenstein. Cube got my number from Candi Ghant of the Mary Jane Girls. I spoke to him, and he was excited to

The Return of Parlet: Shirley Hayden, Mallia Franklin, and Jeanette Washington reassemble Parlet in 1996 for the upcoming Mothership Reconnection twentieth anniversary tour.

talk to me. I worked with Ice Cube for over a year and a half and sang on Coolio, YoYo, Del the Funky Homosapien, and other projects he produced. I was also featured on a song called "How to Survive in South Central" for the film *Boyz n the Hood*. Ice Cube offered me a contract on his Street Knowledge record label. He said he wanted to do an album on The Brides.

One day in the summer of 1992, I walked into Ice Cube's studio, and to my surprise, George Clinton and P-Funk staff member Archie Ivy were in the control booth. They saw me and threw up the P-Funk sign. Ice Cube was excited because his hero, George Clinton, was in the house. George kept throwing me the P-Funk sign repeatedly, and I felt in my spirit that whatever I had established with Cube was about to be squashed. I was right. After that visit from George, my participation in Cube's productions became less and less, and then nothing at all.

MALLIA FRANKLIN People in the industry were telling the new Hip-Hop Generation that we [P-Funk] were out of our minds, we were through, and nothing else would happen for us. But that's not how God planned it, and when sampling began, it brought all of us who were shoved out of the way back to the forefront. Rappers looked up to us because P-Funk is what their parents, grandparents, aunts, and uncles were bumpin' to. That's the music that they grew up with.

Then people like Dr. Dre, Snoop Dogg, and others reached back for some of us. That was the only way we would ever get our piece of the rock in the record industry. I recorded with many West Coast artists like Ice Cube, Nate Dogg, Da Lench Mob, and RBX. Snoop and I were very close. I did his first album, *DoggyStyle*. We spent a lot of time together and did a lot of work. We did a great song for Death Row that wasn't released called "Funk Wit Yo' Brain."

NANCI FLETCHER (VOCALIST, DEATH ROW RECORDS) I can't remember how Dr. Dre found Mallia Franklin. I just know that she showed up in the studio one day. I was told that she sang with George Clinton's Parliament-Funkadelic and was in one of the groups called Parlet.

That day, we recorded "W-Balls" for Snoop's debut album. She worked with the one and only Bootsy Collins and wrote songs with Snoop. Mallia became such a mentor to me after we met in the studio. She would advise me about the industry and give tips to care for my voice, like this thing called "ear coning." I used to go over to her house all the time and kick it with her just to soak up knowledge and hear all of her stories about her wild times in the biz.

BRUCE PETERSON I started managing Mallia in 1991. After a year in Minneapolis with her, we moved to North Hollywood and started hooking up with the West Coast rappers. Mallia worked with Dr. Dre, training the girls who sang with Death Row harmony and phrasing to get the P-Funk sound. They were paying Mallia pretty well and revered her history.

I also knew Ice Cube. He wanted to work with George Clinton, so we flew him into town. We brought him to work on the rapper Del the Funky Homosapien, Ice Cube's cousin. A few months later, Bootsy flew into Los Angeles. Mallia and I were hanging out at Cube's studio and invited him to come by. Ice Cube was excited because he hadn't met Bootsy.

Bootsy, Mallia, Ice Cube, and I sat in his office. Cube talked to us about how his mother went to a Parliament-Funkadelic show when he was twelve and didn't take him. He said that he had been ruined ever since.

My manager's hat went on, and I said, "Well, if you take P-Funk out on tour, then you'll have the tour you missed out on at twelve."

He said, "I'll do it on one condition . . . I'm on the show."

He was ready to put it together and would finance the entire thing.

I told him, "I'll help you put this tour together. Now I need something from you . . . to get Mallia a record deal."

Pat Charbonnet, Ice Cube's manager, was at the studio. Cube talked to Pat, and she called one of her friends, Sylvia Rhone, the senior vice president at Atlantic Records, and put her on speakerphone.

Ice Cube said, "I need a deal for Mallia Franklin, one of the Parlets."

Sylvia said, "One of George's girls . . . yeah, we can do that."

Ice Cube said, "Mallia is here with her manager, Bruce. Bootsy's here with us too. He's going to produce on the project."

Sylvia wanted me and Bootsy to come to New York the next day on her dime. She wanted a guarantee that he was going to be on Mallia's record. Bootsy said, "Girl, I'm on this one! This is my gal pal, Mal. We ain't got no problem here."

We knew we had Prince, who offered to produce while she was in Minneapolis, George, and Ice Cube, and could get Dr. Dre and Snoop. Everything Mallia had done in the music business was about to culminate in this solo project. Everybody in Ice Cube's office was excited; Mallia sat quietly, which was unusual.

We left the studio to pack for New York, and Mallia said, "I'm uncomfortable with this. I don't want to be on a record label run by a woman. I don't get along with *bitches* . . . period!"

I pleaded with her, "We're talking about Sylvia Rhone. You don't even know her! This isn't some P-Funk girl bullshit!"

Mallia wasn't fazed. She flatly said, "NO! I can't do this record deal!"

I said, "Mallia, you're my last shot with the funk. If you don't do this deal, I'm done." She refused.

I hung in there with Mallia for a little longer but never recovered from her turning down Sylvia's offer. I kept my promise and left the management game.

MALLIA FRANKLIN One day after a session in 1994, I was at Dr. Dre's beautiful mansion in Calabasas, complete with waterfalls. His success was a sign of the times. Dre called me "Momma Funk."

We played pool and talked about my time with P-Funk, particularly with Roger and Zapp. He said that he wanted to meet Roger Troutman. In the past, he was told that Roger was hard to work with. He wasn't into drugs, and Dre's claim to fame at that time was *The Chronic.*

He asked, "How am I going to be able to work with him?"

I told Dre, "If he can work with George, he can work with you. Always handle business because Roger is all about business. And if you aren't, Roger will walk."

Dre said, "Momma Funk, can you put us together?"

I called Roger and got him on the phone with Dre. They talked, and he started playing Dre some new music. The next thing I knew, Roger was in the studio with Dre. I brought together Dre and Roger, and they recorded the Tupac song "California Love."

The success of hip-hop and sampling formed mountains of new money from compositions created by Parliament-Funkadelic and its attached spin-offs. It also opened old wounds, ignited new wars, and ushered in court battles between partners to get revenue from the original songs. Sampling was a new pot of gold to fight over. The lack of money shared with the P-Funk artists and songwriters created more financial tensions that many people thought had died with the first crash of the Mothership.

George Clinton's former cohorts, Nene Montes and Armen Boladian (owner of Westbound Records) became his biggest legal enemies. Within five years, there would be a myriad of lawsuits between Clinton, his former co-conspirators, and a group of former P-Funk managers, Bruce Peterson, Raymond Spruell, and Ron Brembry, under the name APF (the Association of Parliament-Funkadelic Members) over various master tapes. If this sounds like a legally confusing, big, fat mess . . . it was.

By 2007, another lawsuit was filed on behalf of George Clinton against Universal Music Group, declaring the right to certain masters released by Casablanca Records for Parlet. George claimed that Universal had no ownership because he had a "Key Man" clause in his original contract. Clinton alleged that he reclaimed his music rights when the former president, Neil Bogart, left the company. Clinton and his legal team contacted Mallia Franklin and asked for a copy of her original contract to aid him in his case because she was the only contracted member of Parlet in the group's existence.

During discovery, Universal Music Group attached documents provided by Nene Montes as "true and correct copies" that Clinton signed in 1980. In the papers, Nene claimed ownership of all Parlet master recordings. Universal tried establishing ownership of the Parlet masters and inferred that Montes was paid $250,000. George testified that he had never seen the 1980 Parlet document until Universal produced it at trial.

In the nineties, Universal, under the PolyGram label, released all three Parlet albums in Japan and a worldwide greatest hits release titled *The Best of Parlet featuring Parliament* as part of their popular Funk Essentials series.

MALLIA FRANKLIN I knew Nene Montes and his partner, Tony Lowe, had all the Casablanca music [Parliament and Parlet]. The contract administration's director at PolyGram, Maurice Russell, confirmed it when I contacted them about my royalties.

He said, "Nene Montes has your money."

When I reached Nene, he was cavalier about it.

I said, "Nene, I don't know about the other girls, but you got to deal with *me* because I have a contract, and I'm due my money. I know PolyGram paid you off. That means you got my royalties, and I want them."

He coldly replied, "Stand in line with everybody else."

In 1994, after the release of *The Best of Parlet*, I got a call from my former fiancé, Donnie Sterling, who was now living and performing in Japan. He told me he could get Parlet some gigs there. My son, Seth, and Cheryl James found Shirley Hayden and Jeanette Washington. As usual, Shirley was ready and down for whatever. But Jeanette was in a whole different place in her life. She was involved with the church and raising her son. But she was also open to making money. We talked about a Parlet reunion. Cheryl and Seth went to George and had him sign an agreement that we could perform as Parlet without interference, but we didn't get much interest.

A year later, Seth suggested calling The Brides, Dawn and Lynn. He felt we could get some gigs if the two groups merged. We repackaged it as the

"She Funk Tour." I was down for it. In the beginning, Jeanette wasn't feeling that idea. She said, "Brides bring problems!" We all still had that residue from those days with P-Funk. Dawn was receptive. Lynn had been successful over the decade as a background vocalist, one of the highest-paid in the music industry at one time. As far as The Brides were concerned, she was over it. Since Lynn declined, I got in touch with Sheila Horne. She'd done shows with George, and I thought she might be interested.

Belita Woods and many other people I had introduced to George over the years were now touring with the P-Funk All-Stars . . . Jerome Rogers, Amp Fiddler, Paul Hill, and Steve Boyd—they all got into P-Funk through my projects or connections. The *crazy* thing was that I couldn't get a gig with George now.

STARR CULLARS (BASSIST) I didn't know any women from Parlet or The Brides when I joined P-Funk All-Stars in 1993. I think I met Sheila Horne first, then Mallia Franklin. I would see Dawn Silva sometimes and rarely see Lynn Mabry, if ever. Through the years, I heard stories about the women from the guys in the band. The overall gist was that two female groups were produced by George and the band.

They started out both being fabulous, with tons of potential. They said that George cut Parlet off before they could even get *close* to success. Still, The Brides of Funkenstein were on their way to being super successful. The guys explained that the personnel of the girl groups were constantly changing. Mallia left Parlet, and then Lynn left The Brides. I asked myself, "Why are these main lead singers hightailing it out of these groups?" Of course, there were other factors, like George's business falling out, drugs, Nene Montes, etc.

I knew when I first met Mallia that she was powerful. She would come to the shows if we were in her town. George would allow her to go onstage and sing. I never understood why they would keep someone with Mallia's talent and ability at bay. I witnessed her come to Archie and George and literally *beg* to return to P-Funk. According to some of the guys, something happened on a previous tour, and they refused to let her return. They would just dismiss her. It pissed me off to see George treat her that way.

I wanted to tell them, "You should *always* be giving her respect because she gave you key personnel that gave you this legacy of music."

George Clinton isn't Prince or Stevie Wonder; he needed these musicians and singers to make this music. It wouldn't have happened if he hadn't met many important people through her. I was amazed that Mallia still had so much love for all of them . . . even George. As bad as she was treated, she always loved him anyway, and most times, he didn't deserve it.

In 1996—after the large resurgence of Parliament-Funkadelic music via West Coast rap, hip-hop, and a stint on the Lollapalooza Festival in 1994—George Clinton acquired a lucrative new record deal with Sony Records due to this young, fresh audience of twenty somethings.

He released his only album for Sony, *T.A.P.O.A.F.O.M.*, an abbreviation for "The Awesome Power of a Fully Operational Mothership." To coincide with the release, the label planned a reunion tour billed as the "Return of the Mothership." The initial idea was to bring everything full circle from the band's heyday to celebrate the twentieth anniversary of the first Mothership Earth Tour in 1976.

This would be momentous, as it marked the return of Bootsy Collins, keyboardist Bernie Worrell, and the two female groups, Parlet and The Brides of Funkenstein. Blueprints were acquired from the original spaceship's designer, Jules Fischer, to re-create the legendary Mothership stage prop. Unfortunately, the reconstructed Mothership was much like the short-lived tour, plagued with problems and missing vital parts. The 1996 replica ultimately landed at its final destination in the Smithsonian National Museum of African American History and Culture in 2011.

STARR CULLARS (BASSIST) When the 1996 Mothership twentieth anniversary tour was planned, The Brides and Parlet members needed to return to reassemble their respective groups. The tour was initially set up like those Funk tours in the seventies. Parlet would do a set. The Brides would do the same. Bootsy would perform, and then everybody would do the Parliament-Funkadelic set together, but that's not how the tour went down.

They got The Brides . . . but not Lynn. She refused to come back. Dawn Silva and Sheila Horne would be The Brides this time. The excuses I heard about Parlet not being on tour were unclear. The only Parlet that I was given a clear answer about was Mallia. The guys said they didn't want to be bothered with her because they felt she would come in and dictate. The main consensus was that it didn't matter, "Mallia will show up to the shows anyway and represent as the leader of Parlet." And at some shows, she did. Ultimately, The Brides' forty-five-minute set was reduced to one song. That was the extent of that tour for the women.

DAWN SILVA When I arrived in New York to start rehearsals, I was informed that I would be sharing a room with Belita Woods. I didn't know Belita at all. I got there a day before her, and the first night was great. Belita came in the next day and was upset because she had to share a room with me. She came in and told me to get the *fuck* out of *her* room. We started to fight. At the time, she was smoking crack. All Belita did was sit in the room and get high. She wasn't going to rehearsals.

George had to get me out of the room with her because I knew I was going to go to jail for hurting her. That's how bad we were fighting. George had a room at the hotel, but he wasn't staying there, so I stayed in that room for a while. Eventually, George showed up, and I started crashing in Garry Shider's room on the couch. I had been out there for a couple of weeks with no room to sleep in. Eventually, Sheila arrived and George got a room for us.

The first show of the Mothership reunion tour was on July 4, 1996, in Central Park in New York. Bootsy came on, and he only did a couple of songs. Then Parliament-Funkadelic came out. Sheila and I stood in the back, waiting for George to call us to the stage. The show was going on, and after a while, I thought, "Oh my God! George isn't going to call us out." I didn't want the fans to believe that The Brides didn't show up. We needed to walk out there so they at least *saw* us. Sheila was afraid.

I looked at her and said, "You go with me, or I'm going alone."

She hesitated, and I started walking. After a few steps, Sheila followed behind. George was out front. He turned around and said, "Oh yeah . . . The Brides." He handed me the microphone, pulled a glass stem out of his pocket, and lit it. He inhaled, blew the smoke in my face, shrugged, and walked off the stage. He went down the ramp and into his trailer. Then rain started pouring down. We got to the end of our song, "Vanish in Our Sleep," but it was horrible. Sheila fought me vocally . . . screaming and wailing over me. I gave the fans the P-Funk sign and walked off the stage, embarrassed and soaking wet. We did a second show on July 5th; unfortunately, it was more of the same.

After Central Park, George continued promoting that The Brides would be on the reunion shows. I'd left but would show up at shows from time to time. I did it as a statement to show the promoters that The Brides

Manager Cheryl James flanked by the reunited Parlet (Shirley Hayden, Mallia Franklin, and Jeanette Washington) in 1996.

were there. George was getting the money for The Brides, but I wasn't being paid, and we weren't allowed to perform any of The Brides' songs. One show was at the House of Blues in Atlanta during the 1996 Olympics. Mallia lived there at the time and came and sang with Sheila and me. I also showed up in Los Angeles at the Universal Amphitheater. I called Lynn and asked her to meet me there . . . and, to my surprise, she did.

LYNN MABRY I received a call from Dawn saying that P-Funk was performing in Los Angeles. I was reluctant because she mentioned that she wanted us to sing "Vanish in Our Sleep." I knew Sheila Horne would not be happy about me returning to sing The Brides' signature ballad. However, Dawn convinced me that it would be fun and the fans would love it. She arranged for me to get a VIP parking pass to go straight from my car directly to the backstage entrance.

I could hear P-Funk performing and heard George yelling and whistling as usual as I entered. The crowd screamed, and everyone seemed to be in pure funk eroticism. As I found my way to the side of the stage, Dawn saw mc, walked over, grabbed my hand, and escorted me onstage toward her microphone. The crowd realized who I was, and I began seeing and hearing the audience react to us. This was the first time Dawn and I, the original

Brides of Funkenstein, had appeared onstage together since 1981. I looked over at Sheila Horne; she was *far* from happy that I was there.

The band struck up "Vanish" as I smiled in appreciation and grabbed the mic to start the first verse. I may have sung four words when production turned off the power. The fans started booing, and I just raised both hands and shrugged my shoulders as if to say, "Sorry." I put the microphone down and walked off the stage. Unfortunately, I wasn't surprised that something like that would happen to us. I also wasn't upset that it *had* happened either.

SHIRLEY HAYDEN After the Mothership Reconnection Tour, we tried to resume She Funk. With Sheila now on tour with George full-time, she was out. Mallia's son, Seth, managed The Warehouse nightclub in Detroit. He financed the first She Funk show in 1998 and got commitments from Mallia, Jeanette, Dawn, and me.

Seth hired a local band and arranged the show featuring Brides, Parlet, and P-Funk songs. He purchased costumes, hired a video crew, bought plane tickets . . . and then the *shit* started. The first to drop out was Mallia. That hurt the worst for Seth and me. My best friend, Ping Spells, came in to help vocally after Mallia bailed. Dawn and Jeanette arrived three days before the show. They hadn't seen or talked to each other since 1981. After our first rehearsal, Dawn informed us that she was changing the show. Oddly enough, Jeanette was cosigning whatever Dawn said.

"Shirley, you don't talk . . . you just sing. We'll do all the talking," Dawn said. Jeanette would just agree.

By showtime, we were totally divided. Everybody was out for themselves. This was a tragic foreshadowing of things to come with She Funk.

We tried again in 1999. Mallia got a show opening up for the Roots in New York at a club called Wetlands. She invited Jeanette, Dawn, and me. We were all going to meet in Atlanta. We got a call that Dawn showed up early with her new boyfriend, who was going to play keyboards. There was already a total breakdown when I arrived two days later. The issue was that Dawn and Mallia were fighting for control. Jeanette was now doing whatever Dawn said, and I was neutral, willing to do whatever was needed. Jeanette and Dawn backed out of the show. Why can't we come together and get along without bullshit?

Mallia and I went to New York and did the show, which was a challenge because Mallia could be a pill as well. There were no more She Funk shows

The Brides of Funkenstein return: In 1996, Sheila Horne and Dawn Silva perform at Central Park in New York for the twentieth anniversary of the Mothership.

after that. We tried other configurations with former Parlets Janice and Gwen and former Brides Jeanette McGruder and Sheila, but the truth was that the P-Funk bullshit ran so deep that every project we *tried* to do went up in smoke because women, some still to this day, are fighting for control.

The new millennium saw more reissues from the Parlet catalog: *Invasion of the Booty Snatchers* in 2003 in Europe and its predecessor, *Pleasure Principle*, in 2013 worldwide, on Universal.

The Brides of Funkenstein album *Funk or Walk* was reissued in 2005 on Warner label Vivid. Both Brides albums were reissued again in 2011 on a Warner subsidiary, Wounded Bird. In 2020, the label released both Brides albums in a double CD offering.

For decades, the women of Parliament-Funkadelic were viewed as mere props for Dr. Funkenstein. They were much more than that. They played an integral part in the success of the band. They were the feminine wall of sound on legendary hits, number-one records, and funk anthems like "Flash Light," "Atomic Dog," "One Nation Under a Groove," "(Not Just)

Knee Deep," "Aqua Boogie," and "Give Up the Funk (Tear the Roof Off the Sucker)."

Their influences have been heard and seen in the formation of interracial and sexually charged girl groups of the eighties, like Vanity/Apollonia 6 and the Mary Jane Girls; in TLC's take on the look of Parlet's *Pleasure Principle* cover in their video "No Scrubs"; and in En Vogue's use of She Funk vocal phrasing in songs or their "Whatever" music video, featuring the group members as updated Brides of Funkenstein.

The women of P-Funk and their legacy have been continuously, but anonymously, in plain sight since their inception.

When Parliament-Funkadelic was inducted into the Rock & Roll Hall of Fame in May of 1997, none of the women were included or invited. Junie Morrison, recruited by Mallia Franklin, was the only member to acknowledge some of the women, thanking Lynn, Dawn, and Mallia.

When the Grammys presented P-Funk with a Lifetime Achievement Award in 2019, again, none of the women were acknowledged. Still anonymous to the masses, the women of Parliament-Funkadelic continue to fight for their right to be acknowledged for their contributions.

WILLIAM "BOOTSY" COLLINS I felt kind of funny about none of the girls being inducted. But who is really in charge of the induction, and who really calls that shot? It was not only some of the girls but some of the guys who weren't inducted. My brother, Catfish, wasn't included. You feel funny about it, but it's like, "What do you do?" I wasn't going to go to George and ask him. I guess this is who he wanted to be there.

I think that Parlet and The Brides changed the singing thing for females and their whole style, attitude, and aggressiveness . . . it was their entire presence. It wasn't a prissy kind of female thing. It was bold. It was a statement they didn't have to say out of their mouths.

They were out front and in your face like, "Bang! Here it is! We're out here, we're singing loud, we're doing our thing, and we're wearing what *we* want to wear! Here we are, and y'all just got to deal with it!"

RON BREMBRY The P-Funk Girls never got the respect they deserved. To this day, *funk* still never gets the respect that it deserves. The girls were special; they influenced many girl groups and didn't get the credit for it. You won't hear their names being mentioned. They were a part of Parliament-Funkadelic, and we were at the top. We were in the top ten groups in the music industry as far as tours. We were selling hit records, platinum records. We were never in the red when it came to record sales. If a record didn't go gold or platinum, it *still* made money. The Brides and Parlet won't get the recognition they deserve . . . just like funk music doesn't.

FRANKIE "KASH" WADDY Girls being with Parliament-Funkadelic was outlandish. That alone revolutionized girl groups. We were ahead of our time, so obviously, the girls would be too. Other groups have something to feed off of when acts like Parlet and The Brides don't go mainstream. To me, successful groups like En Vogue are Parlet and The Brides combined. They have a classy thing like The Brides, but at the same time, they have that raw, gritty thing like Parlet. Many girl groups copied the P-Funk Girls.

Parlet and The Brides were unique. It was almost unrealistic for that time frame because they went against the grain in many different areas. They weren't trying to be super sexy . . . but they were. They weren't trying to be too hard, but at the same time . . . they were hard. They were female radicals.

STARR CULLARS I want people to understand that Parliament-Funkadelic was a male misogynist-based group filled with talent and different abilities. Knowing this, you must realize that Parlet and The Brides were all fantastic, beautiful singers with amazing ability, but these women were galvanized entirely in the P-Funk male system.

For the blood, sweat, and lives that they laid down for the funk, for their beauty, talent, and sacrifice, we can't let it end with the tragedy of what their careers *should* have been. We're changing that story with them being entirely dismissed by the group and not acknowledged by the Rock & Roll Hall of Fame or the Grammys. Telling their story in this book is changing it right now!

EPILOGUE

LONG WAY AROUND

The women of Parliament-Funkadelic made a difference in how the world heard music. Right next to the Supremes, the Marvelettes, Labelle, and Destiny's Child, the P-Funk women made their mark, changed the game, and left pieces of musical and visual DNA in the molecular makeup of many modern-day divas being downloaded, streamed, shared, tagged, and trending on a minute-by-minute basis.

With the availability of music via technology, the legacies of Parlet and The Brides of Funkenstein will expand larger, grow wider, and sing louder, one megabyte at a time. I hope their story, finally told, will carve them an undeniably flamboyant heart decorated with essential glitter in the thick bark of the mammoth oak tree that is music history.

DEBBIE WRIGHT After I left P-Funk and Parlet in 1978, I tried returning to a "normal" life. My mother got me a job working with her at the post office, and I hated it. All I knew was music. I didn't know a regular life. I just knew how to pop my fingers and sing.

I continued to have mental breakdowns for some time. My medications caused me to shake, walk funny, talk funny, and foam at the mouth. I had many years of rough times. I lost my only child, Charles, to gun violence when he was a teen in Detroit. I continued to self-medicate with drugs, putting me in bad circumstances. I was beaten, raped, and robbed because of the places I chose to be due to my drug addiction. I was eventually readmitted to the hospital. After ten years of being prescribed the wrong things, a doctor finally got me on the right medication. I moved back in with my mother and have been doing well ever since. I made music here and there, but never professionally again.

I never blamed anyone for my breakdown. I didn't blame George. I didn't blame any of the guys or the other girls. If anything, I blame the drugs. I indulged heavily in that life and couldn't handle it mentally, so I had to go. I have no regrets about my days in Parliament-Funkadelic . . . not one. They were the best days of my life.

On October 15, 2017, Debbie Wright died in Detroit from a brain aneurysm. She was sixty-six years old.

SHIRLEY HAYDEN People always ask me, "Why were we not recognized at the Hall of Fame or Grammys?" I don't have an answer. I can imagine that the answer can only come from George Clinton. The beautiful work that the women did during the band's most successful time had value. Our sense of style influenced costuming. The energy and attitude that we brought to the stage speak for themselves. We have a great deal to do with the success of P-Funk. What we did back then is what George and the touring members of Parliament-Funkadelic are *still* eating off over forty years later.

My time with P-Funk taught me that I have value . . . there's value in my voice. It taught me that I had all I needed then because I was chosen to be a Parlet and a Parliament-Funkadelic member. It gave me a big stage to perfect my craft. It allowed me to focus, grow, and strengthen musically. It helped me find joy in sitting in the studio for hours, waiting to record one line, and watching the whole creative process. I gave 100 percent to what was larger than myself.

I also learned that everyone is not your friend. As young women, we were all still learning who we were. I experienced that females typically don't build you up; they tear each other down. I leaned toward my funk sisters for support. Mallia supported me, and she recognized my talent. She urged me to be big and bold. Lynn Mabry was that type of sister as well. Other women were intimidated. Having to work with women that rejected me was disheartening. To this day, we still can't get together and perform. Mistrust and control are big factors. I'm OK with it today. It helped to further build my character, endurance, and patience.

I'm grateful for the time I spent with P-Funk perfecting my talent. It's my passion, and it was just getting good when it all folded. I am deeply grateful that I gave my all and that the world responded positively. We were all singing and dancing for the fun . . . and the *funk* of it.

Shirley Hayden cultivated a music career on the theatrical stage in shows like *Ain't Misbehavin'* and *Ma Rainey's Black Bottom*. She headlined legendary jazz clubs and toured Japan twice as a featured vocalist.

In 1998, she joined Kid Rock and the Twisted Brown Trucker Band. After appearing on *The Tonight Show with Jay Leno*, *The David Letterman Show*, and the American Music Awards with Kid Rock, Shirley received a two-time platinum award for the album *The History of Rock*, a five-time platinum award for the album *Cocky*, and an eleven-time platinum and diamond award for the album *Devil Without a Cause*.

Shirley still records and performs, most recently with the Blackman Revue featuring Shirley Hayden. She still plans to perform and celebrate the music of Parlet.

She has a loving daughter, Shelley, and one beautiful and talented grandchild, Ezra.

DAWN SILVA During my time with P-Funk, I didn't know my destiny or journey, and I was long gone from the group when I did. I never really wanted to be a star. I just happened to be in a situation. It was the right place, or maybe the *wrong* place at the right time. But I did have goals. I achieved being up on that stage. I achieved putting a platinum record on my mother's wall. I wanted a hit record and a gold single, and I achieved that. I can say that all the goals I asked God to help me achieve were reached.

If there is one thing I would change regarding my career, I would have never gotten into relationships with men I worked with. Love relationships create a dynamic that can ruin a great business relationship and friendship. The intensity of creating and doing business with someone that you love is one of the hardest things. You would think it would be easy, a perfect scenario, but it's not. Some pitfalls in my career are directly connected to my personal relations with men and love. That's my biggest takeaway.

The women of P-Funk weren't one-dimensional singers. We weren't just funky . . . we were *the* funk. And, of course, because we were Black, we were categorized as R&B. We were far beyond R&B. We were a combination of different art forms under one umbrella. We did country, jazz, blues, rock, and new wave and succeeded in every last one. Not every female singer is talented enough to have those ingredients. George was unique in picking the right people to flesh out his concepts. But as women left, those elements were missing. It's like cooking a pot of gumbo. When you start changing ingredients, the taste will change. The sweetening, the thrust, and the flavor are missing.

It was disrespectful when the Rock Hall and Grammys didn't recognize us. I think I felt worse for Debbie, Mallia, and Jeanette. They worked with P-Funk way before Lynn and I came. I know the feeling of winning. The Brides won awards, even if the organization didn't tell us about it. I knew what it was like for my name to be called. Parlet didn't, they should have, and that's sad.

We were innovators of sound and style. Everybody wanted what George Clinton had. They wanted the sound, the look, and the women. That's the real reason why we weren't inducted into the Rock & Roll Hall of Fame . . . fear. The fear was that we would rise above them. You were a threat if you could stand shoulder to shoulder with the men, which we did every night onstage.

We were considered a threat then, and, to this day, we still are.

Dawn Silva went on to tour with the legendary guitarist B. B. King in the United States and South Africa. She toured South America multiple times as a member of The Platters through most of the nineties. Dawn frequently performed with P-Funk keyboardist Bernie Worrell and his band, The Woo Warriors, including a momentous show at Woodstock '99.

In 2000, Dawn independently released her first solo album, *All My Funky Friends*. The album was licensed in European territories, and sales in the US and overseas garnered her headlining spots at the 2002 North Sea Jazz Festival in Den Haag, Holland, and the Long Beach Funk Festival in 2009.

Dawn Silva leads a version of The Brides of Funkenstein with former Parlet, Jeanette Washington, and Graham Central Station's Gail Muldrow.

Dawn is the mother of a son, Justin; grandmother of two, Hannah and Sienna; and great-grandmother to two girls.

LYNN MABRY While being a member of Parliament-Funkadelic, we were one big happy family onstage. However, women were the lowest on the spectrum. To this day, I have never gotten a royalty check for my part in The Brides of Funkenstein or Parliament-Funkadelic. Many years after I'd left the group, I would see George from time to time. He'd tell me that he was getting his catalog back and that I would see some funds coming. This was compensation owed to us from decades ago. I didn't expect it, but I was hopeful. To date, nothing.

In 2019, I received a call from George Clinton's daughter Barbarella, informing me that the Grammys would finally honor George and P-Funk with a Lifetime Achievement Award. My daughter was invited to accept a Grammy on behalf of her father, Junie Morrison. Because Junie produced many hits, it made sense that he was included as one of the recipients. At the very least, I assumed Parlet—Mallia, Debbie, and Jeanette—would receive honors, as they were the *first* women to sing with the group when it became a popular force in the industry. Again, no women were honored. It took me back to the Rock & Roll Hall of Fame induction. Junie knew this was an injustice and verbally acknowledged a few women—Mallia, Dawn, and me—by name when he accepted his award. Unfortunately, that was all the acknowledgment we were going to receive.

Other band members at least received a Grammy certificate acknowledging their contribution. Even a couple of The Brides' original band members. The women got nothing. We didn't even get an honorable mention from George.

Sometimes I look back at those Parliament-Funkadelic days and laugh. Other times, I can be depressed about it. After thinking about what happened, I realized everything was a stepping stone to getting where I am today. It took me being irresponsible for me to mature.

I always knew that funk wasn't my whole life. In my mind, funk was a pit stop, and that was my only saving grace. Seeing talented musicians create this amazing sound and movement allowed me to explore other areas of my music career. I saw how drugs and physical abuse could affect one's livelihood. I learned the lessons. It helped me avoid those probable pitfalls and taught me to honor myself first.

About ten years into my career, I realized there was a vast difference in how men and women were acknowledged. Regardless of our equal contributions, I started to accept it, the same as I did as an African American woman. Not often being seen as beautiful often, making less money than my male counterparts, and doing the same job. This was, and to this day is, the norm. There aren't many advocates on the side of the female artist. I at least fought whenever I could to make a difference.

Personally, I realized that my life is not about me but about being the best servant I can be. Professionally, I want to create a balance where I can prosper in this business, leave my mark, and have someone say, "What you did was wonderful." Eventually, I'll reap my reward because I am serving people. However, I have committed to doing what I do unto *God*, not man. My focus now is on becoming a more healthy and whole human being. And for that, I am forever grateful.

Lynn had appearances in the film *Stop Making Sense* in 1984 and in the films *Tapeheads* and *The Night Before* in 1988.

Lynn Mabry and business partner and friend Sheila E. formed a nonprofit organization, the Lil Angel Bunny Foundation, later renamed Elevate Hope. Sheila E. and Lynn also had a three-month run in the summer of 1998 as the house band for *The Magic Hour* with basketball legend Earvin "Magic" Johnson as host.

In 2012, Lynn and Sheila E. parted ways in business but maintained their friendship and continued to work on countless projects.

In 2013, Lynn was featured in the Oscar award–winning documentary about music's most influential background singers, *Twenty Feet from Stardom*.

Lynn has also appeared in special projects, recordings, and award shows with other world-renowned artists, such as Elton John, Steve Perry, Namie Amuro, Eric Clapton, Aaron Neville, Dave Koz, Dave Stewart, Daughtry, Hozier, and Mick Jagger.

She is the proud grandmother to Junie Lynn and Osbourn Lennon, from her daughter with producer Junie Morrison, Akasha Mabry.

MALLIA FRANKLIN Parliament-Funkadelic changed the face of music as the world, and the galaxy, knew it. We were the first African American alternative band. We could literally cross over and be as big as white artists And, at that time, the record industry was not ready for that. Like in real life, there is discrimination, bigotry, and wanting to *own*. We weren't going to be commercialized. We were revolutionaries, and we scared the *shit* out of the government when we came out onstage in army fatigues, singing about "One Nation Under a Groove." That was too radical. Too much "Black Panthers" for that ass!

We are also a family. We cried together, fought together, lived, and loved together. Not just bodily but godly . . . spiritually. Music lives on forever . . . it's infinite. So participating as far as the music of Parliament-Funkadelic is truly a blessing.

People have asked me over the years about this title . . . the Queen of Funk. I'm humbled that George would put that out in the universe. He regarded me as a great funk singer, but it's more about my contributions to the funk. The accomplishments of a queen are her deeds and duties to her nation. I did many things that made P-Funk what it became and, in turn, funk music as we now know it to be. I was like Betsy Ross sewing that One Nation flag. It made me feel good as a woman back in the day, knowing I could get the ear of men in power and assist them in ultimately becoming music icons themselves. So, my *deeds* bestowed the title Queen of Funk upon me . . . I earned it.

George always said, "Mallia's a Geiger counter. She feels it and knows when the universe moves." I can say that I found some of the greatest people for over twenty years and brought the *best* to George Clinton and P-Funk. I brought Bootsy. He took it to a higher level musically. Then Junie took it to that next level. Donnie Sterling and David Spradley took it to another. I was a vessel for them all, aligning with the stars and moving through love, light, and the truth . . . never faking the funk. Every top ten hit record that Parliament-Funkadelic or George ever had was achieved with a collaborator I brought . . . that's a fact!

As women in this family of Parliament-Funkadelic, we made our own history. We will always be a huge part of George's and this group's success. People can overlook us as much as they want, but the proof is in the *funk*. You can't erase our voices. You can't erase us from pictures and videos. We were originators and rebels in an era when women were supposed to be quiet, look pretty, and sing.

We, as women in Parliament-Funkadelic, never played it safe.

We're not gonna *ever* play it safe.

We're gonna ride these Motherships.

> Other women will say that about themselves . . . that they are a Queen of Funk. And Mallia always worried about that. But she shouldn't ever worry about being the only "Queen of Funk." She's *our* Queen . . . she'll always be P-Funk's Queen.
>
> GEORGE CLINTON

Mallia Franklin's solo album, originally recorded in the early eighties, was finally released on the Japanese label P-Vine in 1995. She continued to tour and record as the Queen of Funk with various artists, including an unreleased song with Lenny Kravitz.

Mallia recorded with Dallas Austin, Too Short, and Organized Noise and continued working with Snoop Dogg and other rap artists. She recorded and wrote for the soundtrack to the movie *Undercover Brother* on Snoop's "Undercova Funk (Give Up the Funk)" and received a platinum award for Snoop's album *Paid tha Cost to Be da Boss.*

In 2004, Mallia performed with Parliament-Funkadelic at the 46th annual Grammy Awards, their first performance ever on the Grammy stage, with many members from the group's heyday in attendance. She shared what she called one of her most "cherished moments" with many people who were a part of this story: Bootsy, Bernie Worrell, Billy "Bass" Nelson, Frankie "Kash" Waddy, and Garry and Linda Shider, as well as members she'd brought into the P-Funk universe like Belita Woods, Jerome Rogers, Paul Hill, and Steve Boyd.

Mallia Franklin suffered a stroke and heart attack in Waukegan, Illinois, while traveling to perform in July 2009. She died from complications on February 5, 2010, in Los Angeles. She was fifty-seven years old.

At Mallia's memorial service and jam session on March 8, 2010, at the Conga Room in Los Angeles, Lynn Mabry, Dawn Silva, Shirley Hayden, and singer Sue Ann Carwell took the stage with P-Funk alumni Blackbyrd McKnight and Greg Thomas. With Sheila E. sitting on drums, Molina Moye on guitar, and a stage full of talented musicians, they launched into a rendition of Parliament's "Up for the Down Stroke." Bootsy Collins took center stage and gave a public testimonial, saying, "We are here to celebrate the life of Mallia Franklin, who actually introduced me to George Clinton . . . and *that's* where P-Funk was born."

Mallia Franklin had one child, Seth Neblett, with Nathaniel "Nebs" Neblett of New Birth.

ACKNOWLEDGMENTS

Special thanks to Jeanette Washington-Perkins, Amuka Kelly (Sheila Horne), Satori Shakoor (Jeanette McGruder), Gail Muldrow, Janice Evans, Gwen Dozier, Jeff "Cherokee" Bunn, Jim Wright, Gabe Gonzalez, Gwendolyn Lanier, Cynthia Robinson, Michael "Clip" Payne, JoAnne Kushner-Abrams, Shaunna Hall, Melissa A. Weber, Tim Kinley and Donna McCoy, Carlon Thompson-Clinton, Marcel Visser, Rickey Vincent, Susan Schader, Paul Justman, Neville Johnson, Apollonia, Derrick Parker, Maxi & Cheri, Miki, Chaka, and Barbarella Bishop.

Because I lived this life every day, it didn't take the writing of this book for me to indisputably realize that funk and Black music, hip-hop, rap, and many forms of contemporary music would not be what they are today without the contributions, forward-thinking concepts, and afrofuturism of George Clinton and the members of Parliament-Funkadelic. But on a more granular level, my mother's death in 2010 and the years of research and interviews for this book helped me realize, beyond a shadow of a doubt, that Parliament-Funkadelic wouldn't have been what it became without the influence of my mother, Mallia Franklin. *Who* and *what* she brought to George Clinton facilitated the shape of the P-Funk sound. Even in her last days, my mother spent so much time proving to the world that she *was* the Queen of Funk. Her foresight, guidance, talent, and instincts were enough of confirmation to the universe that, indeed, whether she recognized it or not, she'd *already* earned her crown.

And at the root of all of it, I'm just a boy telling the world my mother's story. I dedicate this book to her.

PHOTO CREDITS

Page 7, courtesy of Seth Neblett; page 10, courtesy of Seth Neblett; page 16, courtesy of Seth Neblett; page 21, courtesy of Cheryl James; page 27, left, and right, both courtesy of Debbie Wright; page 33, courtesy of Bootsy Collins; page 37, courtesy of Jenifer Franklin; page 44, photo by Herbie Greene, courtesy of Dawn Silva; page 47, courtesy of Seth Neblett; page 52, photo by Warren Paul Harris; page 55, courtesy of Lynn Mabry; page 61, courtesy of Lynn Mabry; page 64, photo © Mark Sullivan (All rights reserved); page 73, courtesy of Debbie Wright; page 75, photo by Bruce Talamon, courtesy of Shirley Hayden; page 85, courtesy of Seth Neblett; page 93, photo by Steve Rosenstock; page 96, photo by Dean Taylor, courtesy of Seth Neblett; page 106, photo by Steve Rosenstock; page 113, art by Shusei Nagaoka; page 117, courtesy of Lee Rosenbloom; page 119, photos by Steve Rosenstock; page 121, left, courtesy of Seth Neblett; page 121, right, photo by Steve Rosenstock; page 131, courtesy of Cheryl James; page 136, photo by Kevan Stewart; page 141, courtesy of Shirley Hayden; page 144, photo by Steve Rosenstock; page 148, photos by Steve Rosenstock; page 151, photo by Kevan Stewart, courtesy of Cheryl James; page 156, photo by Diem Jones, courtesy of Dawn Silva; page 161, courtesy of Seth Neblett; page 170, photo by © Diem Jones (All rights reserved); page 171, photo by

Steve Rosenstock; page 174, photo by Steve Rosenstock; page 177, photo by Steve Rosenstock; page 180, courtesy of Dawn Silva; page 181, courtesy of Seth Neblett; page 188, top, courtesy of Marcel Visser; page 188, bottom, courtesy of Seth Neblett; page 190, courtesy of Seth Neblett; page 191, courtesy of the Kinley-McCoy/Groove Maneuvers Archives; page 192, courtesy of Lynn Mabry; page 195, courtesy of Lynn Mabry; page 198, photo by Steve Rosenstock; page 200, photos by Christian Rose; page 207, photo by © Diem Jones (All rights reserved); page 211, photo by Steve Rosenstock; page 216, courtesy of Seth Neblett; page 220, courtesy of Seth Neblett; page 224, top, courtesy of Dawn Silva; page 224, bottom, photo by Kevan Stewart, courtesy of Shirley Hayden; page 227, photo by Diem Jones; page 235, courtesy of Seth Neblett; page 239, courtesy of Seth Neblett; page 241, courtesy of Dawn Silva; page 245, courtesy of Seth Neblett; page 262, photo by Henry Mayers, courtesy of Seth Neblett; page 266, photo by Diem Jones, courtesy of Seth Neblett; page 271, photo by Henry Mayers, courtesy of Lynn Mabry; page 275, photo by Sho Kikuchi, courtesy of Seth Neblett; page 278, courtesy of Lynn Mabry; page 292, courtesy of Dawn Silva; page 295, photo by Idella Madison; page 299, courtesy of Lynn Mabry; page 302, photo by Seth Neblett; page 310, photo by Seth Neblett; page 312, photo by Andre Zimmerman.

INDEX

Page numbers in *italics* indicate an illustration.